IMAGES
of America

NORTH CAROLINA STATE PRISON

I0806457

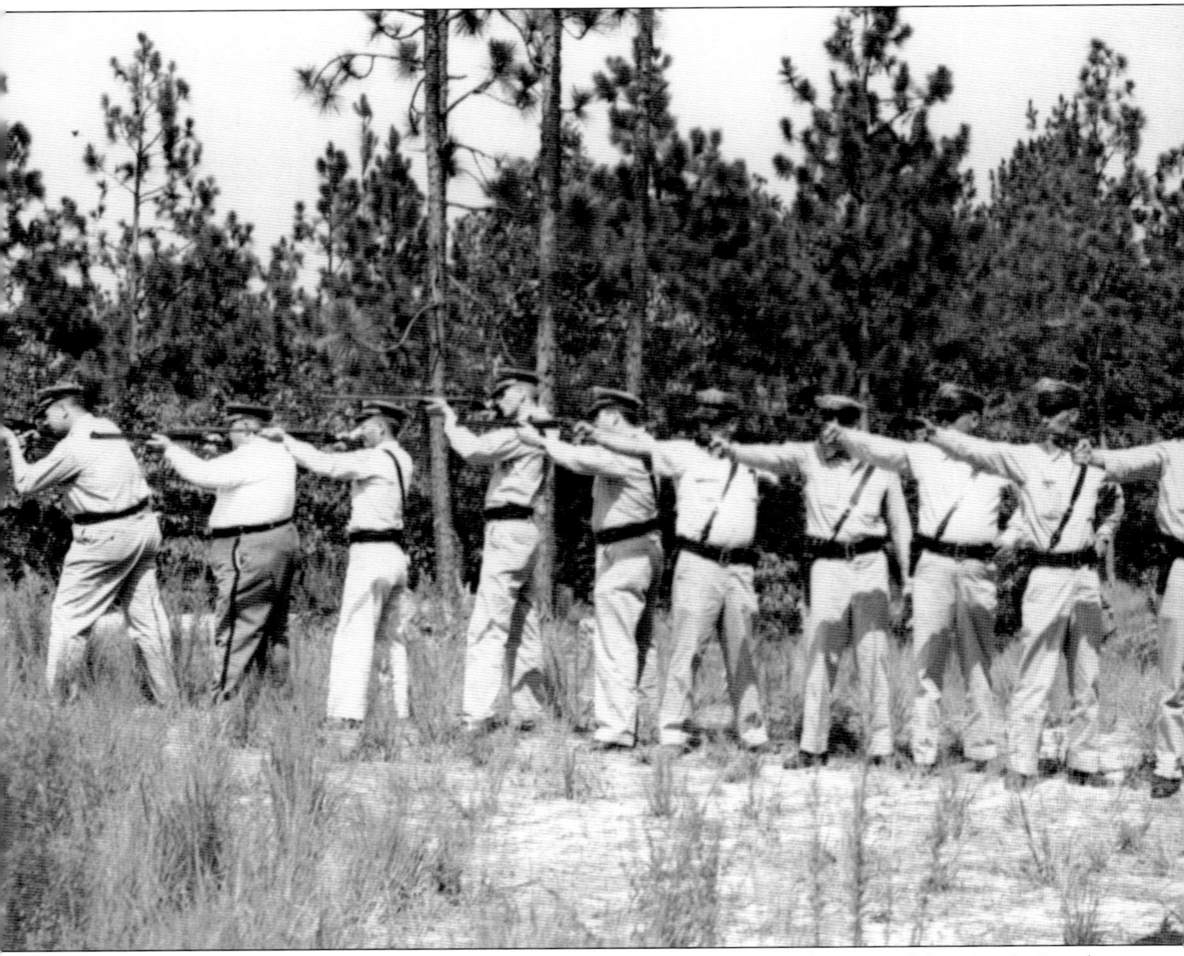

Officers Train with Firearms, 1961. George Randall became director of the North Carolina Prison System in 1960. In an effort to improve the quality of prison operations, he established more stringent criteria for the hiring of correctional officers and improved their training by requiring frequent sessions at the firing range. (Courtesy of the North Carolina Department of Public Safety.)

On the Cover: Inmates are pictured here doing yard work inside the prison walls in 1910. (Courtesy of the North Carolina Department of Public Safety.)

IMAGES
of America

North Carolina State Prison

William G. Hinkle, PhD,
and Gregory S. Taylor, PhD

ARCADIA
PUBLISHING

ISBN 978-1-4671-1516-2

Published by Arcadia Publishing
Charleston, South Carolina

Printed in the United States of America

Library of Congress Control Number: 2015948909

For all general information, please contact Arcadia Publishing:
Telephone 843-853-2070
Fax 843-853-0044
E-mail sales@arcadiapublishing.com
For customer service and orders:
Toll-Free 1-888-313-2665

Visit us on the Internet at www.arcadiapublishing.com

This book is dedicated to my friend, mentor, and colleague Dr. Stuart Henry, professor and director, School of Public Affairs, San Diego State University, 2015.
— Dr. William G. Hinkle

This book is dedicated to my students, who continue to inspire.
— Dr. Gregory S. Taylor

Contents

ACKNOWLEDGMENTS

The authors gratefully acknowledge the following people for their contribution to this book: Beverly A. Mizen for putting the proposal together and working on the photographs and text; communications officer Keith Acree, representing the North Carolina Department of Public Safety; Kim Andersen, representing the North Carolina State Archives; and Katherine Beery, representing the North Carolina State Museum of History. Special thanks to J.D. and Judson Manly from Manly Steel in Dalton, Georgia, for their generous contribution of material and information about the convict cars.

We also wish to thank our editors at Arcadia Publishing, Lily Watkins and Sarah Gottlieb, for their expertise and encouragement throughout the entire process.

Finally, we wish to thank our student coauthors: Ashley Jane Tackett, Donald Melvin Lewis, Divoria Shakee Williams, Jerrell D. Ralph, Kevin Ishmael Wilson, Ciara Agnes Brown, Dillion Kyle Chappell, Torrian Reshad Edmonds, Zachary Diego Green, Jack Adams Jones, Makayla Rose Mizell, Michael Paul O'Brien, Tyson Lamont Terry, Calvin Jerome Bowe, and Mesha Le'Sane.

Unless otherwise noted, all images appear courtesy of the North Carolina Department of Public Safety.

INTRODUCTION

North Carolina lacked a statewide legal and penal system for much of its early history. Counties were expected to enforce laws and punish lawbreakers, but both concerns often fell to vigilante groups. When counties did act, they rarely employed imprisonment. Instead, they resorted to fines, public humiliation, corporal and capital punishment, or banishment. In 1741, the colonial legislature sought to change that when it authorized the use of county tax revenue for the construction of local jails. Most counties ignored the law, and those that complied generally constructed ill-equipped buildings unsuited to long-term imprisonment. As a result, those housed in early prisons remained only briefly until their court hearing.

Most states had a similar history but began to centralize law enforcement and punishment, in the form of penitentiaries, in the late 18th century. North Carolina was not part of that trend. In 1801, state leaders had their first discussions about building a penitentiary, but those proved short-lived, as concerns over cost and placement subverted any perceived need for the state to handle incarceration. Formal legislation to construct a state penitentiary failed 10 times between 1805 and 1845, and by 1861, only North Carolina, South Carolina, and Florida did not have a state penitentiary.

As a result of the Radical Reconstruction period following the Civil War, Southern states were required to write new constitutions. North Carolina's constitution, ratified in 1868, abolished corporal punishment, public humiliation, and banishment and reserved the death penalty for murder, rape, burglary, and arson; all other crimes were punishable by fines or imprisonment. Appreciating that this meant an increased prison population the county-based system could not handle, the constitution called for construction of a state-run self-sustaining penitentiary that served "not only to satisfy justice, but also to reform the offender." Subsequent laws created a penitentiary commission to oversee the construction and administration of the institution and required it to segregate inmates by race and gender and put inmates to work.

With the parameters set, in September 1868 the commission authorized Gov. William Woods Holden to spend $100,000 on the purchase of 8,000 acres of land in Chatham County, just east of Raleigh, as the penitentiary site. Almost immediately, charges of corruption arose, and a legislative investigation found the land poorly situated and worthless. State officials put the debacle behind them and, in 1869, located a more useful 20-acre plot just outside of Raleigh, for which they paid $10,000.

In January 1870, as construction bids were being evaluated, the first inmates moved to the penitentiary location. They erected a wooden stockade and temporary buildings and prepared to work with construction crews to build the permanent establishment. The first permanent buildings were occupied by 1875, but not until 1884 was construction on the entire penitentiary complete. The final complex, the North Carolina State Prison, also known as Central Prison, encompassed 22 acres and had 450 cells.

Although the state finally had a functioning penitentiary, few offenders were incarcerated within its walls. Instead, administrators leased inmate labor to private companies or employed inmates on chain gangs, in labor camps, or on farms. Many prisoners thus worked and resided outside the penitentiary walls. Concern about having convicted felons beyond the secure penitentiary eventually led the state to return inmates to its confines, where they labored in on-site industries. Wherever they worked, the labor policy served two purposes. First, the state was required to run the penitentiary as a self-sustaining institution, and employing inmate labor seemed a cost-effective means of achieving that requirement. Their labor produced revenue to offset the costs of running the penitentiary or reduced expenditures, as inmates produced goods for their own consumption. Second, a penitentiary, by definition, houses criminal offenders sentenced to incarceration at hard labor. Putting inmates to work at menial jobs that provided few useful or transferable skills and offered little edification or uplift fulfilled that definition.

The purpose of inmate labor changed little during the penitentiary's history, but its physical plant evolved remarkably. In 1935, the original 19th-century construction was modernized with new fireproofing, modern plumbing, advanced cell door locks, and transparent barriers in the visitors' center. In 1938, it received additional improvements when hot and cold running water, electric lights, and ventilation systems were provided to each cell, while new HVAC units, showers, and steel doors were added to the institution at large. In the 1980s, even more dramatic changes occurred when the original structures were razed and replaced by modern facilities. The modernized state penitentiary still stands, and with a capacity of 750, it houses death row and high-security inmates as well as all those sentenced to terms over 20 years.

The prison not only evolved structurally during its long history, it also attempted to change to fit emergent theories of penology. There are at least four rationales for the punishment of criminal offenders that do not require capital or corporal punishment. Restraint, as embodied in the penitentiary, is based on the idea that people have free will and are rationally motivated to maximize pleasure and minimize pain. Punishment, therefore, serves at least two utilitarian purposes. First, it provides specific deterrence, which requires the offender to suffer for his crimes to the extent that he will never break the law in the future. Second, it promotes general deterrence among non-offenders based on their knowledge of the suffering of those who have been incarcerated. Reform, as it emerged in the reformatory, asserts that individuals commit crimes as a result of internal forces beyond their control. Curing the physical, mental, or moral defects that led to criminal behavior is the purpose of incarceration. In a similar vein, rehabilitation, as it appears in the form of the correctional institution, equates crime with both internal and external forces such as poverty and unemployment. Incarceration is seen as an opportunity to diagnose and treat inmates in order to overcome social and personal problems. Finally, reintegration is a rejection of the penitentiary, reformatory, and the correctional institution altogether as major sources of crime in and of themselves. Semi-custodial community-based facilities for the treatment of nonviolent, youthful, and first-time property and drug offenders are consistent with the reintegration rationale.

Designed to deliver punishment, Central Prison attempted to employ reform and rehabilitation over the course of its history. At its inception, the prison followed the restraint model. Despite the constitutional assertion that the prison was to reform the inmate, in practice it focused almost solely on punishment. Inmates faced strict regulations, suffered punishment for violations, and received only limited job training, education, or moral uplift. Despite this strict sensibility, early wardens implemented the reformative methods through classification systems using merit-based promotions and behavioral incentives. Among the most important incentives was the indeterminate sentence, by which inmates could earn time off for good behavior and hopefully internalize the benefits of obedience. More recently, the prison incorporated elements of the rehabilitative approach by offering job training, educational programs, and counseling.

Regardless of the evolving theories of penology and the consequent changes in policy, administrators never forgot that punishment was the primary reason for the penitentiary's existence. Officials thus focused their administrative agenda on six basic issues.

First, they ensured that the penitentiary's physical grounds and layout helped maintain order and prevent escape. Maximum-security prisons are generally surrounded by high brick walls or multiple banks of fences capped with razor wire. This is because it is assumed that serious offenders will take any opportunity to escape. They are also assumed to take any opportunity to break institutional rules and thus present a threat to staff as well as other inmates. Consequently, offenders should be moved from one building to another only as required, such as for meals and work. Other than that, movement is problematic because it provides an opportunity for prisoners to come into physical contact with staff and other inmates. As a result of this concern, prison authorities develop what has been termed lock psychosis. Numbering, counting, checking, and locking make up their daily routine. Beyond that, they were not designed to facilitate reformatory, rehabilitative, or reintegrative treatment programs. Such activities require the frequent and often irregular movement of prisoners from one location to another. In the 19th century, penitentiaries were designed to move inmates en masse and only when absolutely necessary to and from the mess hall and work.

Second, officials classified, ranked, and assigned inmates to specific cell blocks that provided the most safety, security, and punishment. In a maximum-security prison, classification involves the assignment of prisoners (given their previous propensities for disruption of prison routine or escape attempts) to housing units (cell blocks or dormitories), work assignments, and if available, treatment programs such as educational or trade training. Different jobs and different cells fit the needs of different individuals; however, an offender's work assignment usually depended upon the needs of the institution. If the bakery needed a man, that is where he went. Offenders with a history of violence and more than 20 years to serve are generally considered high risk for escape and causing disruptions. An offender classified as high risk might be assigned to a segregation unit, locked in a cell for 23 hours a day, coming out for an hour each day for a shower, supervised phone call, or light recreation in a very limited area under constant surveillance. On the other hand, an offender with a history of serious property or drug offenses would likely be assigned to a dormitory rather than to a cell block, a job assignment that requires the use of tools, and perhaps a GED or other educational or vocational program if available.

Third, officials assigned inmates to specific forms of labor to fulfill the twin task of punishment and financial self-sufficiency. The definition of a penitentiary is a place where criminal offenders are sent for imprisonment at hard labor, in lieu of corporal or capital punishment. Thus, work should be painful, backbreaking, and meaningless, such as breaking up stones, in essence, "making little ones out of big ones." An alternative view, and one that is much more common in practice, is to force prisoners to earn their keep through hard work without compensation. According to deterrence theorists, making license plates is an example of an appropriate type of work for prisoners. Moreover, prisoners can be trusted with only a very limited range of work activities. Creative or purposeful work would, in any case, present an unnecessary security risk.

Fourth, officials enforced inmate behavior and maintained discipline through the use of rewards for good behavior and punishments for bad behavior. Offender breeches of institutional rules in maximum-security prisons are more problematic than at lower levels of security. This is because the offenders incarcerated within maximum-security prisons are assumed to be more dangerous than offenders housed within medium- and minimum -security facilities. Indeed, serious offenders can be expected to commit serious infractions of institutional rules. Only the coercive restraint of such offenders in segregated disciplinary units will ensure the safety of staff and inmates alike.

Fifth, officials maintained conditions of confinement that included only those things absolutely necessary for survival in terms of food, clothing, shelter, and medical care. In this connection, correctional administrators are precluded by the Eighth Amendment to the US Constitution from the use of cruel and unusual punishment. The food should be adequate enough to preserve satisfactory health. Prisoners should not be permitted to own any unnecessary property or possess personal amenities that might make their time in prison more tolerable. Under no circumstances should they have it "too good" in prison, as personal degradation is an implicit part of punishment. The Eighth Amendment, however, is subject to broad interpretation on the part of prison managers. Violations do occur and are occasionally brought to the attention of the public or government officials. Challenges to the conditions of confinement are routinely filed in federal courts by prison inmates.

Sixth, if one assumes, as proponents of deterrence do, that people choose to break the law, any other explanation for crime is pointless. Most people have an intuitive sense of what treatment means relative to prison inmates. Educational and trade training come immediately to the mind of the layperson. However, within a maximum-security prison, treatment is not the primary reason for imprisonment. Punishment is the primary reason for imprisonment, and any other type of treatment is inconsistent with deterrence theory. People choose to break the law and change only if they want to change in a positive manner. Hardened and serious criminals are assumed to be irredeemable, so no staff member is responsible for trying to change anyone. Moreover, treatment programs require offender movement for reasons other than feeding or labor and are considered risky at best.

Throughout its history, the penitentiary sought to punish lawbreakers in a safe and secure manner. In the process of doing so, the institution attempted to apply three of the four penological theories, focused on the six administrative considerations, and evolved to serve the needs of the state. In the process of so doing, the institution applied the four penological theories, focused on the six administrative considerations, and evolved to serve the needs of the state. This study offers a visual overview of how the North Carolina State Prison affected that punishment, implemented those theories, addressed those considerations, and fulfilled that service.

One

Building a Penitentiary

Construction work on the North Carolina State Prison began on January 6, 1870, when 33 inmates joined a larger civilian crew at the worksite. A wooden-pole stockade went up first and gave the penitentiary its original nickname, "the Poles." With the prisoners secure behind the wall, their numbers increased, and 12 temporary inmate quarters were built. The 19-square-foot buildings had a central hallway running down the middle and were covered by one continuous roof. The hallway, a walkway atop the stockade, and sentry boxes stationed around its exterior provided custody officers vantage points from which to watch the inmates, who worked alongside skilled craftsmen to construct the permanent structures.

As construction on the formal penitentiary buildings began, administrators revised their plans and called for a permanent structure with 450 cells, a 50 percent increase from the original blueprints. With that increase incorporated into the new design, work on the permanent structures proceeded. Making use of a neighboring quarry, which the prison purchased in 1873, and on-site brick kilns and tin shops, inmates and workers laid the foundations, slowly raised the first stone and masonry buildings, built the cell walls, and hung the cell doors. They also erected a permanent stone barrier to surround the penitentiary and, in 1872, laid tracks to connect the site to a nearby railroad.

In 1875, the first permanent cell buildings were occupied, the main administrative building was complete in 1880, and the entire eastern cell house of the penitentiary was populated in 1881. Final work was complete in 1884, when the main intake building and the western cell house were occupied. With the permanent buildings complete, the temporary quarters were converted into stables for horses and cattle. Construction took 14 years and cost $1.25 million, a figure that would have been higher without the savings resultant from the use of inmate labor. Although among the last of states to construct a penitentiary, North Carolina eventually had one of the most architecturally advanced penal facilities in the nation.

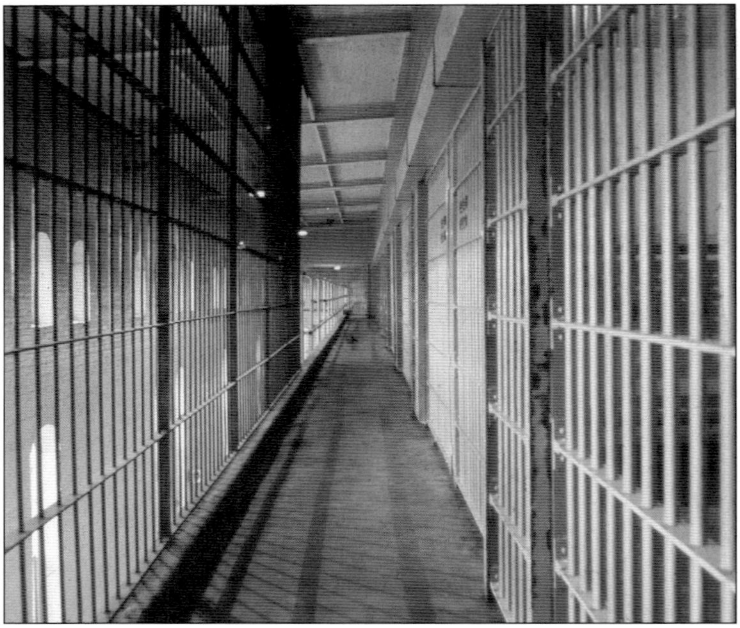

Cell-Block Corridor, North Carolina State Penitentiary. A penitentiary is a public institution in which those convicted of crimes are confined for definite or indefinite terms. Confinement is regarded as more humane and effective than corporal or capital punishment, but it is administered to cause enough unpleasantness to affect both specific and general deterrence.

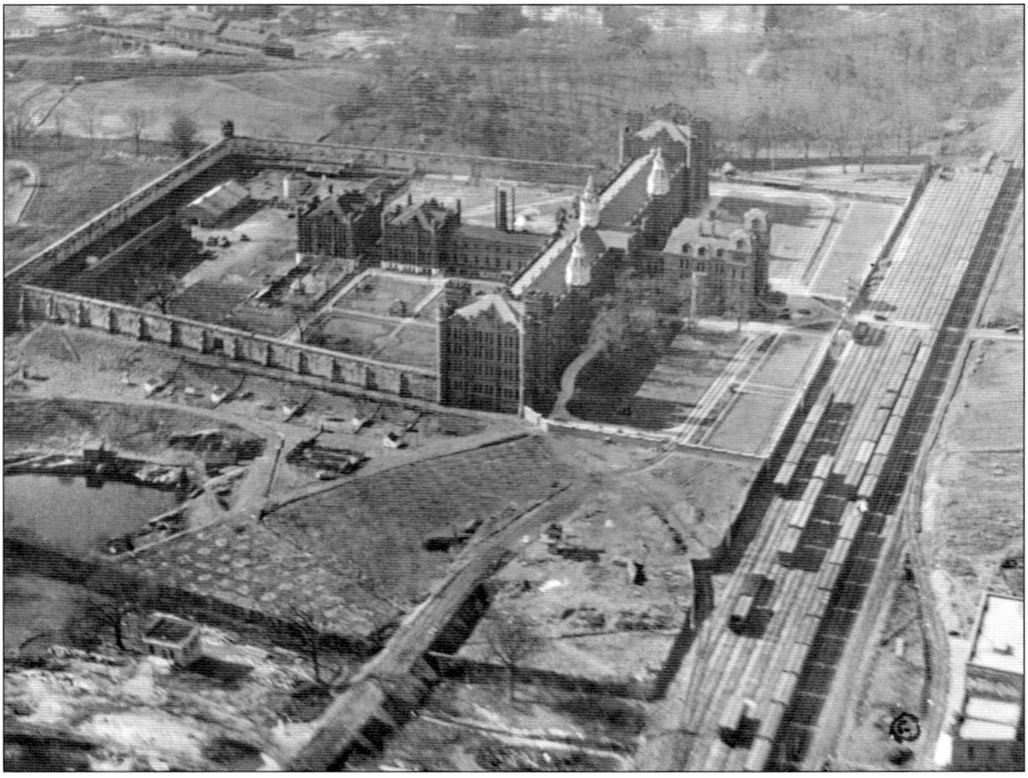

Aerial View from the East, 1900s. On April 12, 1869, the North Carolina General Assembly passed "An Act to Provide for the Erection of a Penitentiary." The act situated the new institution one mile west of the capitol on the extension of Morgan Street near Hillsboro Road in Raleigh. The railroad track in front of the prison, visible on the right of the image here, and the proximity of the stone quarry, evident in the lower left, were essential to the site choice.

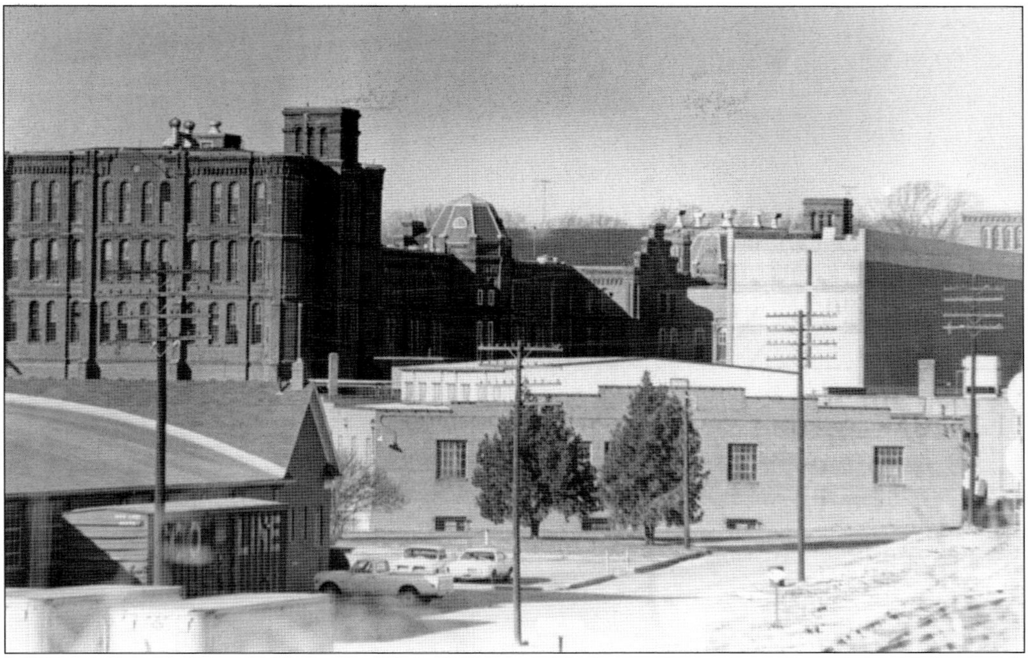

View of East Pavilion, Hospital, 1970s. The penitentiary commission created to oversee all elements of the new institution first addressed matters of judgment, taste, and economy as well as the management and discipline of the inmates. Since the state had never before undertaken a penal program, debates on these issues often proved contentious.

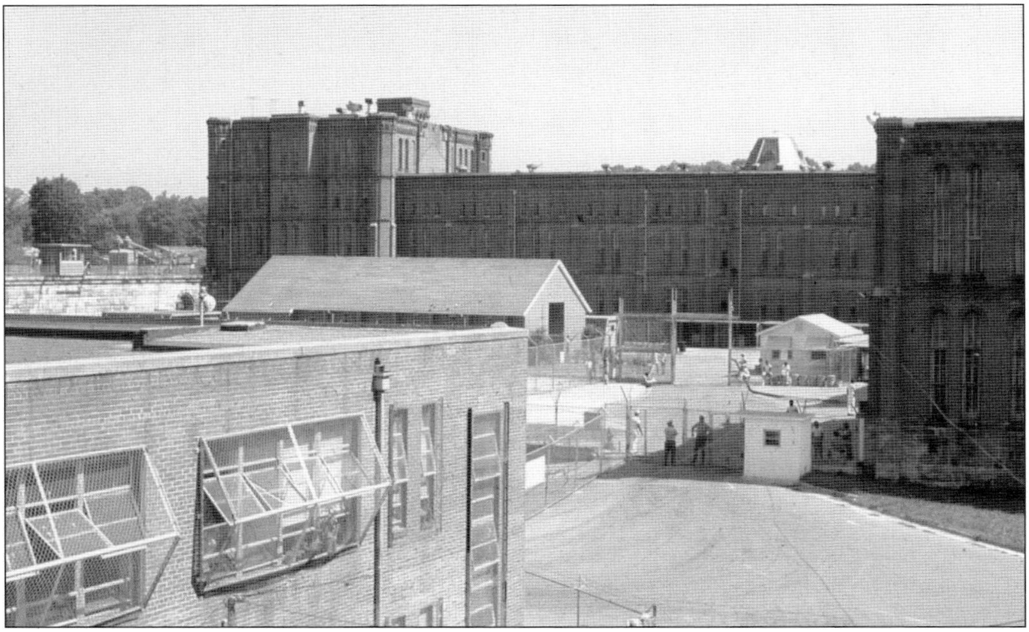

Rear View of West Pavilion, Location of Dangerous Insane Inmates, 1970s. The commissioners, in keeping with the constitutional prerogative that the penitentiary be self-sustaining, eventually decided to employ inmates in as much of the original construction as possible. Doing so would achieve the punitive element of their punishment while saving the state the burden of additional construction crews.

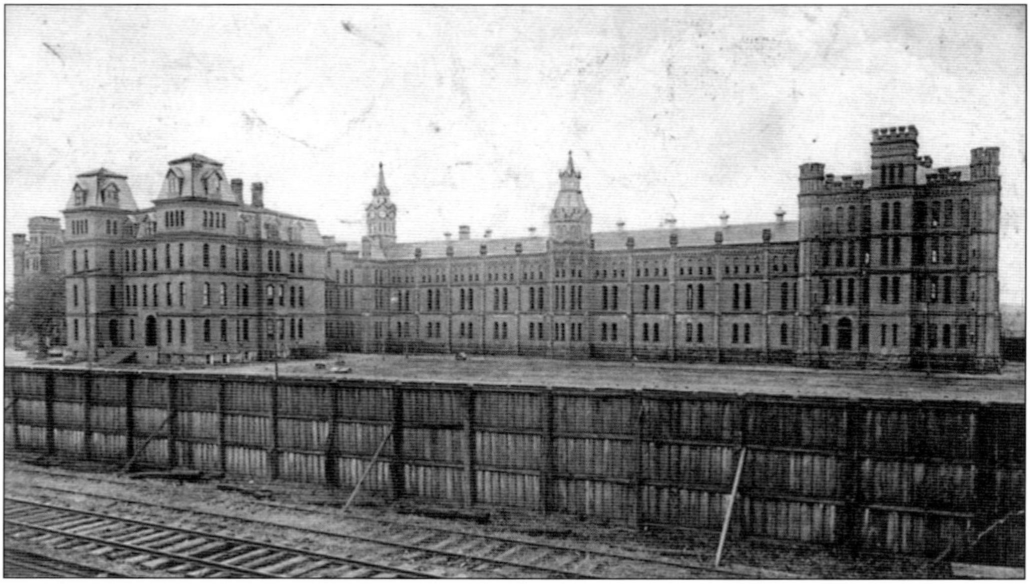

WOODEN STOCKADE AROUND THE COMPLETED PRISON, 1900S. First constructed was the 2,965-foot-long pine pole stockade, which rose 15 feet and had its base buried four feet deep. The stockade included two wagon gates, one railroad gate, and one small personnel gate. By November 1, 1870, the stockade and temporary buildings were complete.

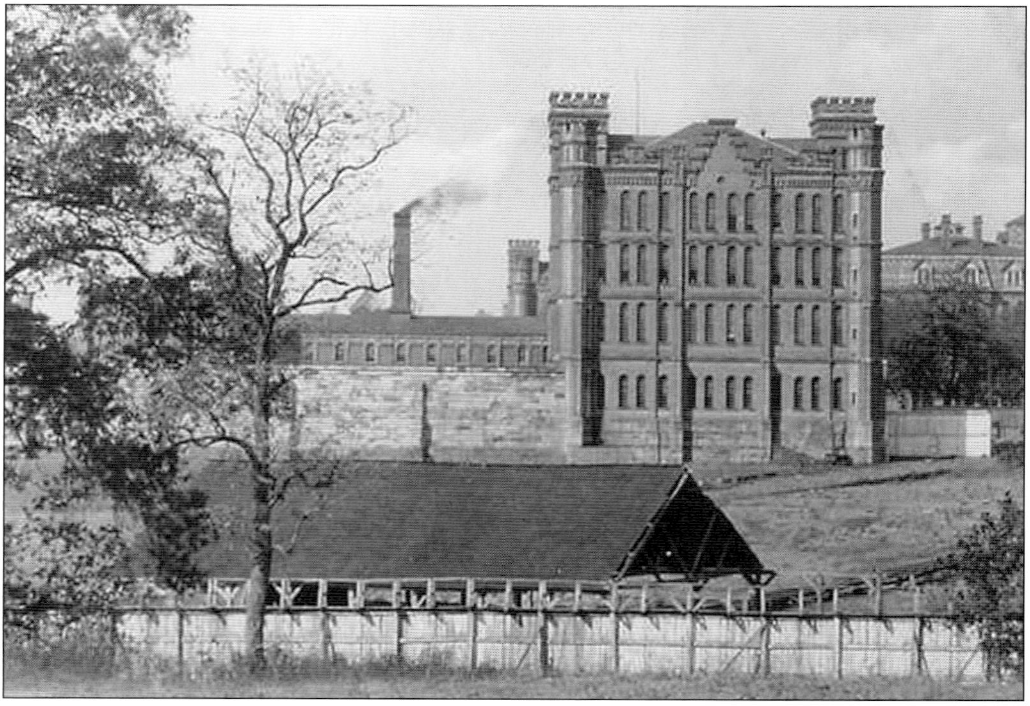

WOODEN STOCKADE, TEMPORARY BUILDINGS, EAST PAVILION, 1900S. Next to rise were the temporary wooden buildings, including twelve prison cells, two hospital rooms, and two rooms for lockup. In addition, there was a 20-by-24-foot bathing room and a 20-foot-by-38-foot washroom, both supplied with tubs furnished with hot and cold water. A 20-by-38-foot kitchen and a 20-by-25-foot bakery completed the inmates' amenities.

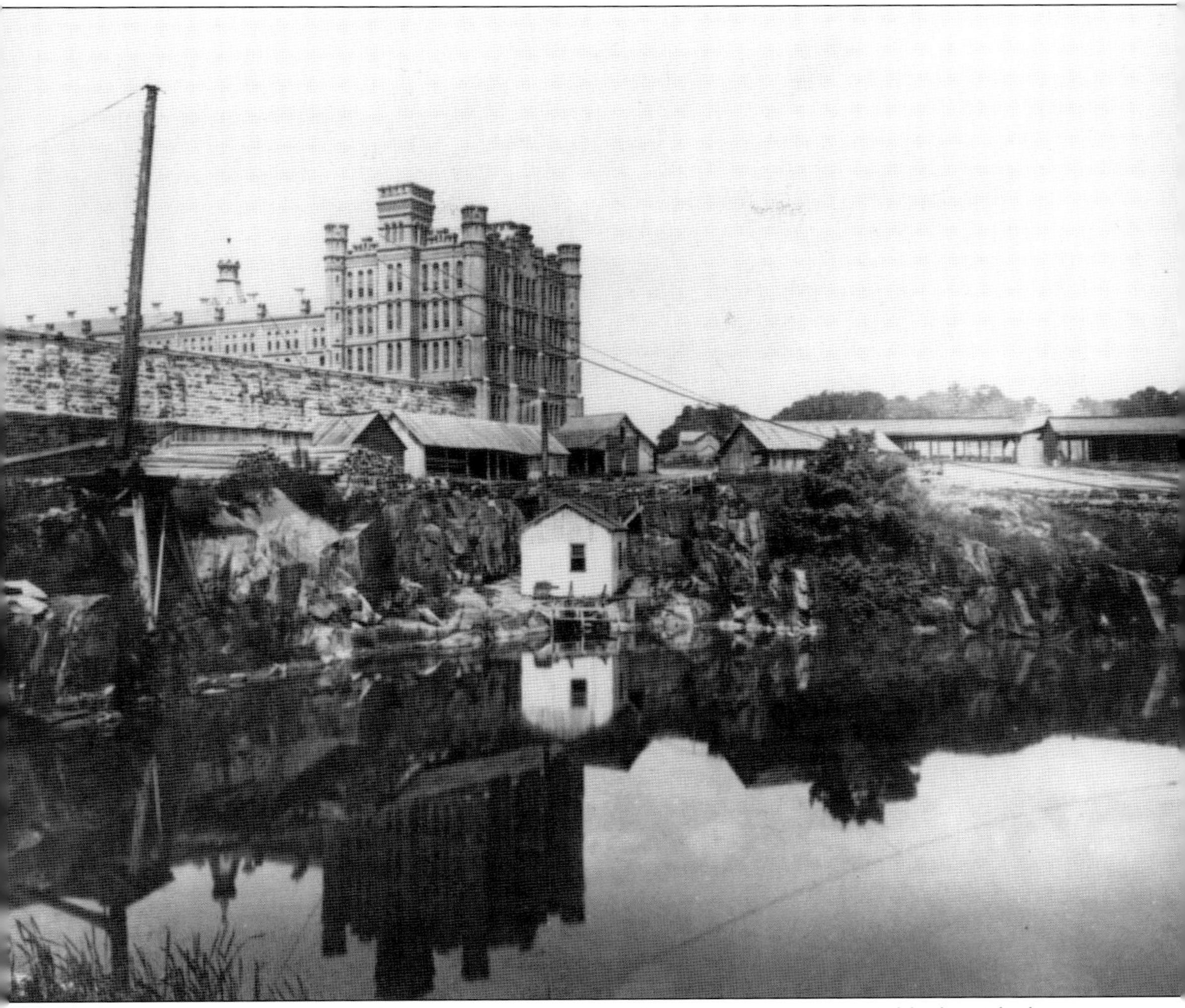

QUARRY POND, TEMPORARY WOODEN BUILDINGS IN FOREGROUND, 1900S. A blacksmith shop, a carpentry shop, a toolhouse, and stables were built next. The inmates, of course, could not be left alone, so the site soon included a three-room guard office, a separate kitchen and dining facility for the custody officers, and 12 sentry boxes. Some of the temporary structures can be seen in the foreground of this photograph. Architect Levi T. Schofield, from Cleveland, Ohio, and Col. William J. Hicks, a Raleigh native who served as assistant architect and project superintendent, drafted blueprints for the permanent structures. The result was a plan for a magnificent brick structure enclosed by a 20-foot high granite wall. Rock for the buildings and wall came from the quarry pictured here, which was surrounded by an 870-foot plank stockade.

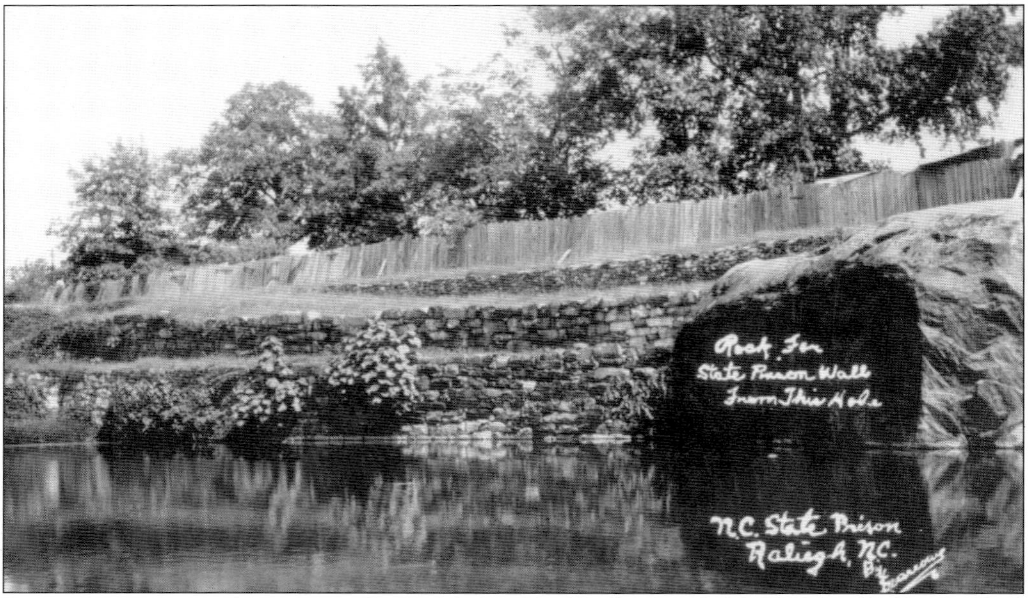

STOCKADE AROUND STONE QUARRY, 1880S. With the blueprints in hand, the commissioners put out bids. The construction process was divided into eight sections, and bids were accepted for each portion of the work, although bidders could put in offers for more than one section. The commissioners believed this system ensured better work would be done, it would be done cheaper, and it would be distributed in the fairest possible manner. As advertising for the bids began, workmen opened more fully the rock quarry to better demonstrate the available resources.

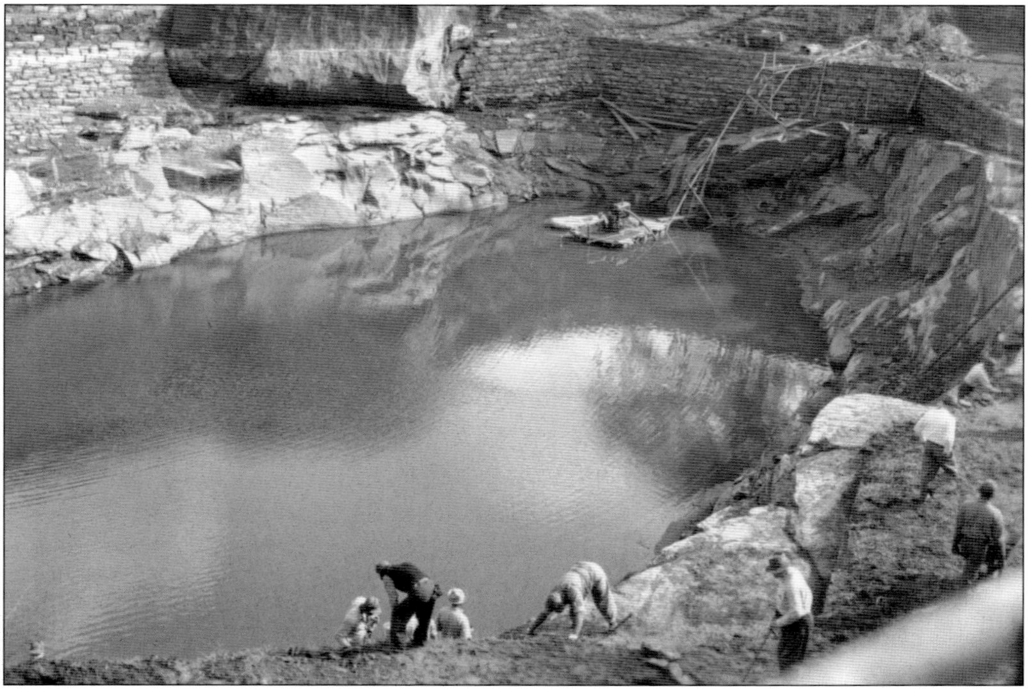

STONE QUARRY POND, 1950S. The opening of the quarry exposed the quality and quantity of stone to such an extent that the Coleman Brothers firm reduced their bid for the stonework by $20,000. Such a savings proved the correctness of the penitentiary's location.

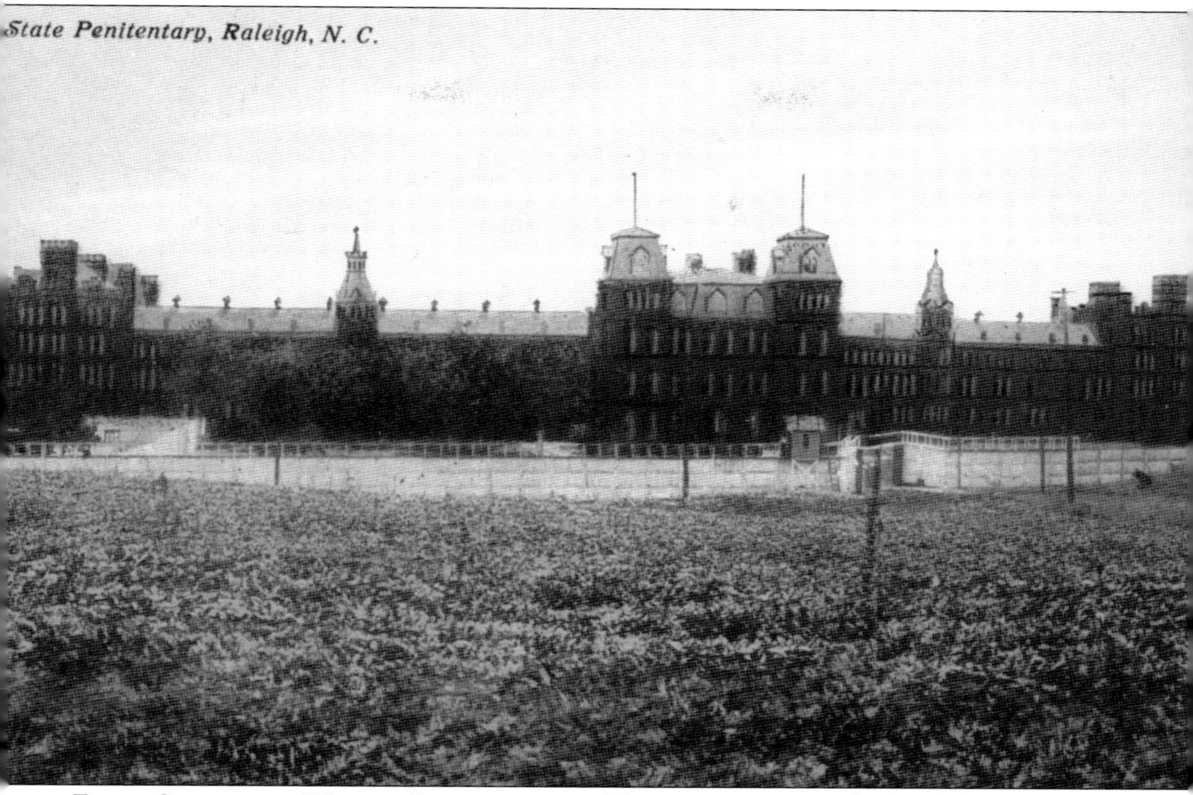

FRONT GATE IN THE WOODEN STOCKADE, 1911. The commissioners judged each bid on cost, capability, and responsibility. By December 1870, the eight bids were awarded. As recorded in the 1870 Commissioners Report to the General Assembly, Contract No. 1, for the stonework, was awarded to Coleman Brothers of Cincinnati, Ohio, at $341,986.65. Contract No. 2, for the brickwork, also was awarded to Coleman Brothers at $77,328.29.

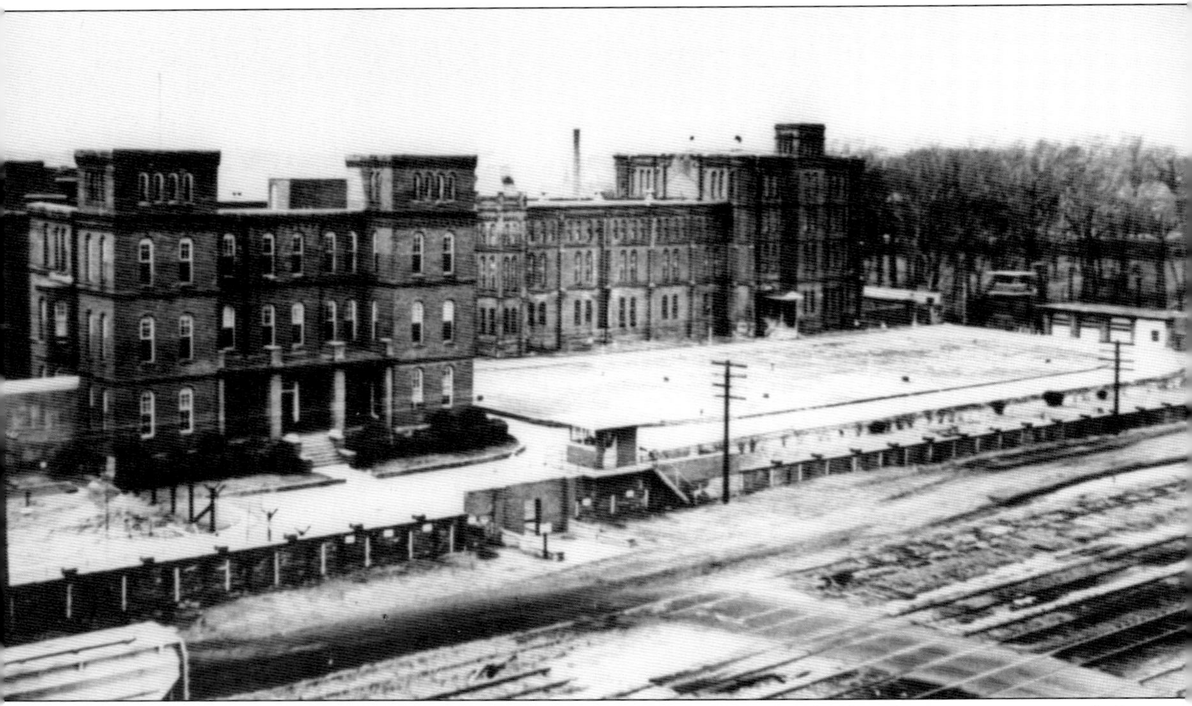

VIEW OF THE PRISON ENTRANCE AND WALL, 1900S. Contract No. 3, for the plastering, was awarded to J. Edward Kirby of Baltimore, Maryland, at $11,809.32. This contract was later transferred to John Hamil, of Raleigh, North Carolina. Contract No. 4, for the wrought ironwork, was divided: furnishing of the cell doors, frames, and locks was awarded to a Mr. Clements of Cincinnati, Ohio, at $30,000, while all other work was awarded to J.P. Stidham & Co. Philadelphia, Pennsylvania, at $70,584.03.

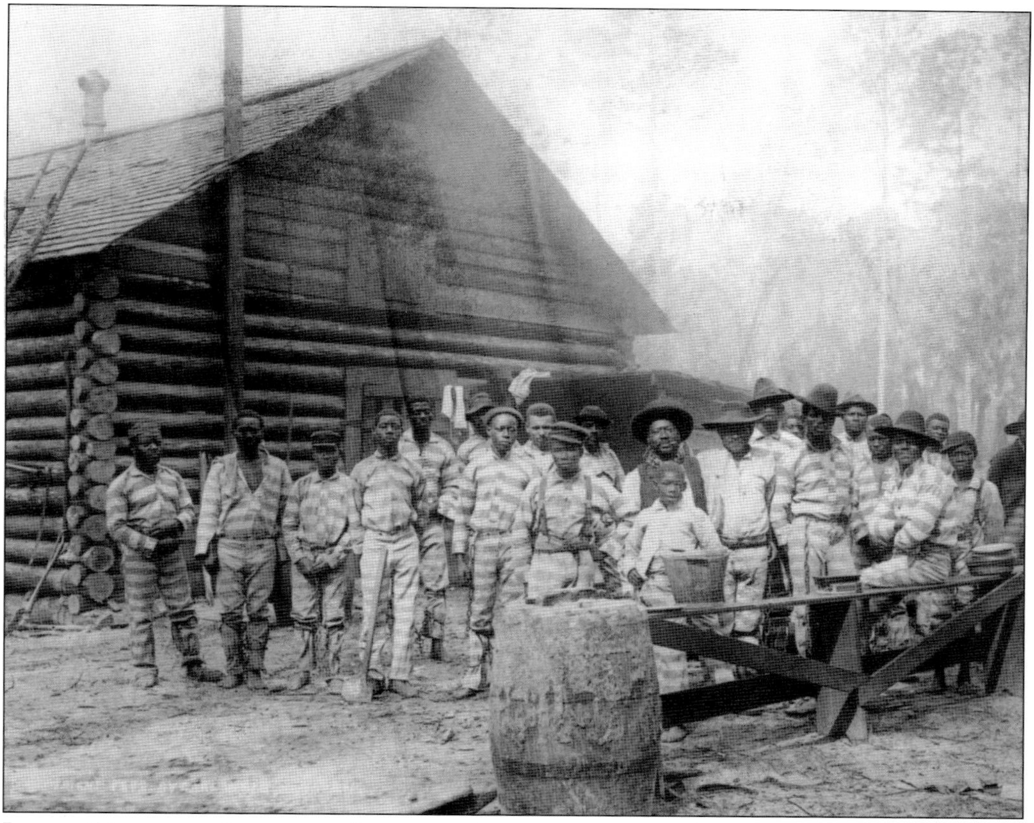

INMATE WORKERS IN FRONT OF A TEMPORARY STRUCTURE, 1880S. Contract No. 5, for carpentering, was awarded to Howard & Thomas of Cincinnati, Ohio, at $37,222.84. Contract No. 6, for painting, was awarded to Davies & Barnes of Cleveland, Ohio, at $6,700.69. Contact No. 7, for galvanized-iron work, was awarded to Dunn & Witt of Cincinnati, Ohio, at $23,718.98. Contract No. 8, for plumbing, was awarded to Murdock & Lacy of Cincinnati, Ohio, at $6,494.37.

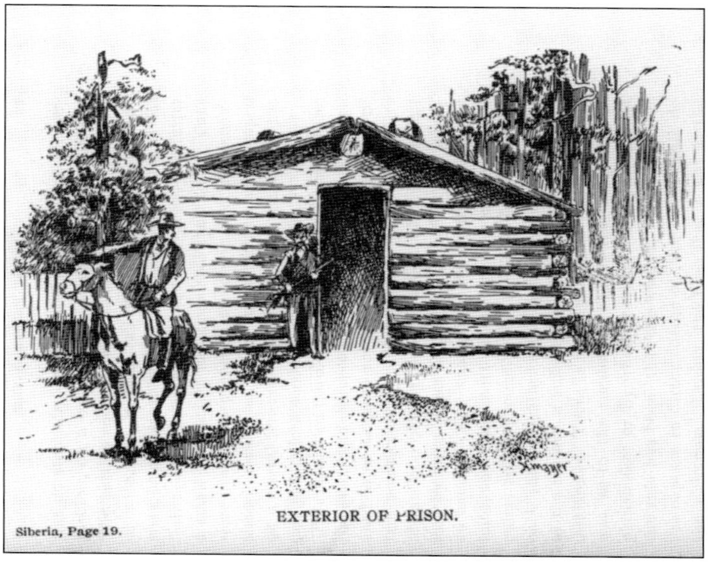

SKETCH OF TEMPORARY PRISON. In January 1870, Coleman Brothers became the first of the outside contractors to begin work on the penitentiary. Using 70 convicts a day, who were housed in crude log structures, the company obtained all the rock needed from the nearby quarry except for cut slabs for the cell floors (the rock from the quarry was too hard to be sawn on-site).

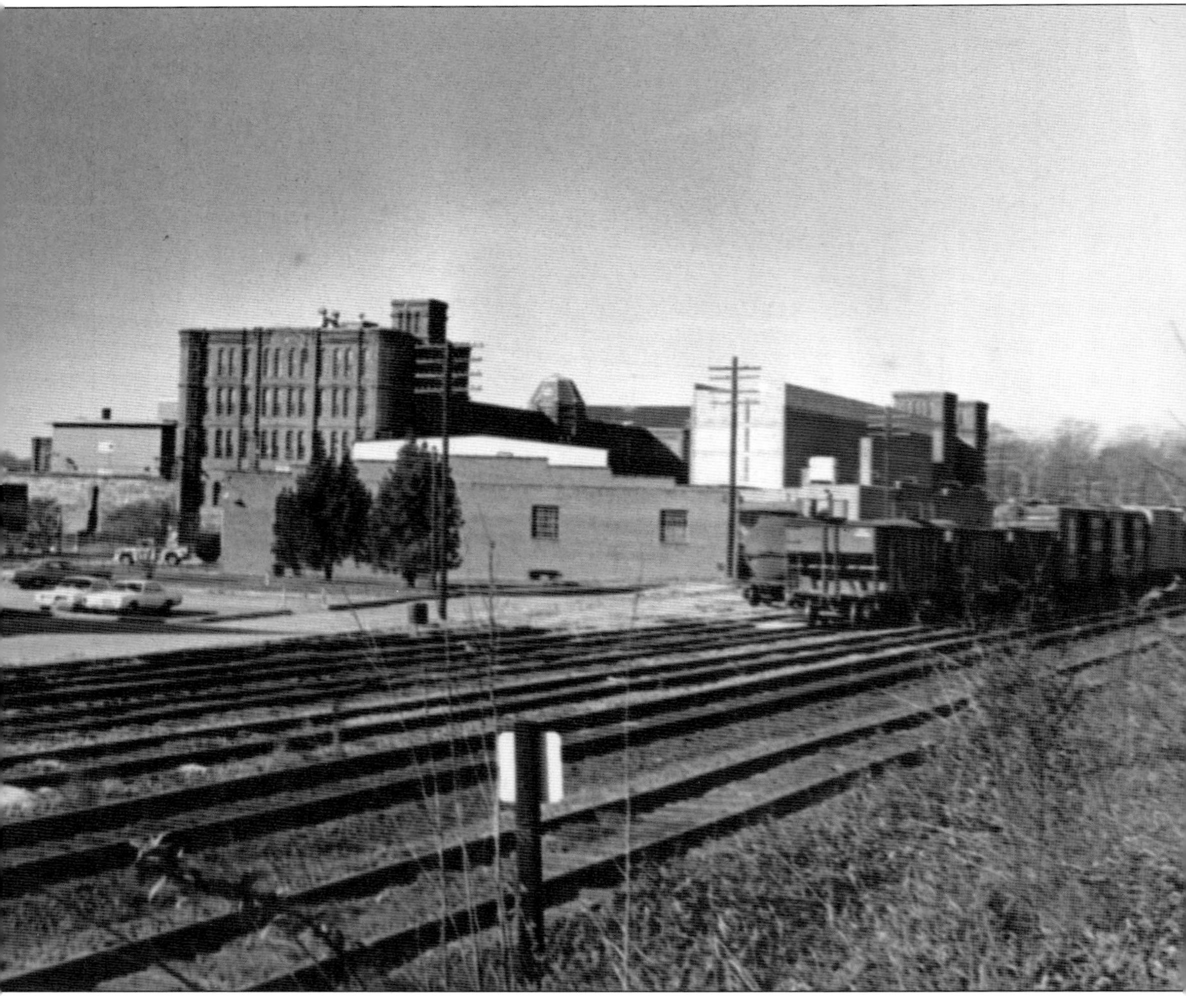

NORTH CAROLINA RAILROAD, EAST PAVILION IN BACKGROUND, 1970s. In 1872, a short turnout from the North Carolina Railroad into the penitentiary site was built. The 850-foot track connected the penitentiary with the railroad and facilitated the supply of building material. Thanks to the tracks, construction of the permanent buildings progressed, and by 1875, the first brick cell block, containing 64 cells, was complete.

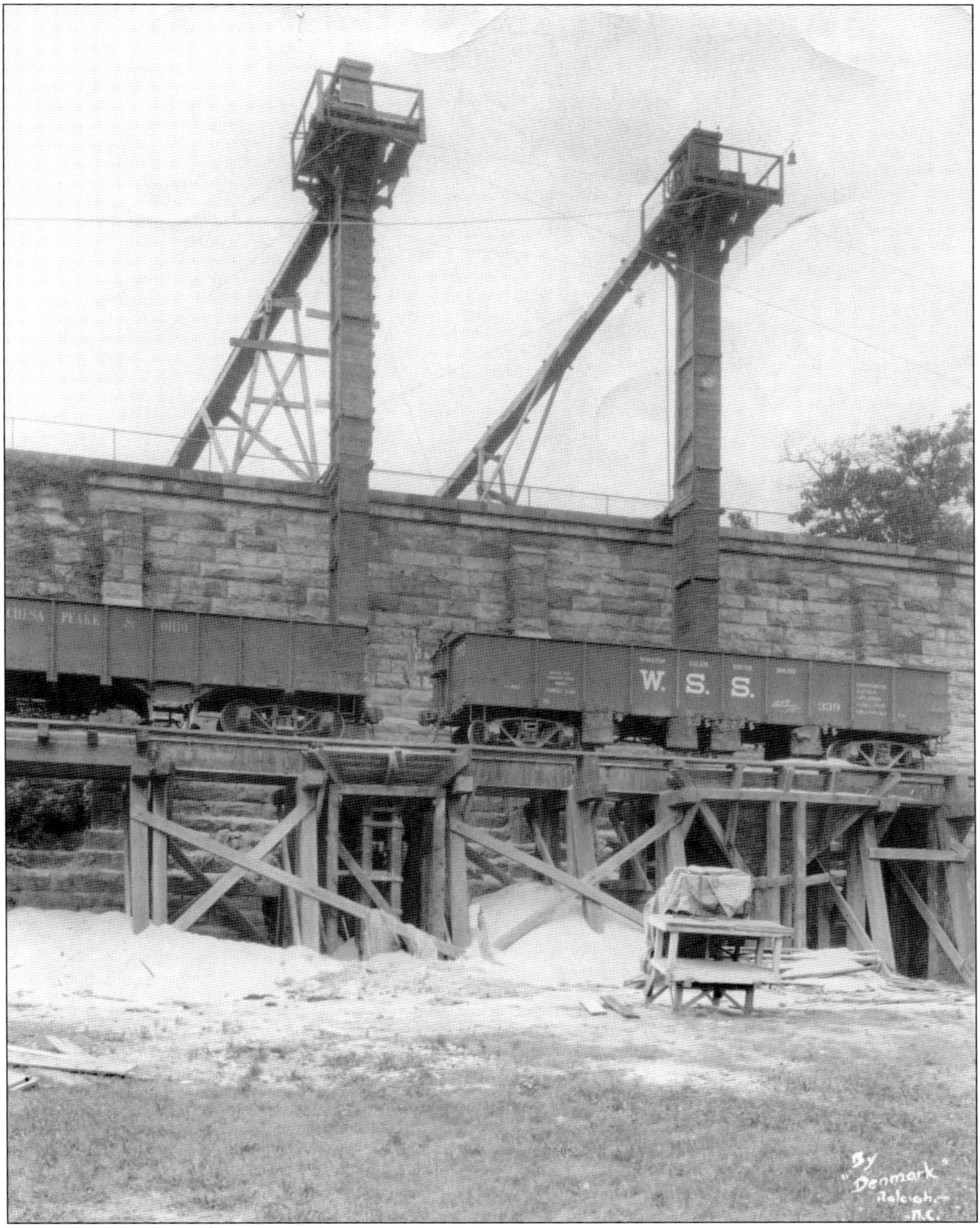

Unloading Point for Materials Entering the Prison. The connection with the railroad not only facilitated the original construction efforts, it also long provided an economical means of supplying the penitentiary and eased several major renovations the facility underwent in the 1930s, 1940s, and 1980s.

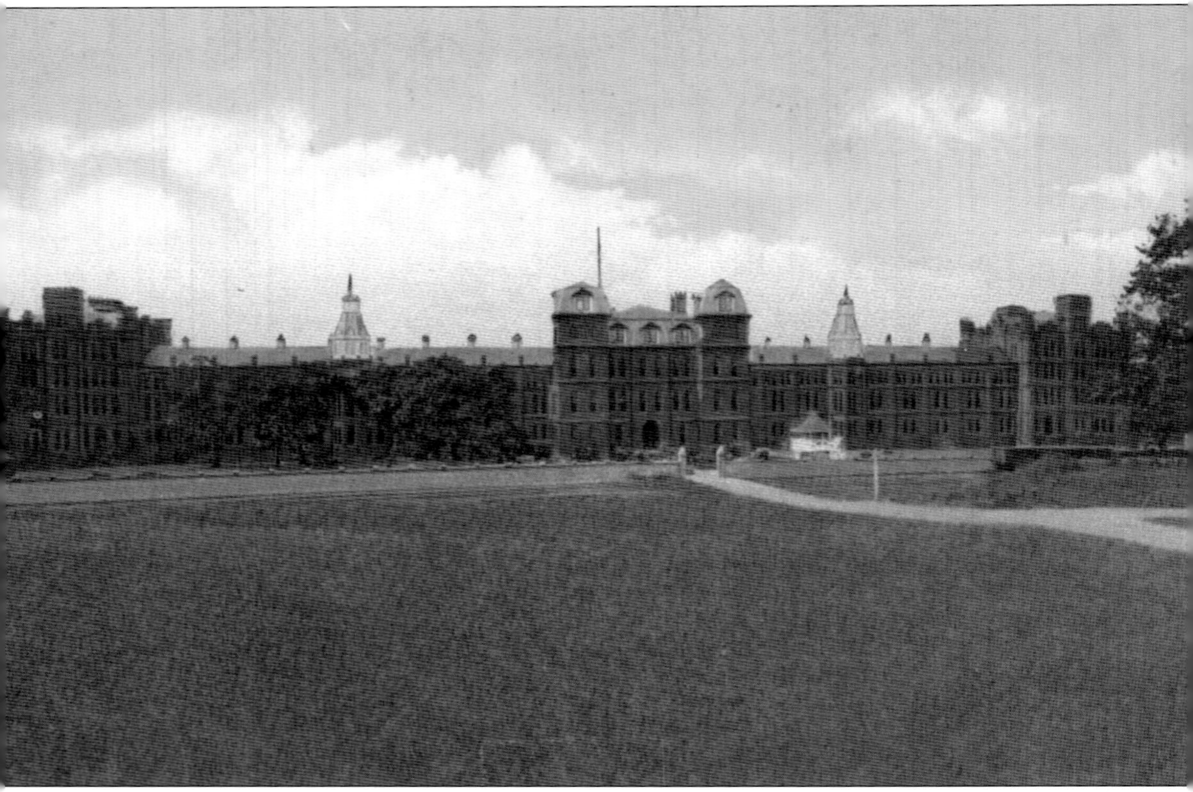

Picture Postcard, East Pavilion at Left, West Pavilion at Right, 1900s. Despite the progress, commissioners grew concerned with the generally slow pace of construction. In 1877, they appointed William J. Hicks architect and warden, thus giving him complete control of the institution and its manpower. Under Hicks's watch, the permanent stone outer wall was completed in 1880, and additional cell blocks, administrative buildings, and assorted facilities were completed over the next four years. By December 1884, some 14 years after construction began, the prison was complete.

Two

The Walls

The need to keep inmates confined within the borders of the penitentiary was obvious, so among the first tasks the administration faced was to complete a wall. The original wooden stockade served the purpose, but the penitentiary needed a permanent stone wall that provided more security. With access to the nearby quarry, construction crews set to work accessing the stone and laying the foundations for the wall.

Due to a lack of funds and the large number of convicts employed on other assignments, construction of the permanent wall progressed slowly. The commissioners requested additional money from the state to speed up the process, but little was forthcoming. On the evening of July 9, 1878, two white and six African American inmates attempted to scale the wooden stockade. Custody officers opened fire, killing one inmate and wounding another; the rest of the escapees fled back to their cells. Although the escape attempt failed, the effort gave proof to penitentiary administrators that the stone wall needed to be completed quickly.

Despite the desire to speed up completion, not until October 1880 was the wall complete. When fully erected, the hard granite barrier stood 20 feet high, was 17 feet thick at its base, and included offsets on every course. It created a forbidding presence that not only enclosed the penitentiary grounds but also set a menacing tone, which demonstrated clearly who held power in the institution. Armed custody officers walked the wall and manned the towers, and access points through the wall were heavily gated and manned by additional guard staff. Referring to the rear wall, warden William J. Hicks reported his satisfaction in the 1880 biennial report, bragging that North Carolina had as good, if not the best, prison wall in the United States. By 1921, a brick wall finally replaced the old and expensive board fence that surrounded the front of the prison.

As the decades passed, the wall was fortified and additional security installed. Internal and external lighting bathed the wall, barbed and high-tension wires made efforts to scale it unlikely, and cleared land on either side provided custody officers clear sight lines and offered escapees no place to hide. High-tech communication devices in the guard towers and the creation of additional posts beyond the original walls offered an added corridor of security. While escapes did happen, Central Prison's wall proved a formidable barrier.

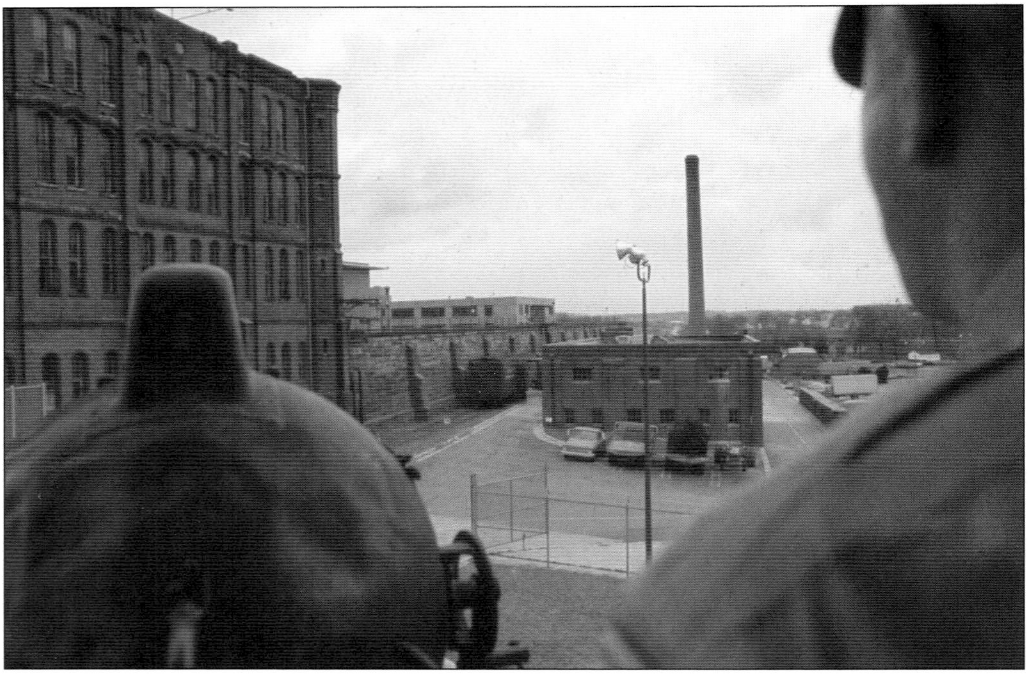

Guard's View from the Northeast, 1970s. By late 1878, the permanent stone exterior wall was nearing completion on the east, south, and west sides. The wall was a minimum of 15 feet high and tall enough for Warden Hicks to remove the temporary wooden pole stockade. The north side of the wall was incomplete, because that section was to be closed in by the main administration building, which was still under construction. The gap created a tempting spot for inmates to escape, as they saw other opportunities varnishing.

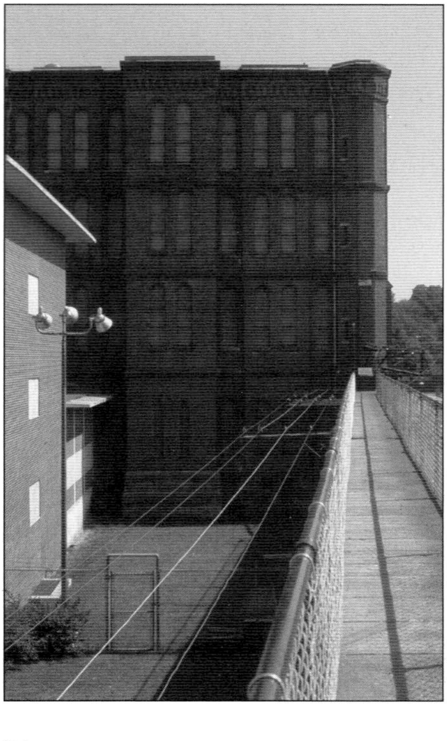

Walkway atop the Southeast, or Rear, Yard Wall, 1970s. This image provides a perspective of the exterior wall behind the main administration building. On the same trajectory, the wall extended beyond the other side of the main building and enclosed the entire northern front yard of the prison. Visible are modern additions to the wall's security, including high-powered lights, electrified high-tension wires running the length of the interior of the wall, and the guarded walkway.

View of the Rear, or South, Yard Wall, 1970s. Despite escape attempts, in 1878, Warden Hicks reported that discipline was good and had been maintained "without frequently resorting to severe measures."

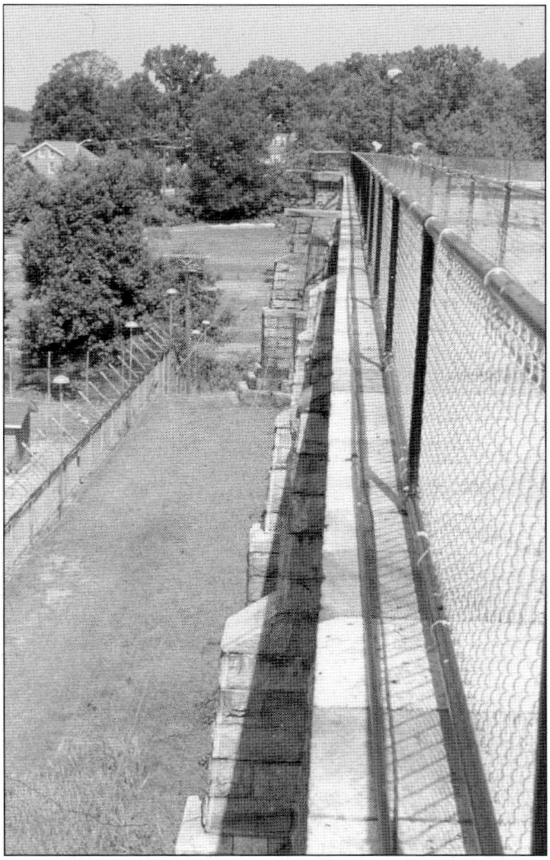

Guard Patrolling the Front, or North, Yard Wall, 1970s. Control of the prison yard and the institution as a whole depended upon the vigilance and close attention of the custody officers. They ensured that rules were obeyed, institutional order was maintained, and the safety and security of staff and inmates alike was secured.

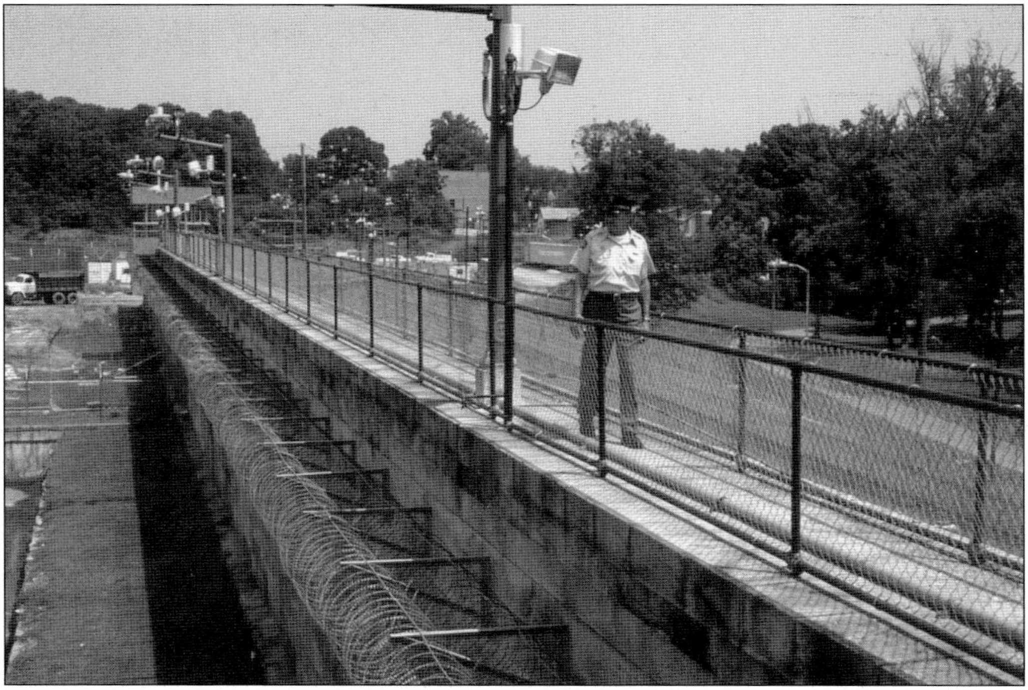

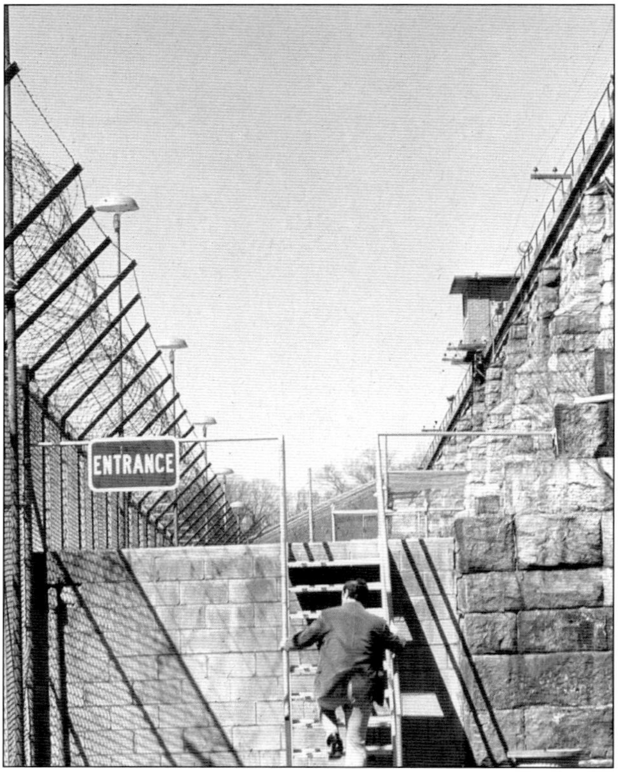

VIEW OF MIDWAY BETWEEN THE WALL AND THE PERIMETER FENCE. Improving prison security remained a constant concern for the administration, and widening the outer perimeter with additional obstacles was a key component of that effort. In this image, the cleared land beyond the stone wall and the exterior lighting are obvious. So, too, is the exterior guard tower as well as the chain-link fence topped with double rows of barbed wire.

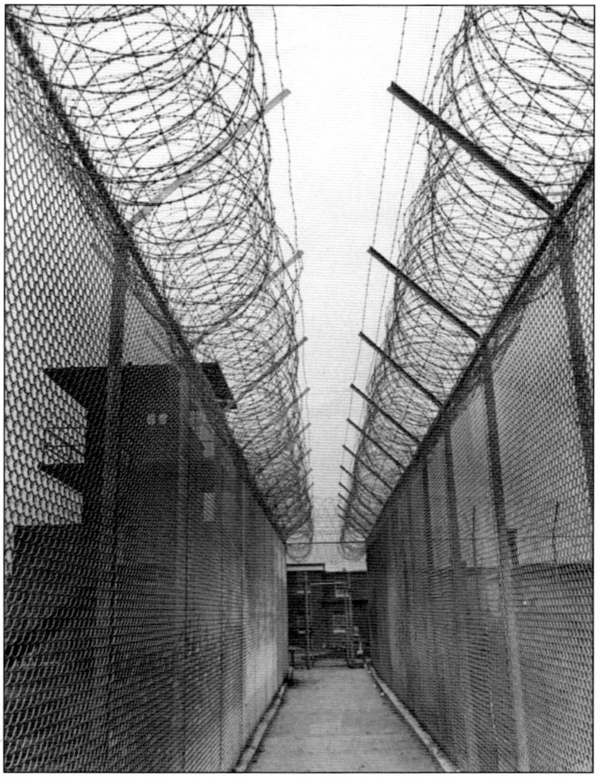

GUARD TOWER. In this image, the cleared land beyond the stone wall and the exterior guard tower, as well as the chain-link fence topped with double rows of barbed wire, is obvious. The exterior towers stood apart from the main wall and provided an extra layer of security. High-powered spotlights provided the ability to pick out inmates who might attempt to escape under cover of darkness.

Penitentiary Officials outside the Wall, 1970s. This photograph offers some perspective on the height of the wall and demonstrates the menacing position the custody officers atop it had over the inmates. As the penitentiary was updated, state officials often visited to oversee the renovations and progress. The wall offered a perfect vantage point to view many of the exterior renovations and was a popular place for administrators and staff to take visiting dignitaries.

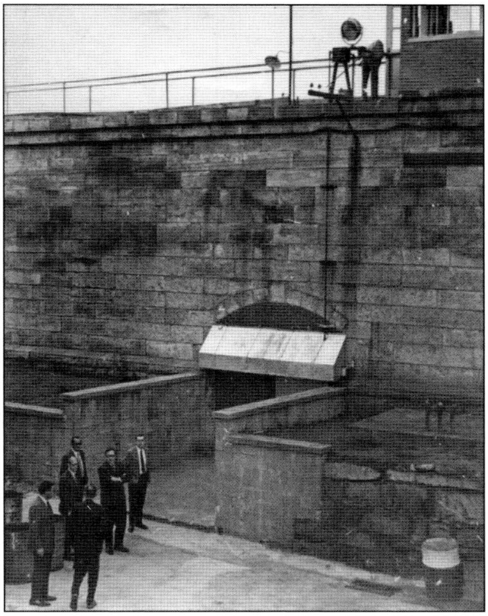

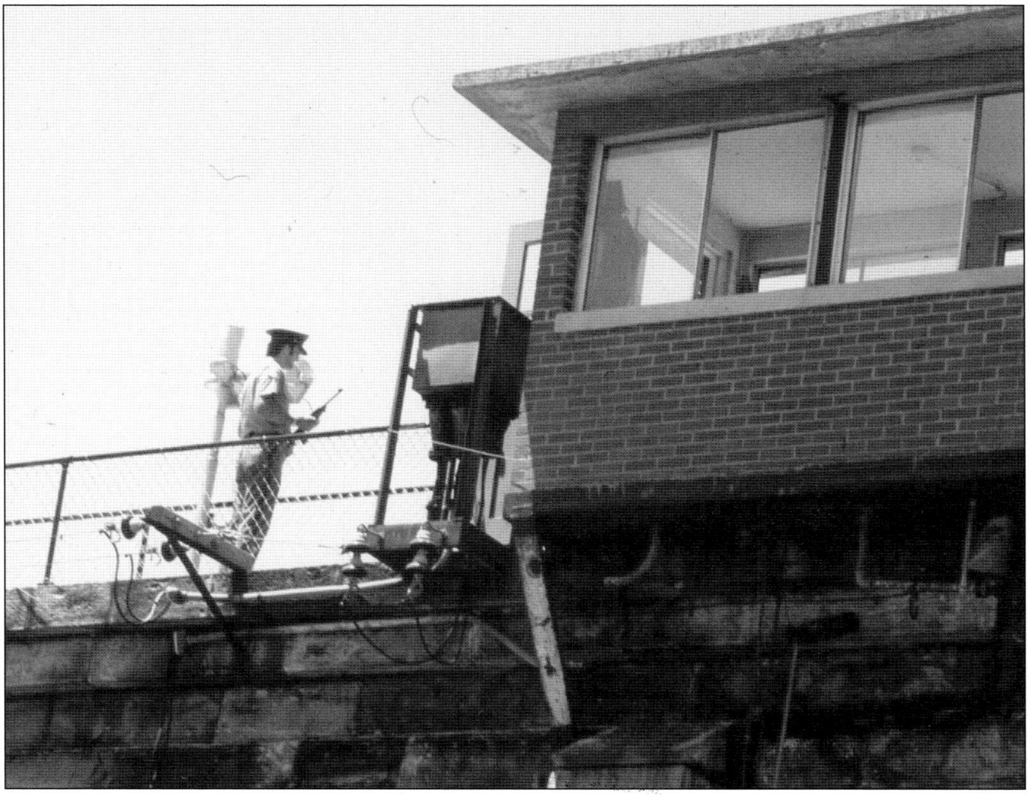

Armed Tower Guard. The wall included evenly spaced towers from which custody officers could pinpoint any unrest on the yard, call in additional officers, coordinate a response, and should the situation require it, provide lethal force. From their posts, they could view activity within the penitentiary walls, spy an inmate who managed to get beyond the walls, and observe suspicious activity in the penitentiary's exterior vicinity.

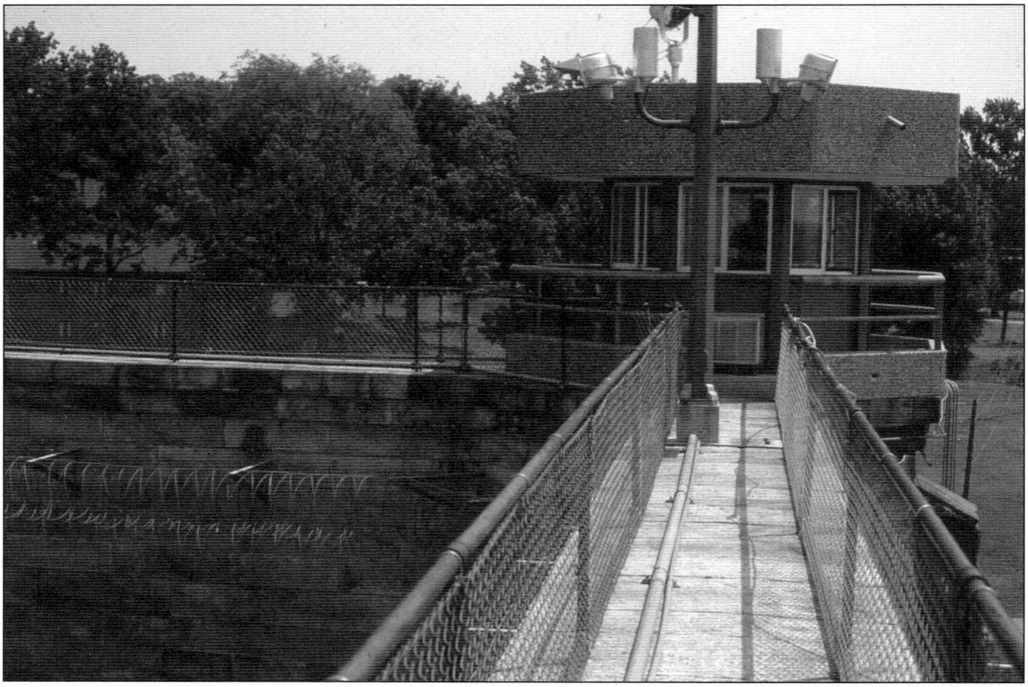

Corner Guard Tower. Each corner of the wall sported a guard tower. In this photograph, the corner tower, the walkway atop the wall, the modern cameras and sensors providing additional security, and the interior barbed wire are apparent. The wall was a multifaceted component that provided both a standing barrier as well as the platform for mobile observation and reaction.

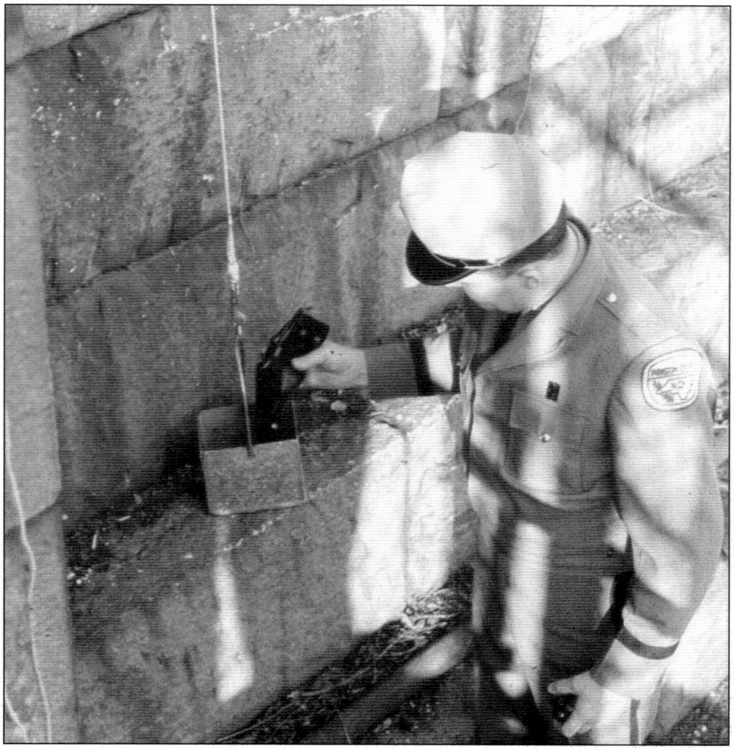

Low-Tech Transfer. Despite the high-tech nature of much of the penitentiary, in some instances, communication between the custody officers on the ground and those on the wall was rather old-fashioned. In an effort to avoid leaving their posts on the penitentiary grounds, custody officers often used a rope and bucket to transfer small items.

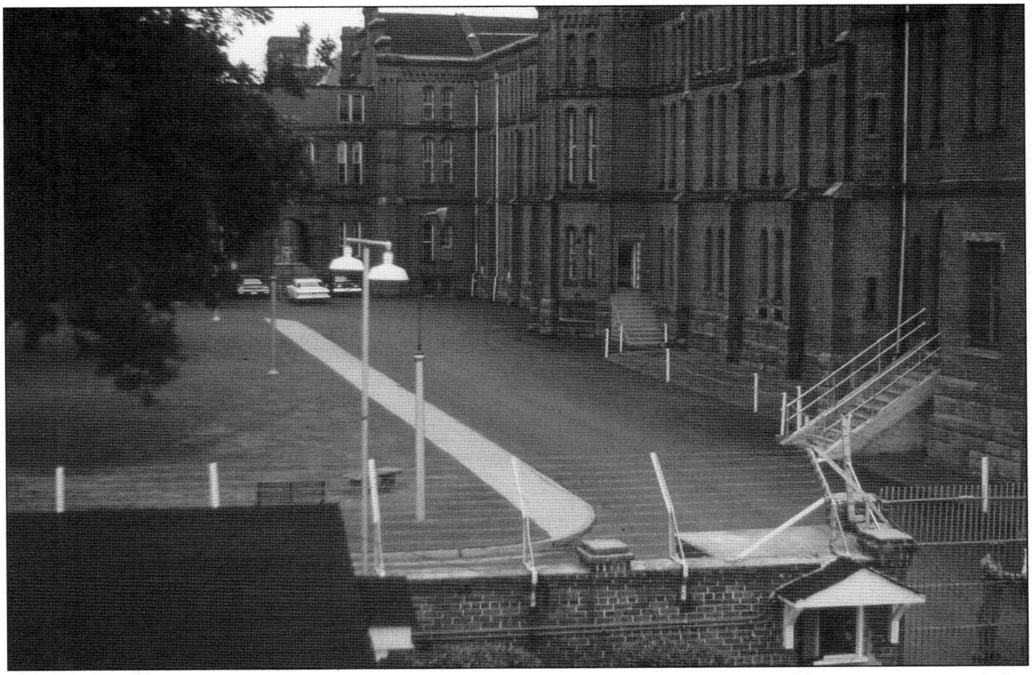

NORTHWEST WALL LOOKING AT THE FRONT ENTRANCE, 1970S. Pictured here is a view of the front entrance to the administration building. Visible on the lower right is a guard attending a steel gate. The guard room to the left of the entrance gate and the high-tension wires atop a brick fence are also seen. This entrance was doubly gated and manned as a precaution against any breach of security.

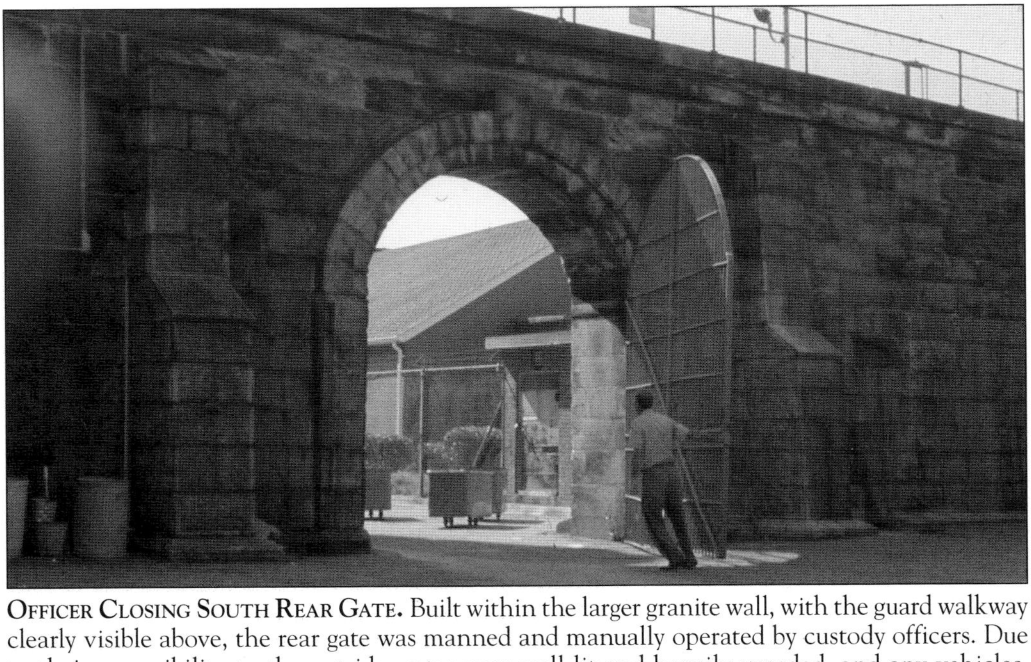

OFFICER CLOSING SOUTH REAR GATE. Built within the larger granite wall, with the guard walkway clearly visible above, the rear gate was manned and manually operated by custody officers. Due to their accessibility to the outside, gates were well lit and heavily guarded, and any vehicles, material, or individuals entering the prison were searched thoroughly and closely monitored.

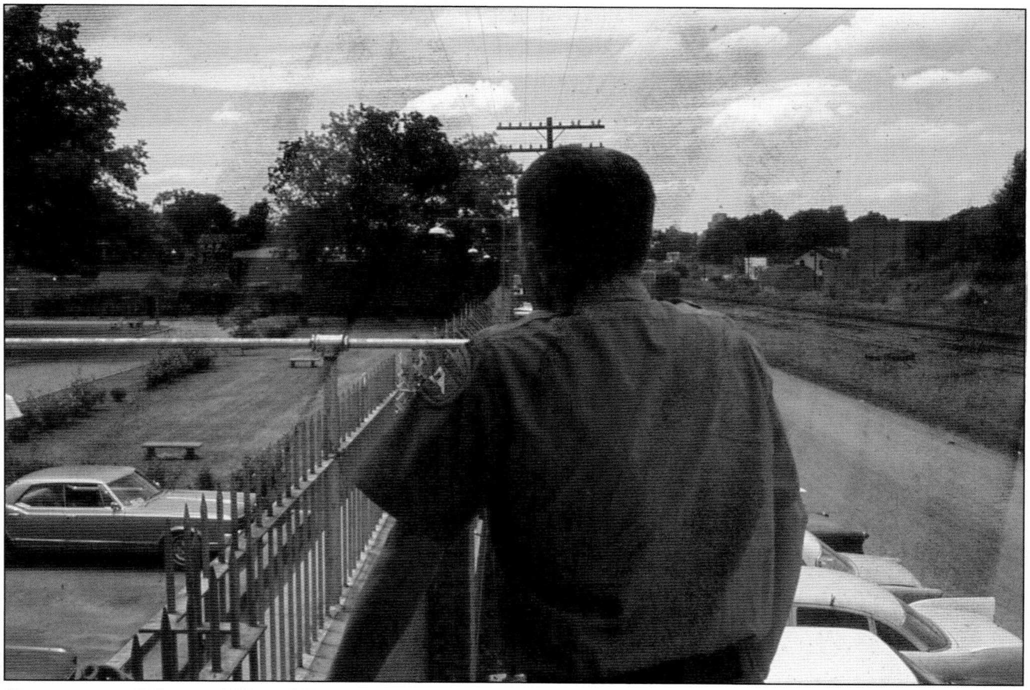

Officer on North Wall Facing the Administration Building. Inmates were not the only ones the custody officers had to watch over and protect. Pictured here is the main entrance parking lot, where custody officers and visitors alike parked.

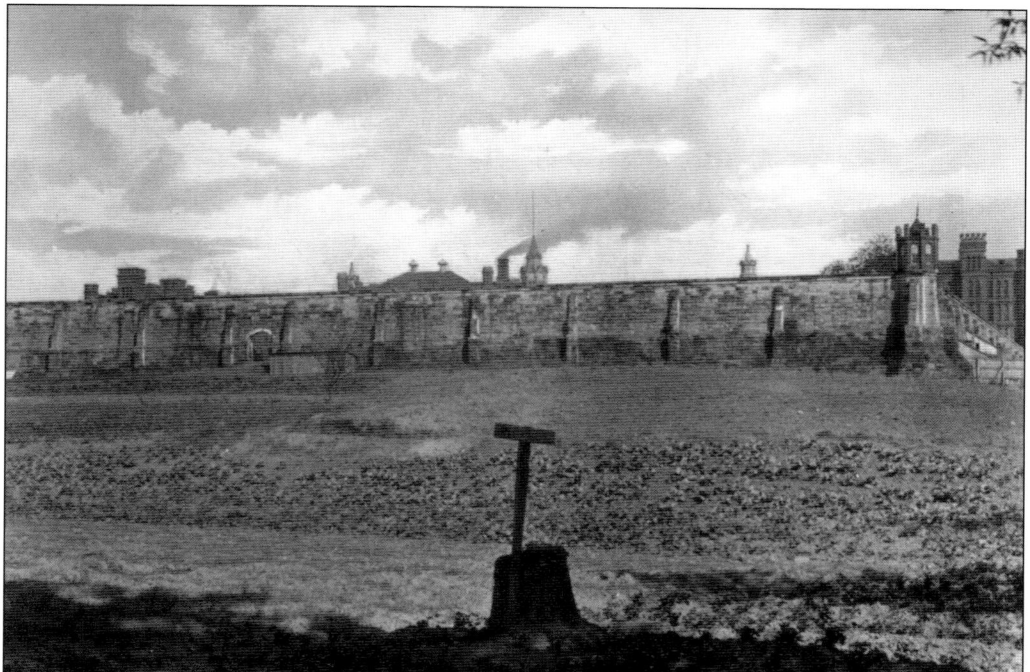

Rear, or South, Wall, 1918. Central Prison's imposing stone wall was one of its defining features, and it stood for more than a century as the final barrier between inmates and the outside world.

Three

THE PHYSICAL PLANT

Central Prison was modeled on the Auburn System, by which inmates were isolated except for their work assignments and at meals; silence was enforced at all times. To facilitate these strictures, the penitentiary consisted of two distinct cell houses divided into four cell blocks of five tiers each. Each tier consisted of 30 cells, situated back to back, with punishment cells located on the lowest tier. Originally, cell blocks and dining areas were segregated by gender and race, but women were moved to their own correctional facility in 1935, and in 1965, the penitentiary was desegregated. The penitentiary also changed its behavioral expectations over the years, as administrators dropped the isolation of inmates and the demand for silence. Those were not the only changes. As the number of inmates grew, the facility eventually became overcrowded. Initially, the penitentiary doubled cell occupancy, but it later constructed dormitory-style housing, in which low-risk inmates lived in an open housing unit. With the total reconstruction of the penitentiary in the 1980s, additional units were added to ease the crowding issues.

However the inmates were organized, their maintenance was of prime importance to the administration, and security was the central focus. Each cell door could be locked individually, each tier could be locked as a whole, and an entire cell house could be closed off from the rest of the penitentiary. When inmates left their cells, custody officers held them under close scrutiny, and with the evolution of the penitentiary, fenced and wired walkways offered further control during periods of movement.

The penitentiary had to do more than contain the inmates. It also had to meet their needs. The institution fed them, cared for their medical needs, put them to work, and offered spiritual and educational opportunities. Beyond the cells, therefore, Central Prison included a kitchen, bakery, classrooms, workshops, hospital, and chapel. By balancing security with the needs of the inmates, the penitentiary's physical plant created a self-contained institutional community.

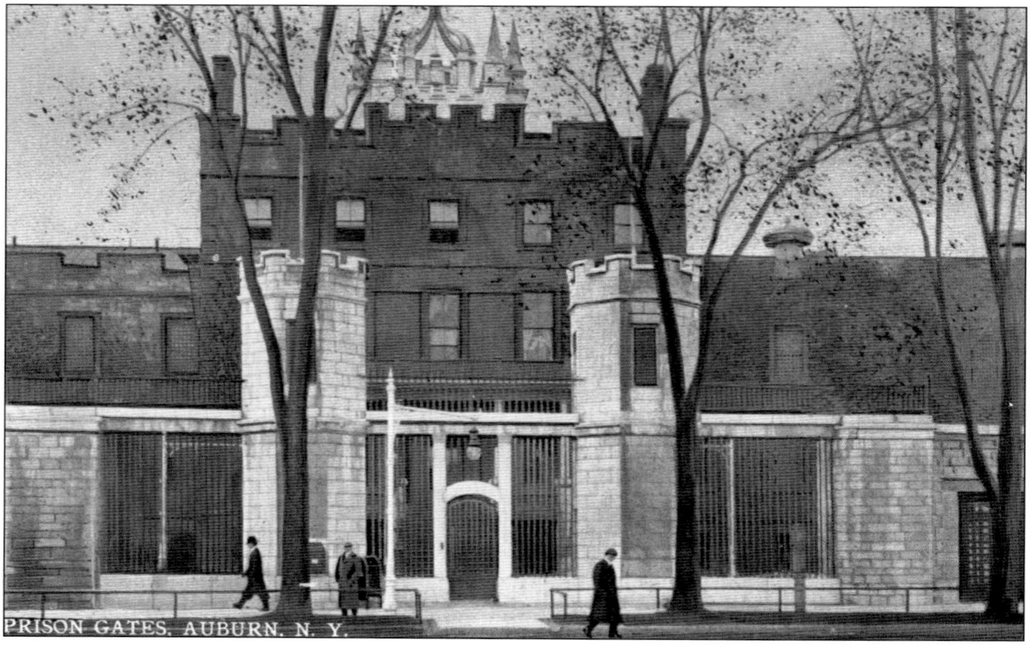

FRONT ENTRANCE OF AUBURN STATE PENITENTIARY, 1920S. The North Carolina State Prison was based on the Auburn system of prison discipline. The Auburn system (also known as the silent system) was a penal method developed in the 1820s in Auburn, New York. During the day, prisoners worked and ate meals together but were forbidden to speak. At night, they returned to solitary confinement in small individual cells. Custody officers enforced silence at all times.

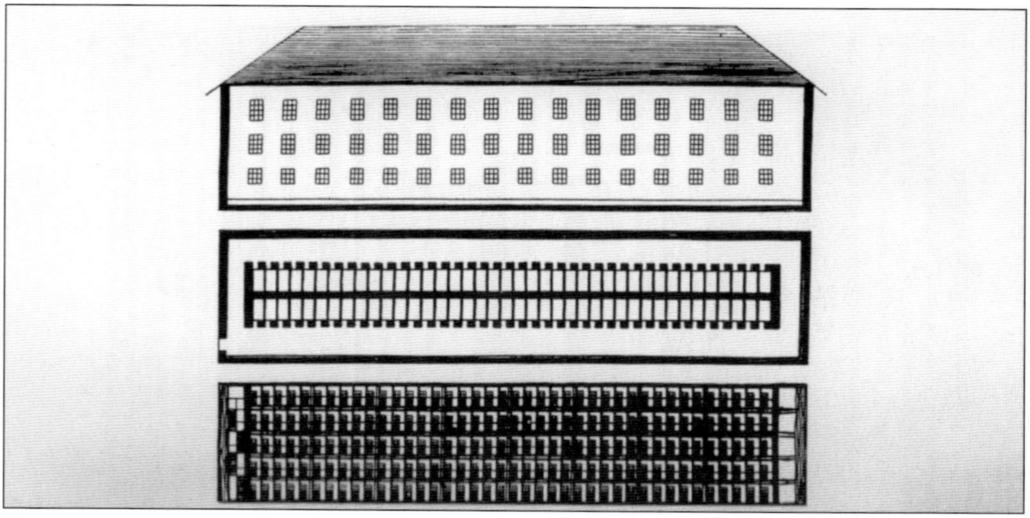

DIAGRAM OF AUBURN CELL HOUSE. In this image, the top illustration shows the Auburn-style cell house from the outside. The middle is an overhead view of the cell block showing the cells arranged back to back with a hallway around the entire block. The bottom is a view of the cell block from the inside showing all five tiers on one side, the doors to all the cells, and a staircase on the left. The North Carolina State Prison copied this classic design.

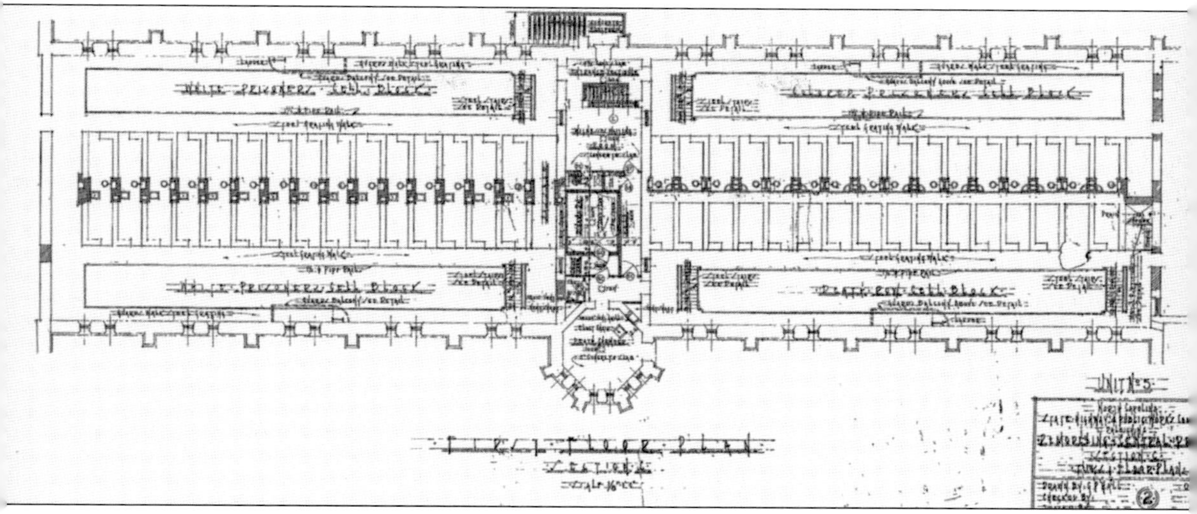

BLUEPRINT OF C- AND D-BLOCK. Each cell house was divided into two blocks (C and D cell blocks in the blueprint above) with 160 cells (on five tiers) on each side. Thus, in the blueprint above, there are 320 cells (160 in C-Block and 160 in D-Block). The cells were eight by six feet and seven feet high with ventilation at the top and bottom and without plumbing. The cells contained strap-iron beds with cotton and corn-shuck mattresses, blankets, sheets, and pillowcases. This blueprint is for the first floor of the east cell house. C-Block, on the left, housed White inmates. D-Block, on the right, housed African American inmates on the far side and death row inmates on the near side. The death chamber was located in the octagonal section in the middle front of the cell house.

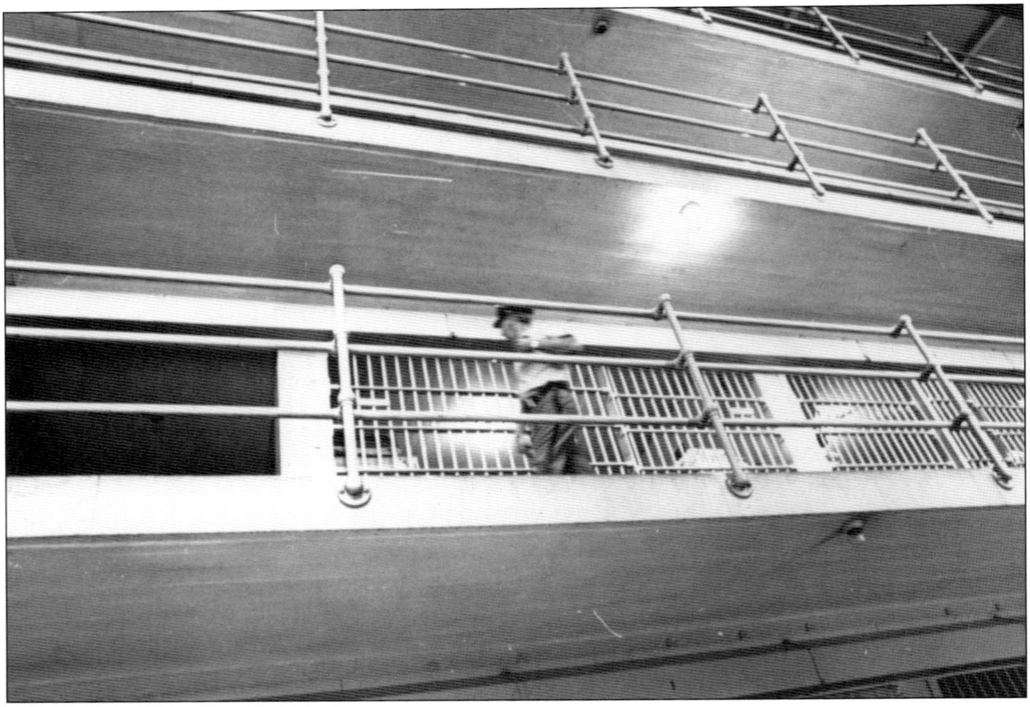

CUSTODY OFFICER TAKING THE COUNT, 1970S. Inmates were counted every two hours. The "in-count" occurred when all offenders were in the cell blocks in the morning and at night. "Out -counts" occurred during the day in the workshops, hospital, and yard.

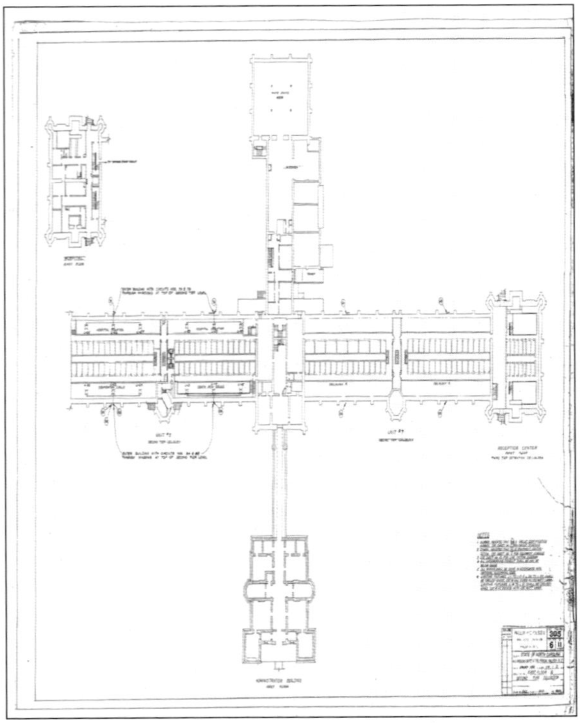

BLUEPRINT OF CENTRAL PRISON. This blueprint shows the entire penitentiary. The front section, extending north from the middle of the blueprint, contained the administrative offices. Moving south along the central corridor led to the cell houses, kitchen, and the dining hall in the rear of the institution. The hospital and chapel, both located in the east pavilion, are depicted separately in the upper left. The "Dangerous Insane" unit was located in the west pavilion.

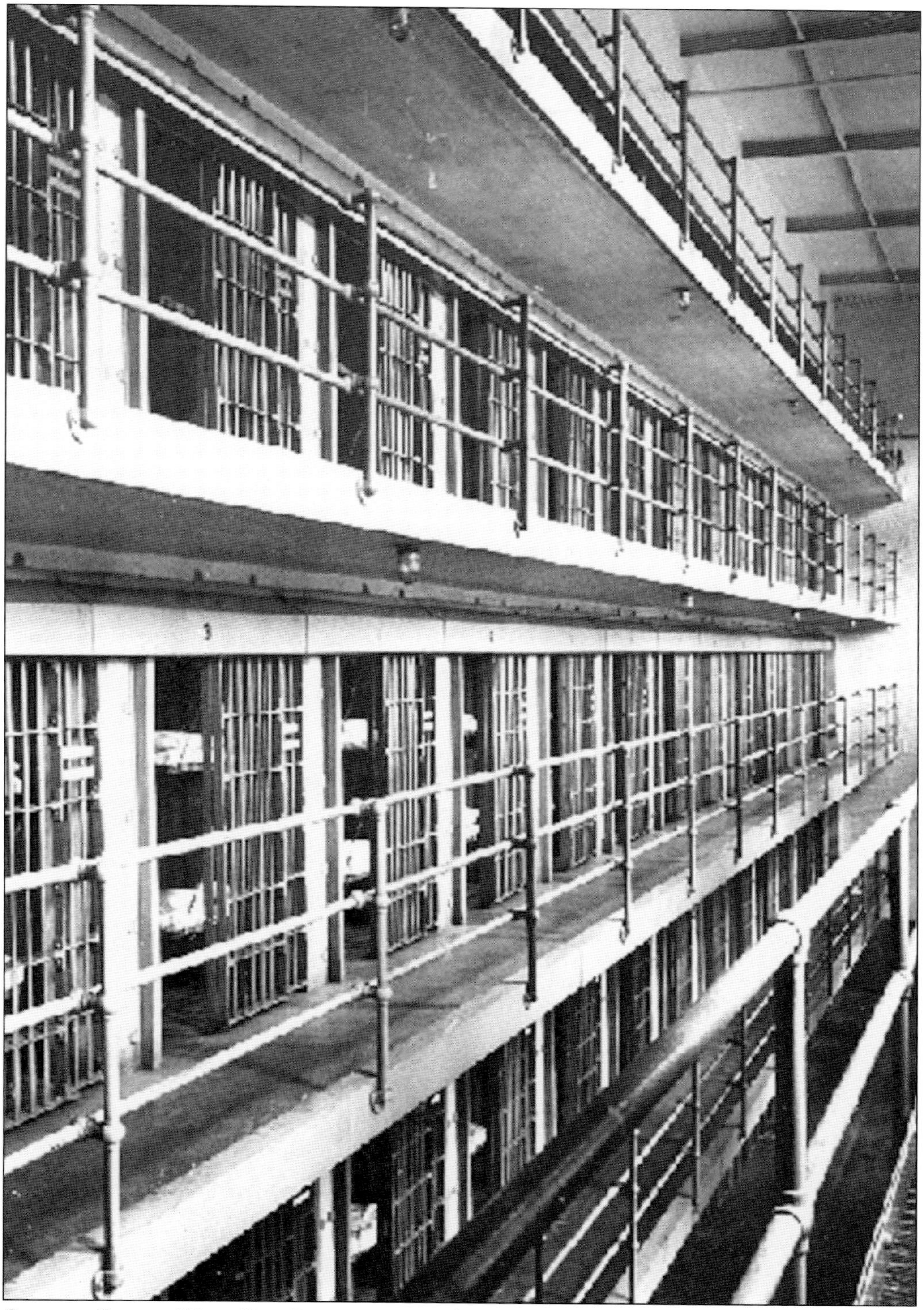

Central Prison, West Cell Block, 1934. In keeping with the Auburn Model, cell blocks were five tiers high and had 32 cells per tier (160 total), located back-to-back with a walkway around each level and a stairway at the east end. Punishment cells were on the lowest tier.

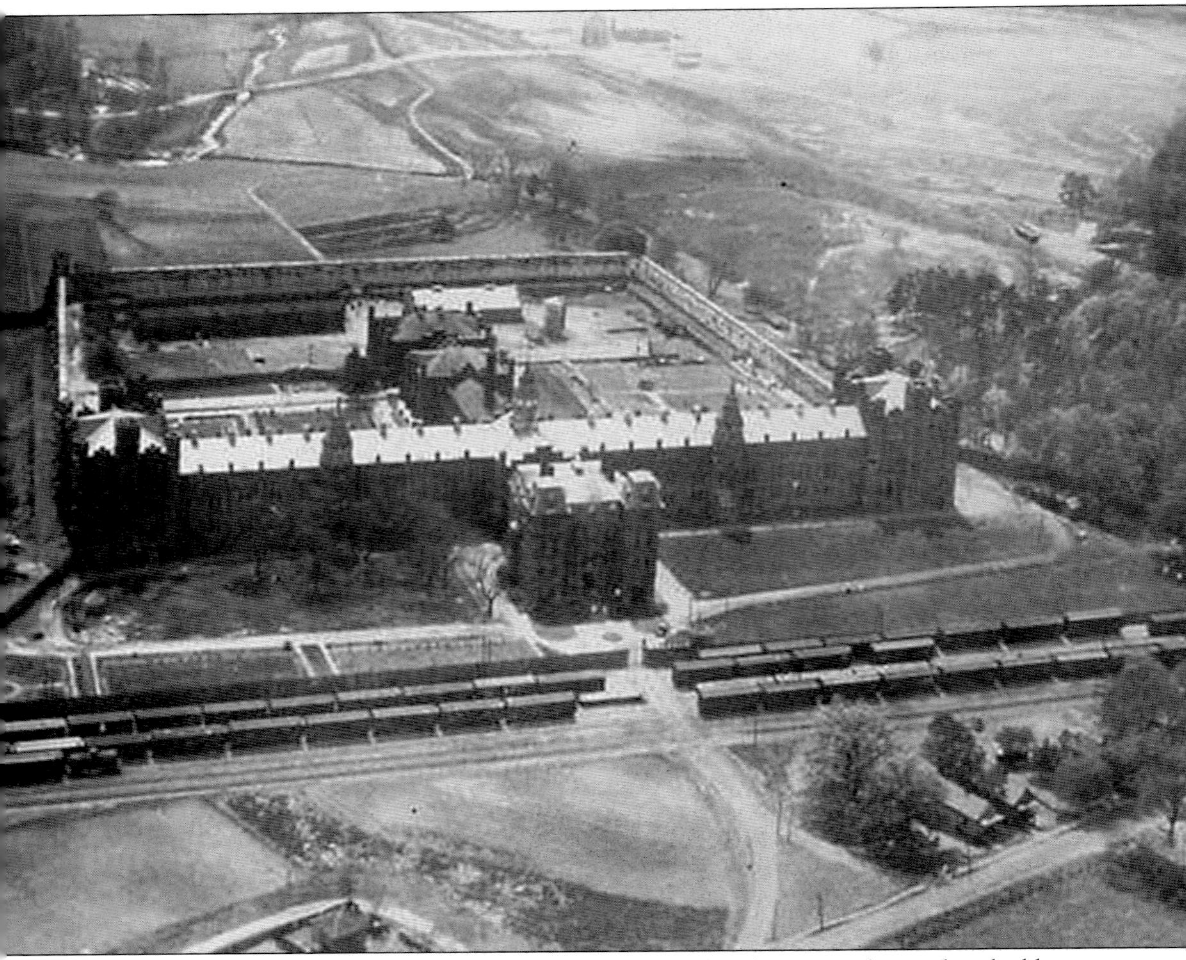

Aerial View, 1900s. This exterior view shows the completed prison as depicted in the blueprints. The administration building is flanked on the left and the right by the cell houses and the east and west pavilions.

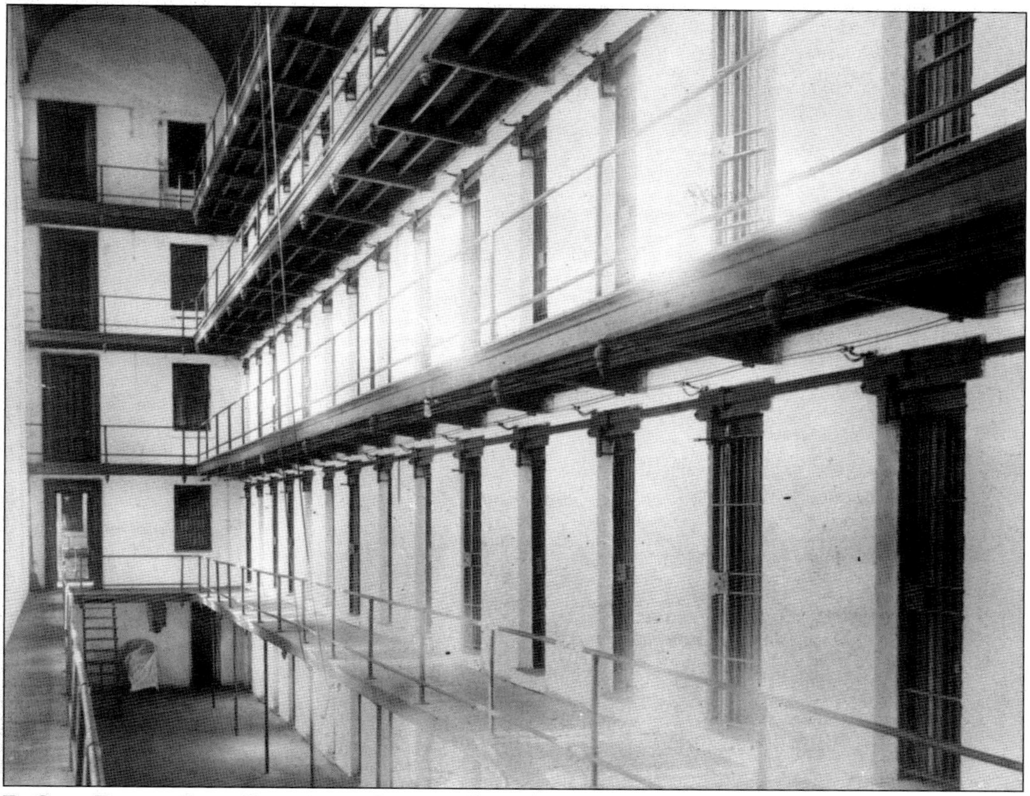

D Cell Block, Iron Bar, 1919. Every cell in the penitentiary was locked with a keyed door lock. This was but the first means of inmate control. In addition, there was a long iron bar, or brake, that ran the length of the tier and allowed custody officers to secure the entire tier at one time. When the bar was rolled forward, none of the cell doors would open even if an individual door was unlocked. Clearly evident above each cell door and running the length of each tier is the brake.

Cell-Block Interior, 1919. The brake was activated by a lever or crank located at the far end of the tier that was securely housed in a lockbox. When the brake was in the forward position, an iron flange extended down over the door frame of each cell. The flanges can be seen extending down from the brake on the upper left side of each cell door. When officers were ready to release the entire cell block, they rolled the bar backward, along with the flange, so that the doors could open. In the event officers did not want a particular inmate to leave his cell, they simply key-locked his door.

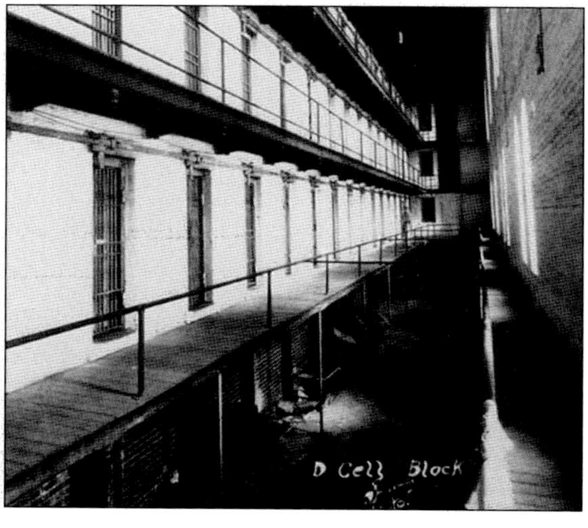

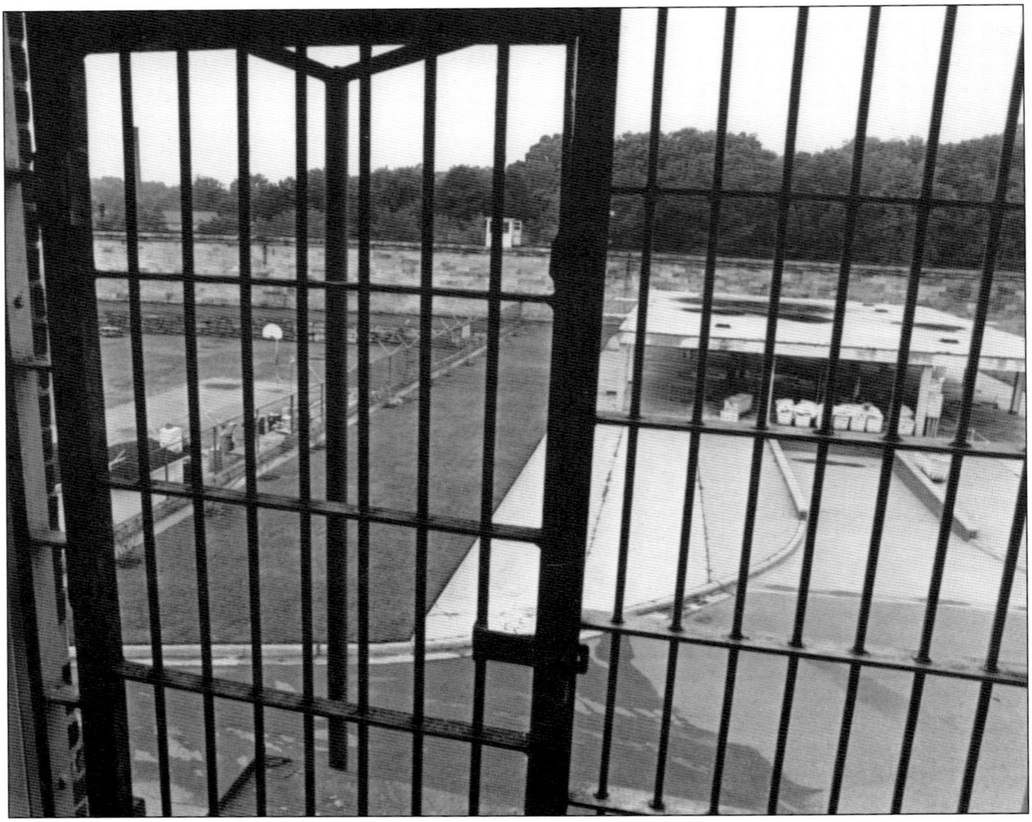

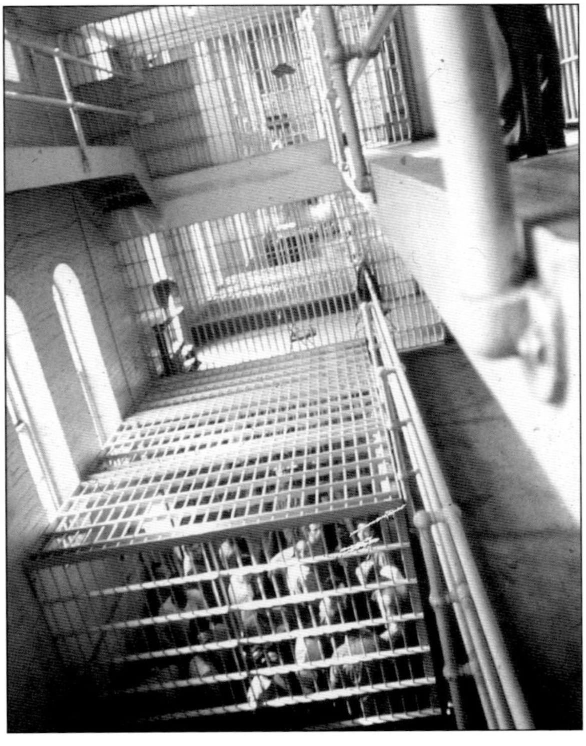

Cell-House Door, 1900s. A third device used to control inmates was the cell-house door. By design, there was only one door in cell houses. Thus, in order to escape from the cell house, much less from the prison itself, an inmate needed to defeat three locks: the one on the cell door, the brake over the cell door; and the door to the cell house itself.

Sally Port, 1970s. Another means of inmate control was the sally port, which was a secure, controlled entryway. When inmates entered the cell house from the outside, they entered this cage first. Only after the exterior cell-house door was closed and locked was the cell-block door opened. This created a choke point and prevented the free flow of inmates into or out of the cell houses.

CUSTODY OFFICER ON CELL-BLOCK TIER, 1970S. Should an inmate defeat all those locks, he or she still needed to outwit the custody officers who walked the tiers and avoid detection by the custody officers manning the towers along the wall.

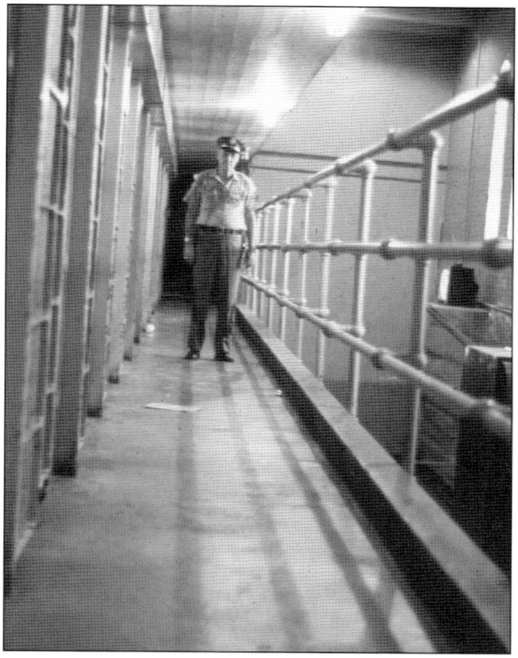

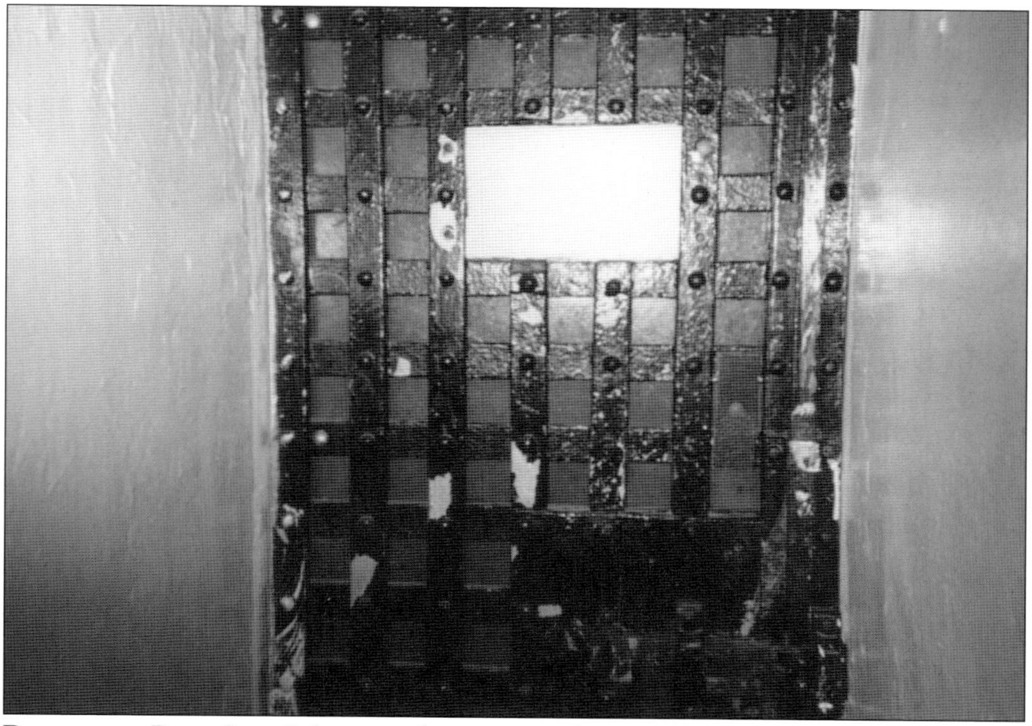

DISCIPLINARY DARK CELL. Solitary-confinement punishment cells like the one pictured here were located on the bottom tier in D-Block on the side designated for African American prisoners. Some of the punishment cells included a solid wood door behind the iron door to shut out all light. On a bread and water diet, the time an inmate could spend in solitary was limited. Those subjected to such punishment were checked regularly for any physical or mental health issues. The dark cell was used as a form of punishment well into the 20th century at Central Prison.

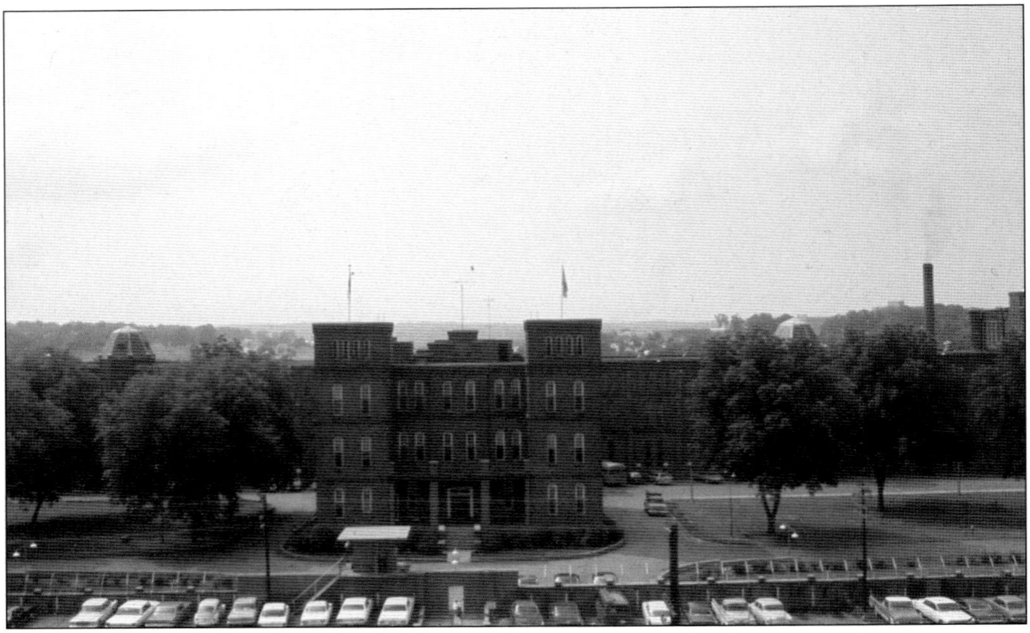

ADMINISTRATION BUILDING, 1950S. The central administrative building stood three stories and opened on an 18-by-20-foot vestibule surrounded by business offices with bedrooms above. It was separated from the main cell blocks by an extended corridor.

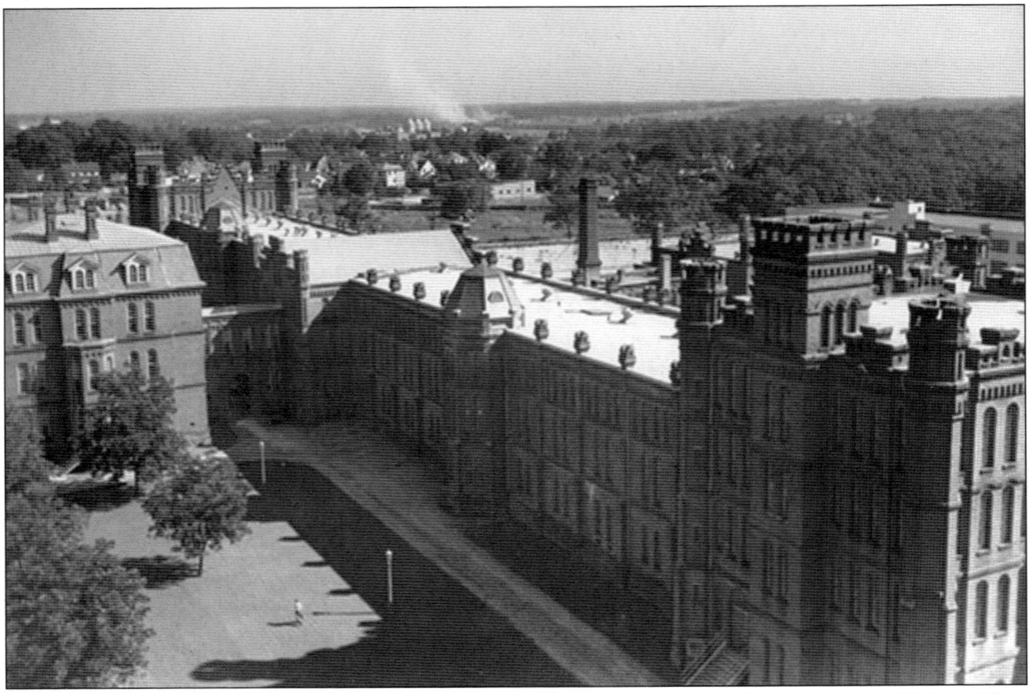

VIEW OF THE PRISON WITH THE TURRETED WEST PAVILION IN THE FOREGROUND, 1940S. This image depicts well the separation of the main administrative building, on the far left, from the cell houses. Also clearly evident is the sense of Central Prison as a majestic castle-like structure, with its brick and stone construction, the several turrets and cupolas, the narrow wall-length windows, and the two prominent pavilions.

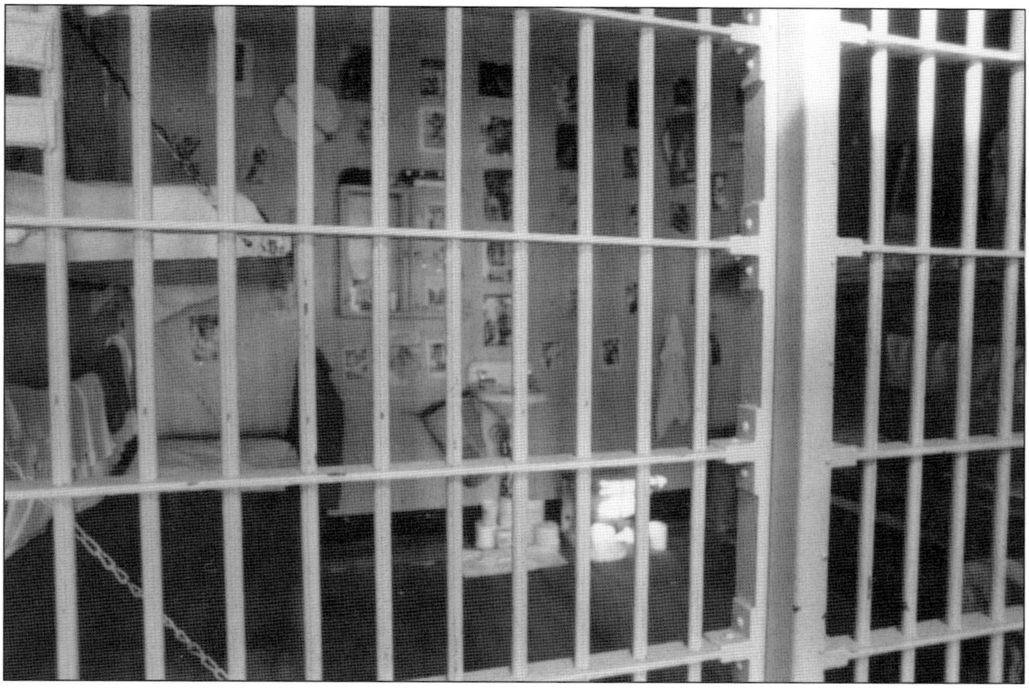

Two-Man Cell, 1950s. In the biennial report for 1932, warden H.H. Honeycutt reported, "Due to the large number of prisoners received during this period we have been overcrowded all the time during the two years. And due to this overcrowded condition and with the equipment we have it has been necessary to place double deck beds in cells originally intended for one prisoner only, consequently we have two men in many cells that were only intended for one."

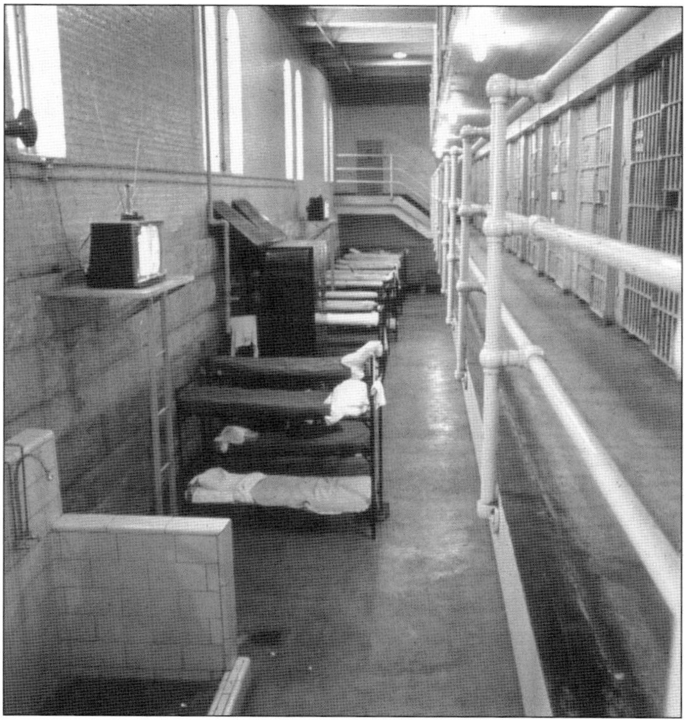

Overcrowded Conditions. Overcrowding remained a problem at Central Prison, occasionally requiring the bunking of inmates in hallways.

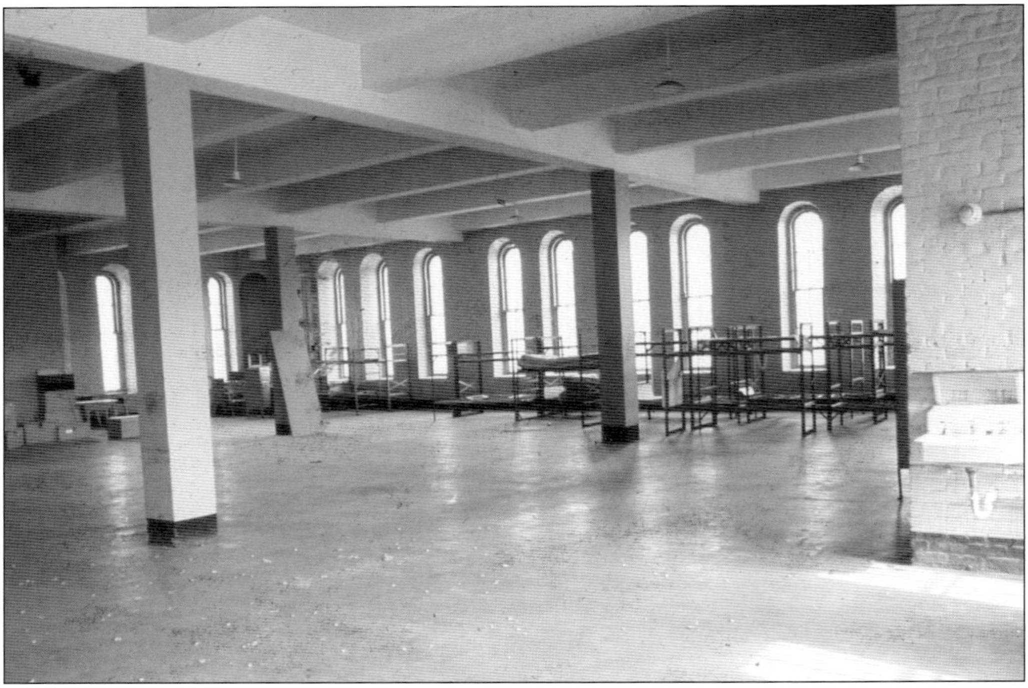

DORMITORY UNDER RENOVATION, BUNK BEDS NEAR THE WINDOWS, 1969. One economical means of dealing with overcrowding was the use of dormitories. Low-risk inmates could escape the confining cells and instead find housing in these larger open structures.

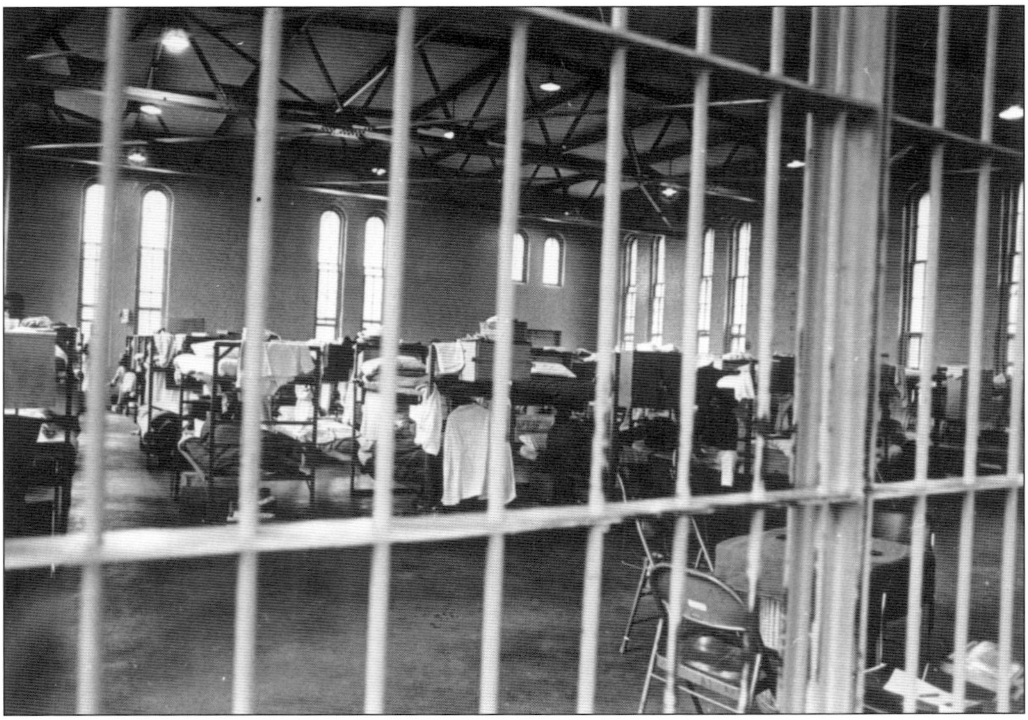

OCCUPIED DORMITORY, 1969. Although the living quarters were still rather close, inmates had more space and freedom of movement than in the cells.

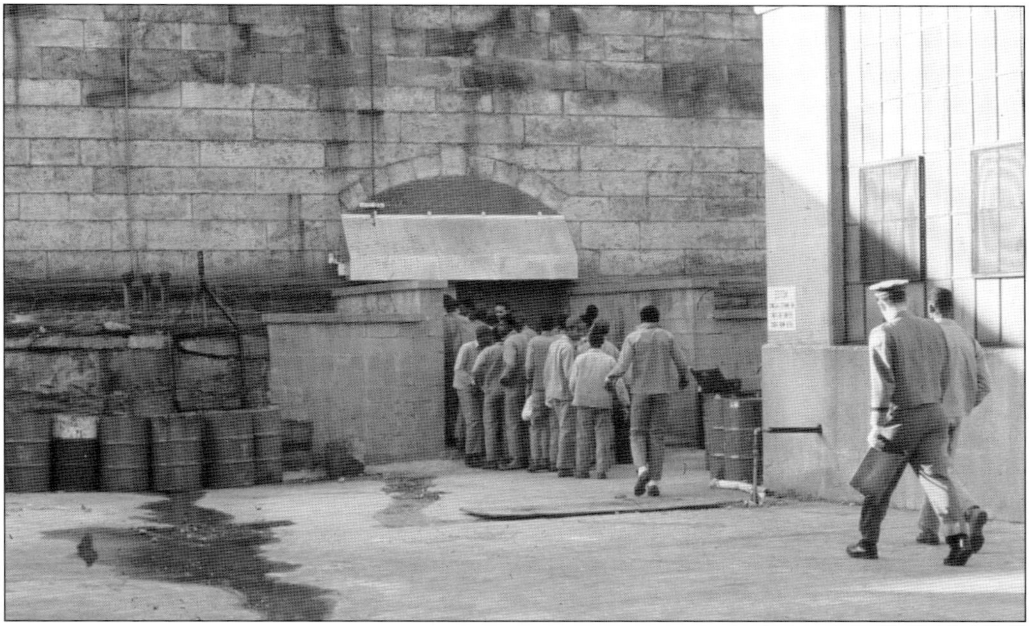

GUARD ESCORTING INMATES. Despite all the locks, brakes, cages, and walls, moving inmates from their cell blocks to meals, recreation, or work was a tense time for custody officers. To minimize the risk of trouble and prevent any unauthorized activities, custody officers were careful to keep inmates in line as they were moved.

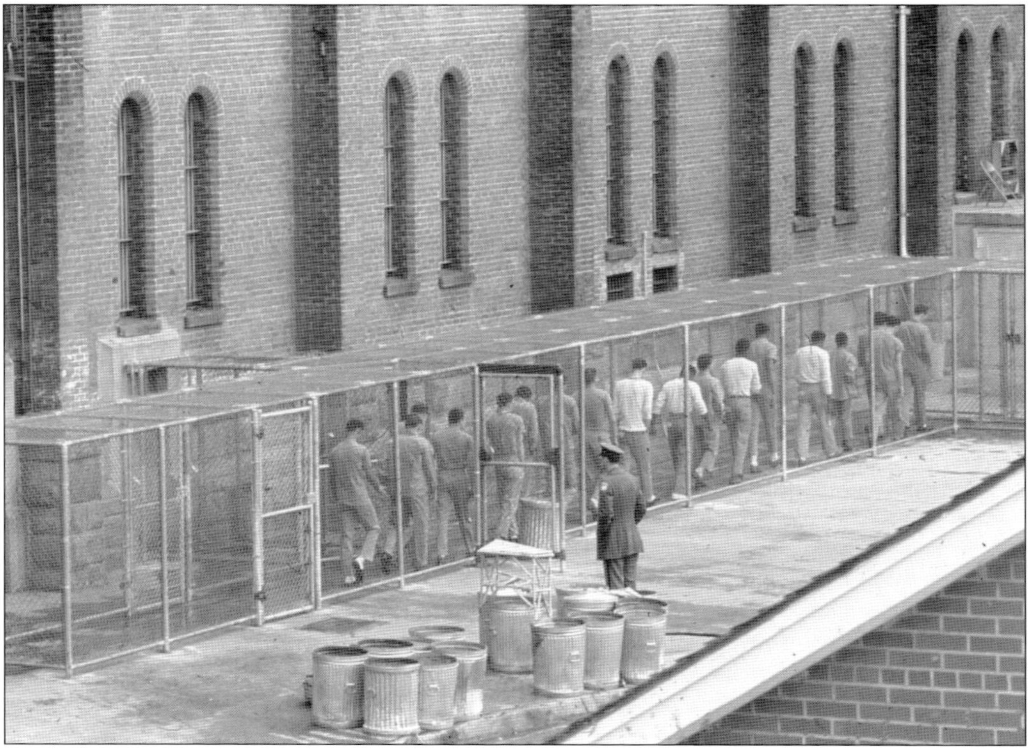

CAGED WALKWAY. By the 1970s, internal caged walkways made controlling inmates as they moved from one location to another much easier and safer for the custody officers.

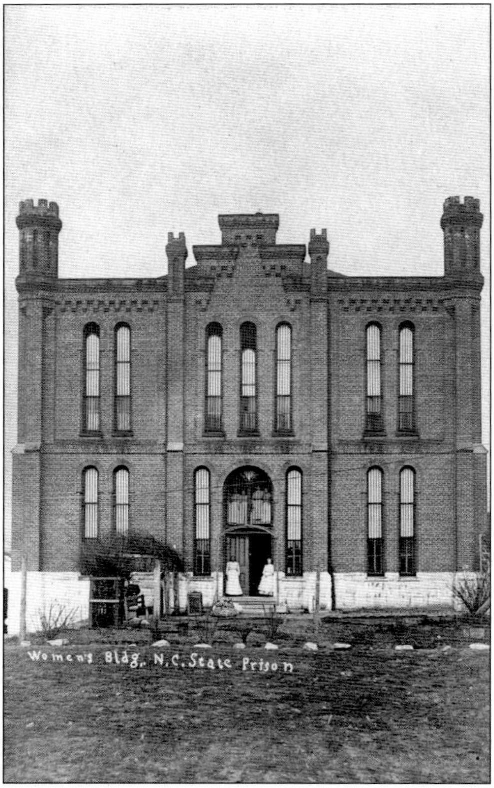

Women's Prison, 1910. Separate from the main penitentiary structure, south of the inmate dining hall, was the four-tiered, 58-by-81-foot women's prison, with 64 cells. The building was fully lighted, heated, and ventilated and included separate female workrooms and a hospital ward. In 1910, there were 49 women confined in Central Prison—10 white and 39 African American. The average number housed throughout its history was 22.

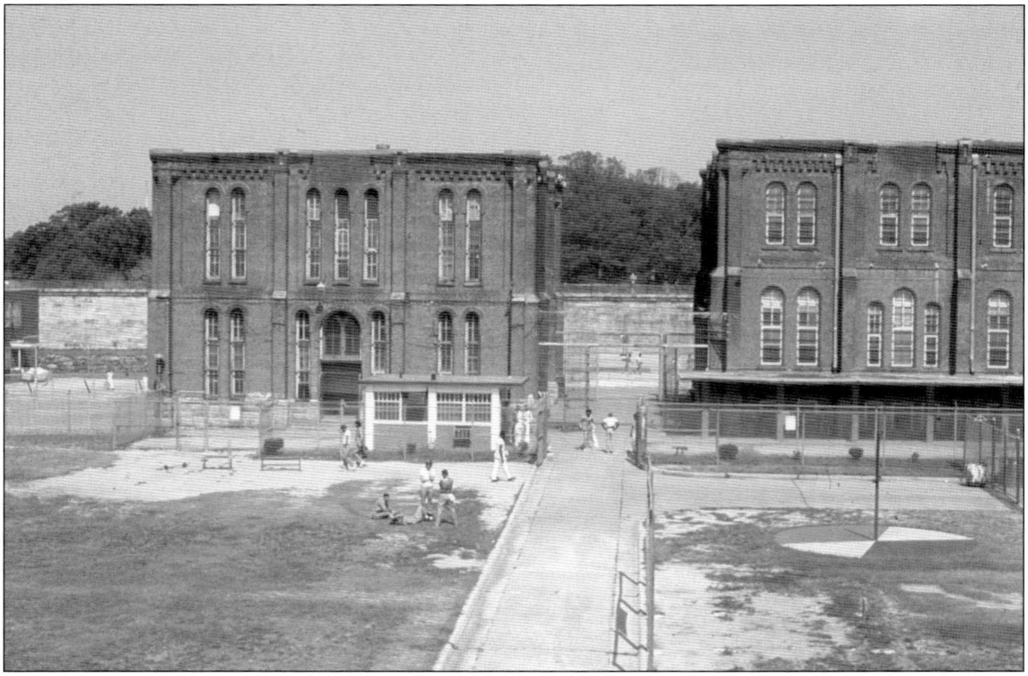

Truncated Women's Prison, Mess Hall to the Right, 1970s. The ornamental turrets were removed in the 1930s when the facility was renovated. Women were housed in Central Prison until 1935, when they were moved to a separate facility.

Four

Convict Prison Labor

Determined to meet the constitutional requirement of a self-sustaining penitentiary, North Carolina put its inmates to profitable labor beyond the prison walls in 1875. Officials signed leases with several railroads, including the Western North Carolina Railroad, the Cape Fear & Yadkin Valley Railroad, the Georgia & North Carolina, and the University Railroad. By 1880, there were 692 of the penitentiary's 993 inmates working as railroad construction crews. That left only 301 inmates actually serving their time at the penitentiary site, another reason for the slow completion of the wall and buildings.

By the mid-1880s, the railroad building boom began to wane, and the state looked for new revenue streams. The result was the development of an extensive system of chain gangs and road camps. By 1912, the penitentiary netted $1 per day per inmate for their work on the gangs and camps. It was this revenue, not any thought of reform or rehabilitation, that drove the continued use of inmate labor. Conveniently, as it turned out, the chain gangs and road camps served as additional forms of specific and general deterrence.

By the 1920s, the condition of many of the camps' facilities was deplorable. In 1925, therefore, the general assembly changed the state's prison system from a corporation to a department of state government. In 1933, the General Assembly passed legislation (S.B. 96 Chapter 172), which enabled the state to take over all the county prisoners on farms and in work camps (about 3,650 in all) and use their labor under the control of the state highway commission. With that control, the state cleaned up and improved the camps. Part of that improvement was the erection of permanent camps of standard design and capacity. The permanent camps solved an additional problem. In many of the temporary camps, segregation proved impossible to uphold, but the new camps were specifically constructed to ensure inmates were segregated by race. With issues of health, economics, and race addressed, North Carolina employed the chain gang until 1972—longer than any other state.

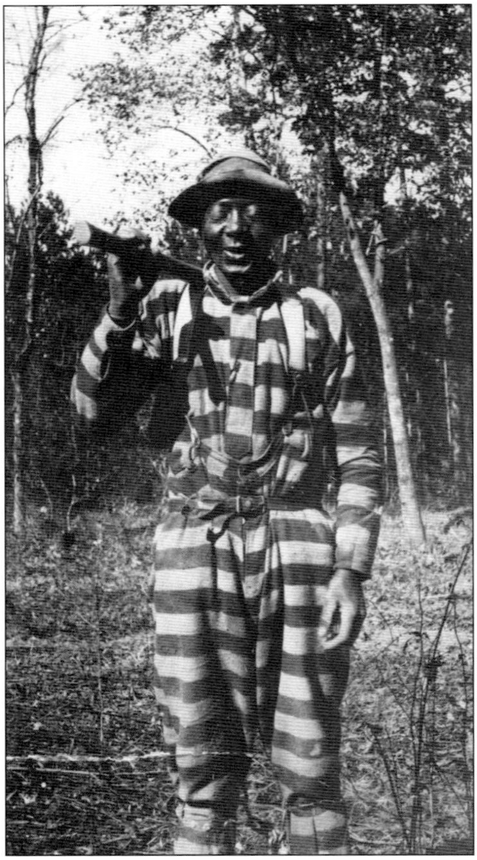

CONVICT LABORER IN CHAINS, 1917. In 1866, the state legislature authorized county judges to sentence noncapital offenders for up to one year of chain gang labor on roads, railroads, or any other internal improvement. Initially, custody officers employed by the county supervised prisoners working on public roads, while officers employed by private contractors or railroads supervised the work of the prisoners.

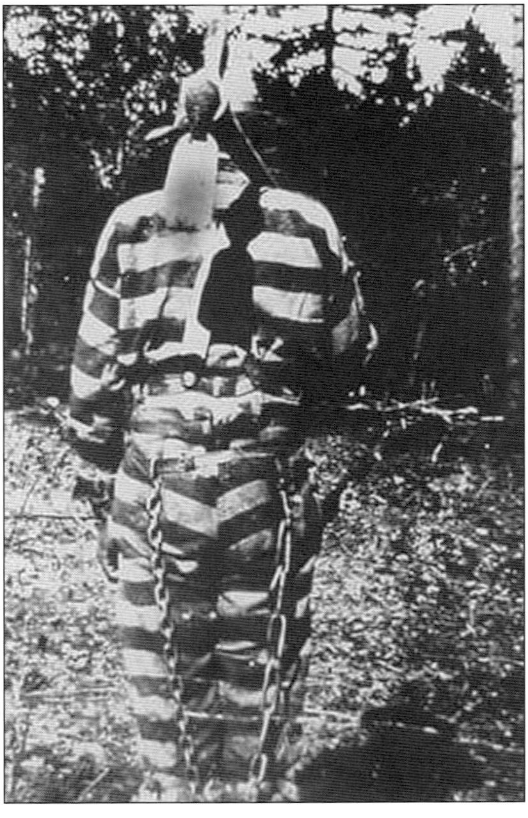

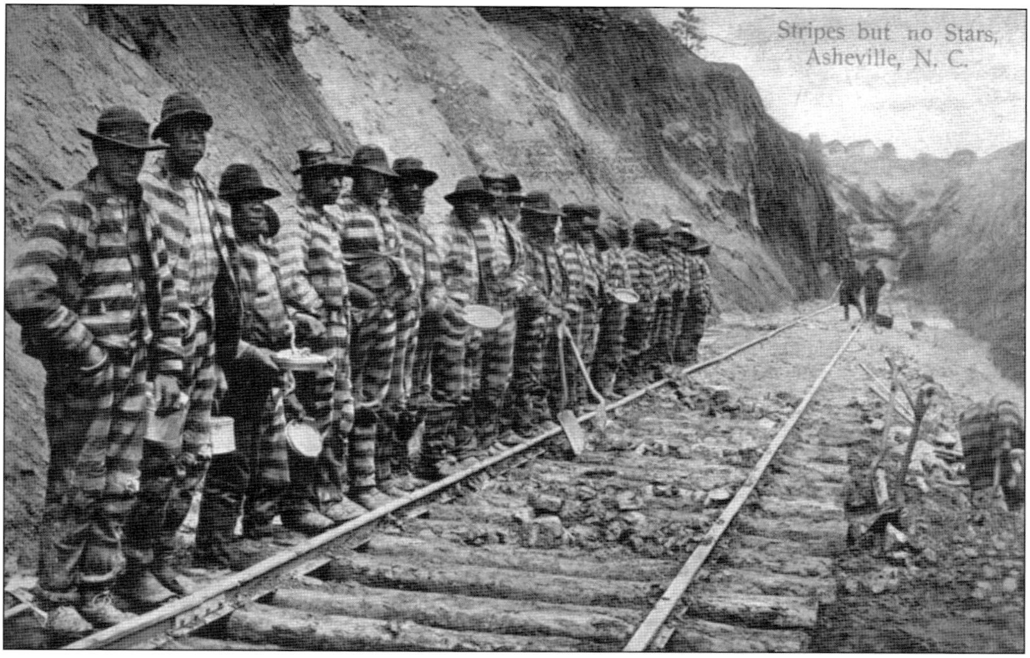

CHAIN GANG, 1915. The state followed a similar course, although it, not the individual companies, guarded the inmate workers in all cases. In 1876, for instance, the penitentiary leased 200 inmates to the Spartanburg & Asheville Railroad Company. The company fed, clothed, and attended to the health of the inmates and paid for the labor of any inmate who escaped.

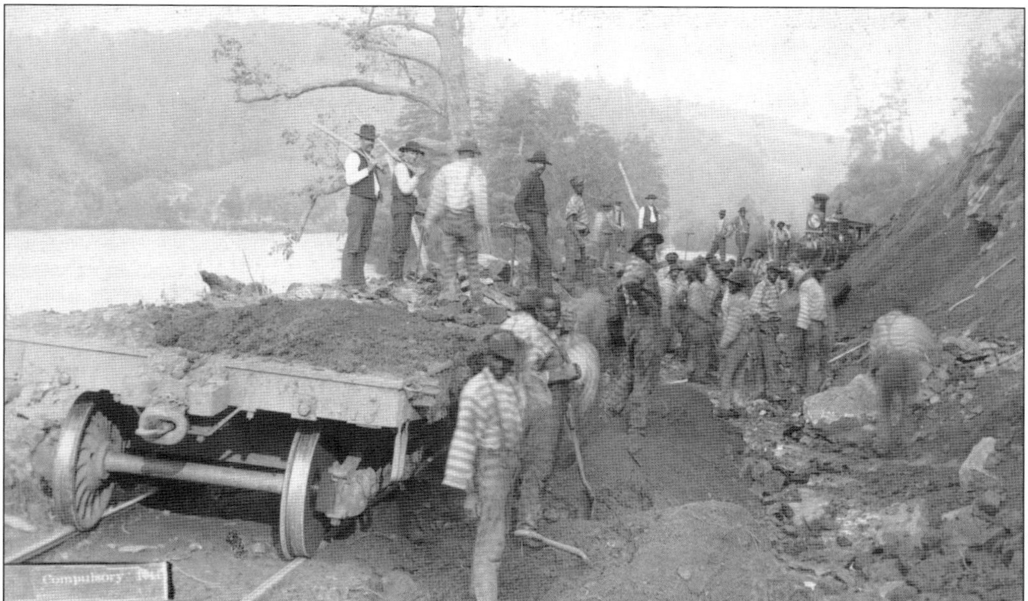

WESTERN NORTH CAROLINA RAILROAD, 1876. In 1876, the penitentiary also furnished 332 convicts to the Western North Carolina Railroad. According to road superintendent Col. S.D. Tate, the value of their labor was between $35,000 and $50,000. The railroad loaned the penitentiary $2,395.70 to cover transportation expenses and the cost of building quarters for the prisoners and custody officers.

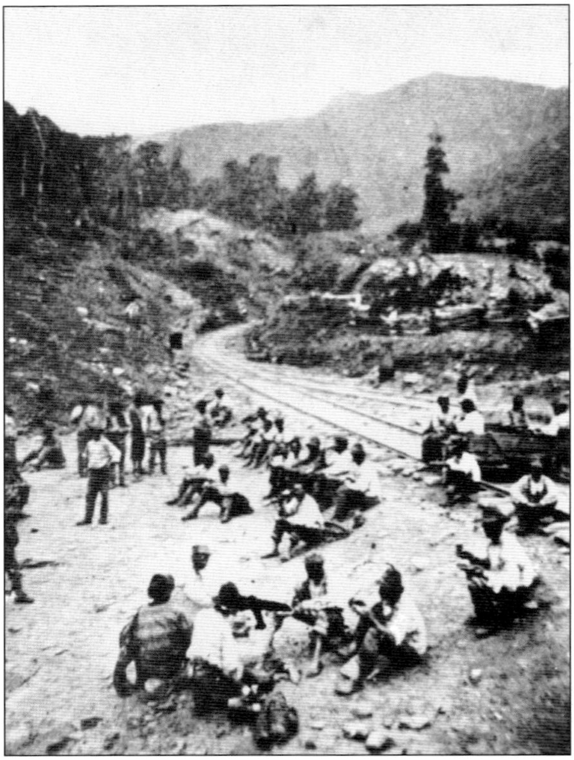

Western North Carolina Railroad at Coleman, 1878. Two years later, the prison provided the Western North Carolina Railroad 558 inmates, and in the year's biennial report, supervisor Maj. R.P. Atkinson wrote, "The convicts upon this great State work are performing a large amount of labor." The labor came at a cost, however, as 94 inmates died and 149 escaped.

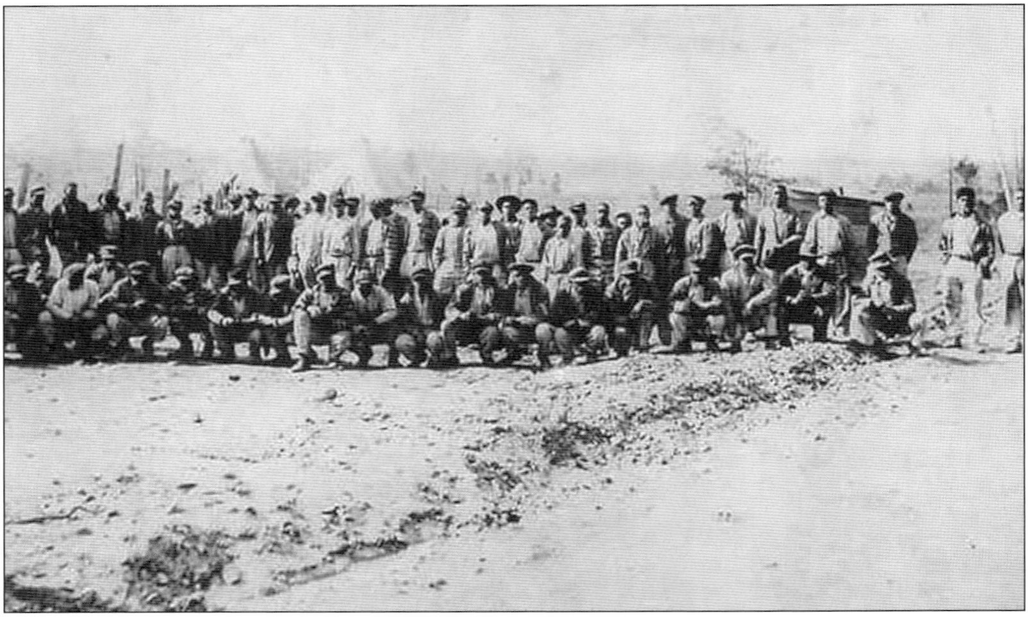

Convict Railroad Laborers, 1880s. Despite the relative success of leasing inmates to the railroads, officials understood such work would not continue indefinitely. This realization became especially resonant with the end of the railroad boom in 1892 and the return of inmates from their labor sites to the penitentiary. The fear of a large, idle, and potentially restive inmate population, combined with the need to support the institution financially, worried warden William J. Hicks, who began looking for new avenues of convict labor.

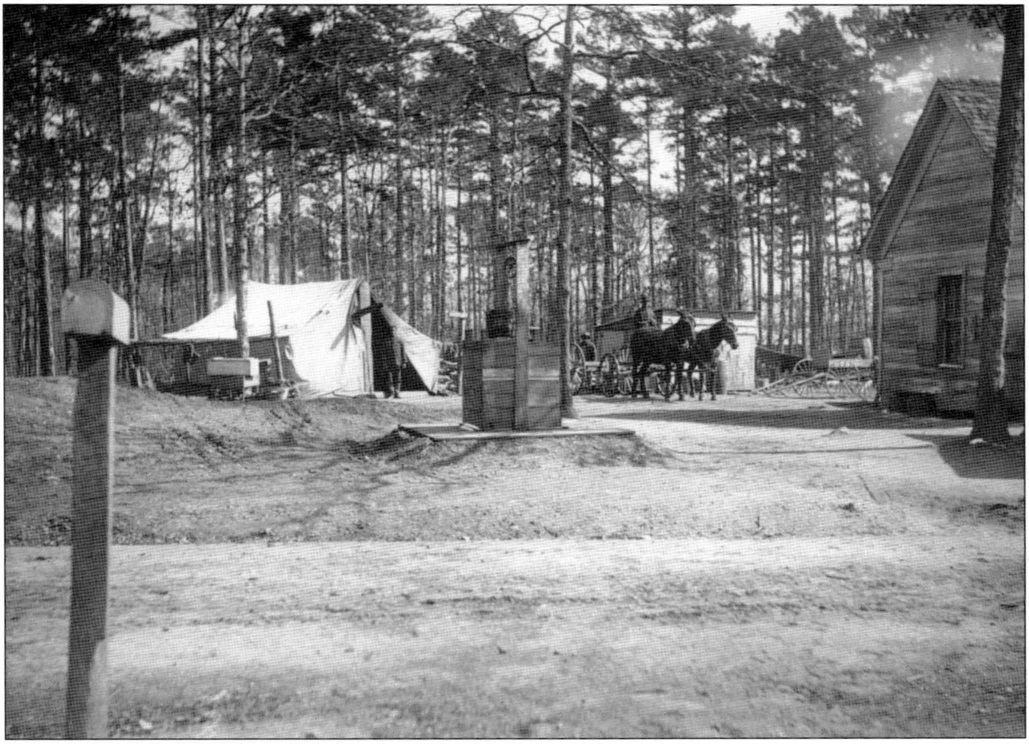

Wake County Roadwork Camp, 1919. The search for new labor opportunities led the state to develop a system of mobile and permanent roadwork camps of between 30 and 80 inmates. This workforce became especially important beginning in 1901, when inmates were employed to grade new roads and maintain existing ones. Beyond roadwork, inmate gangs worked in rock quarries and on bridge building.

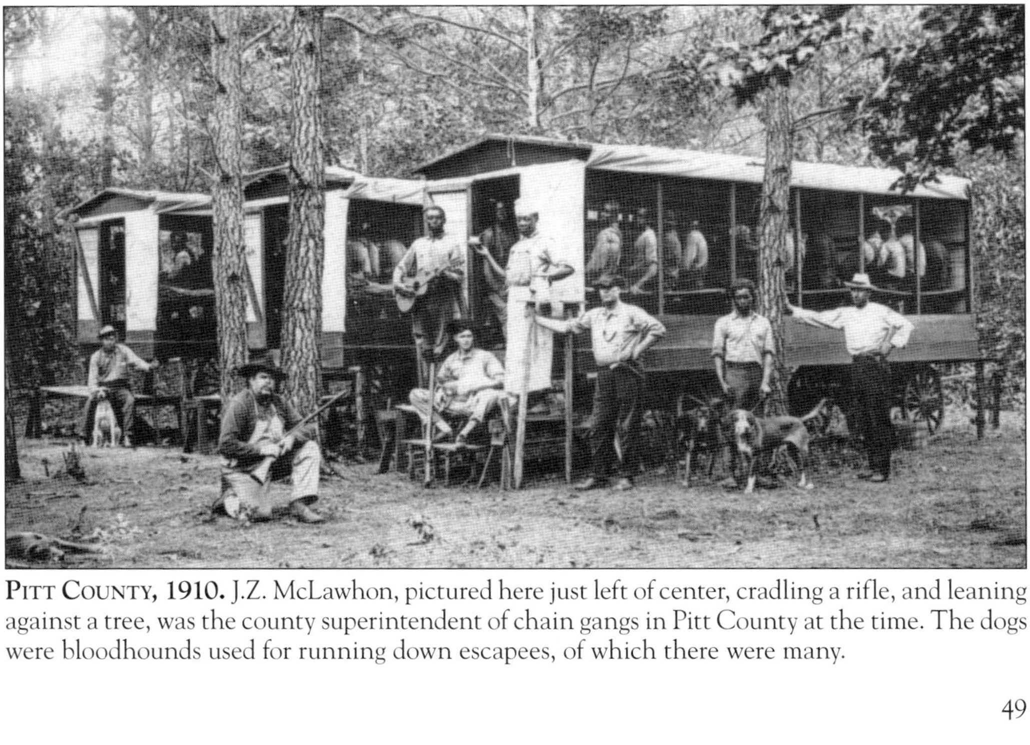

Pitt County, 1910. J.Z. McLawhon, pictured here just left of center, cradling a rifle, and leaning against a tree, was the county superintendent of chain gangs in Pitt County at the time. The dogs were bloodhounds used for running down escapees, of which there were many.

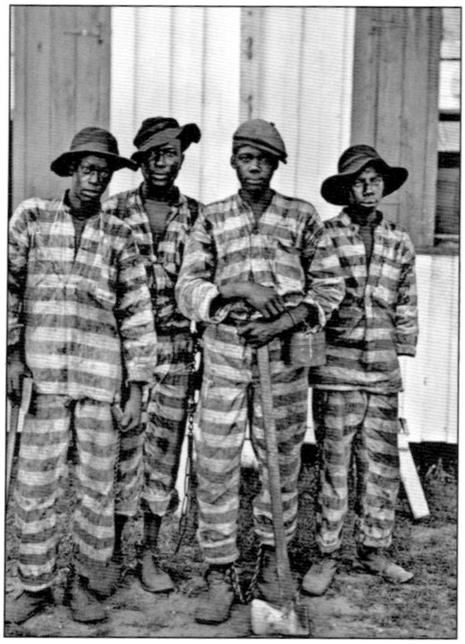

Georgia Chain Gang, 1900s. While this new form of prison labor solved the inmate idleness problem to some extent, the next issue was how to control the prisoners at dozens of scattered worksites. The answer was the chain gang. Georgia was the first state to use chain gangs, in 1908, and North Carolina soon followed suit. Various measures ensured inmates could work but not escape.

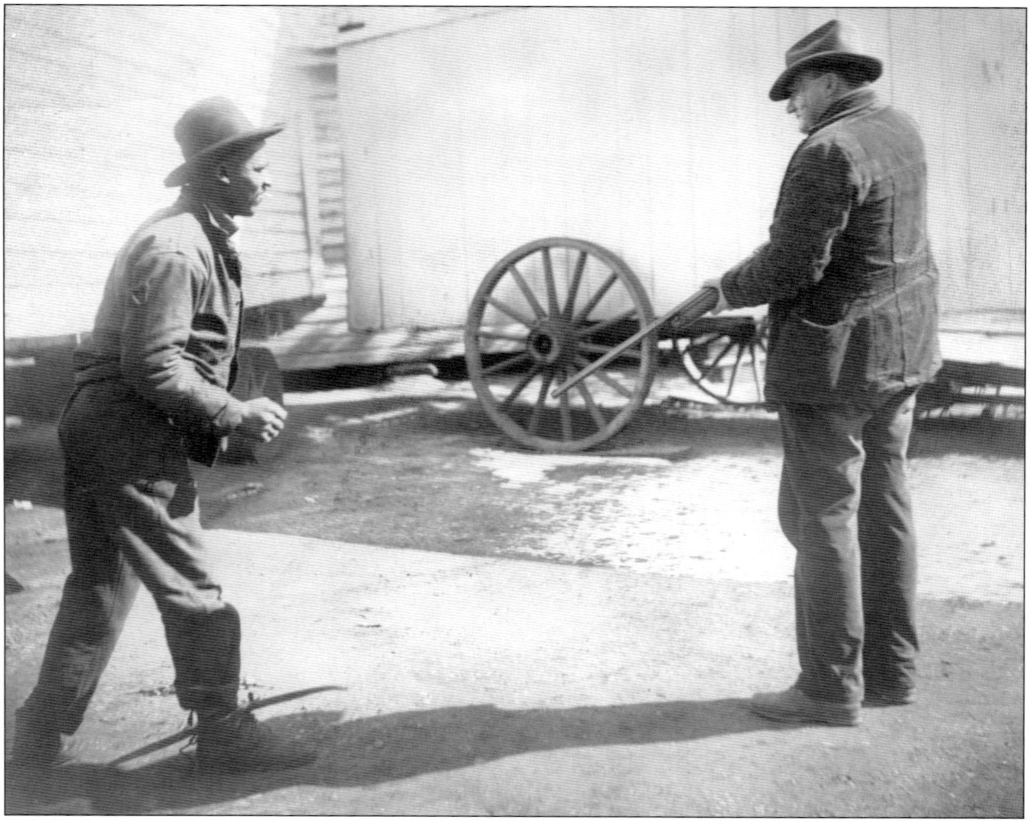

Hobble-Spike Chain on Legs, Wake County, 1919. In this photograph, a prisoner is wearing spikes. Spikes consisted of steel bayonets riveted around the ankles; 10 inches of steel in front and 10 inches behind made it so the convict could hardly walk without tripping or sleep without waking when he turned. The cuff between the two steel prongs fitted closely around the ankle and was typically applied to a prisoner after an escape attempt. During the day, they rubbed against the legs, creating sores that often became infected. Such infections were known as shackle poison.

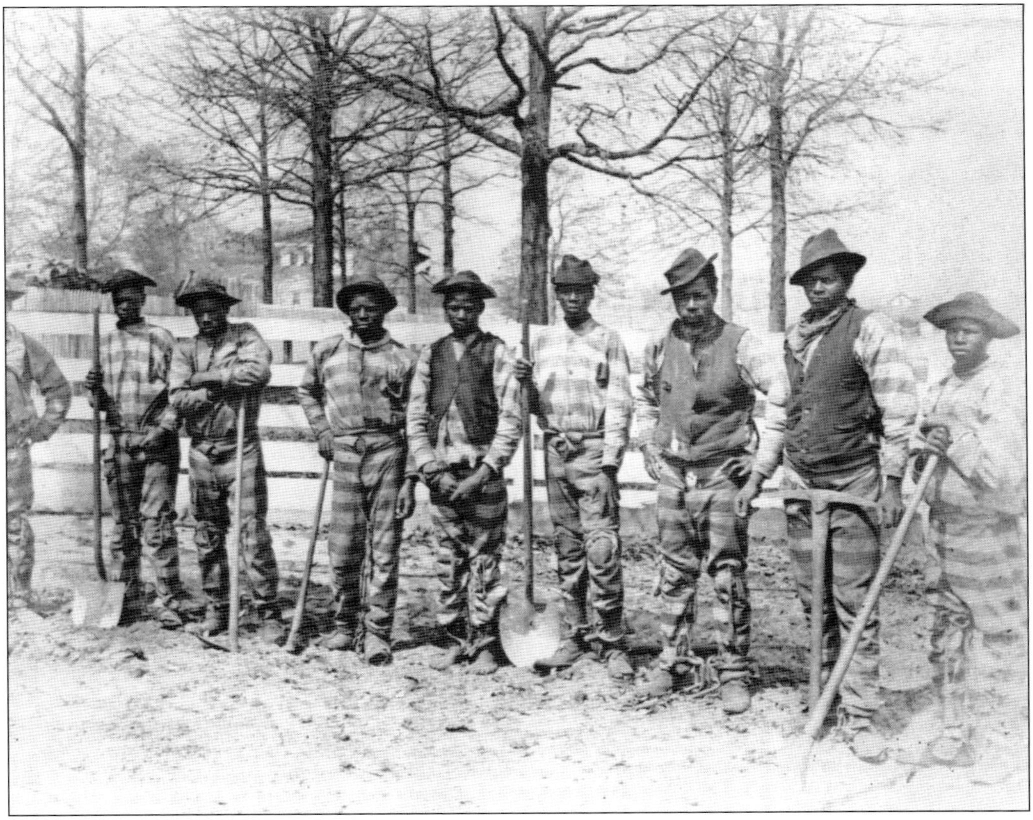

Chain Gangs, 1900s. The more common chain was the "strad" or stride chain, which was attached to the ankles and, depending upon its length, could make taking a full step impossible.

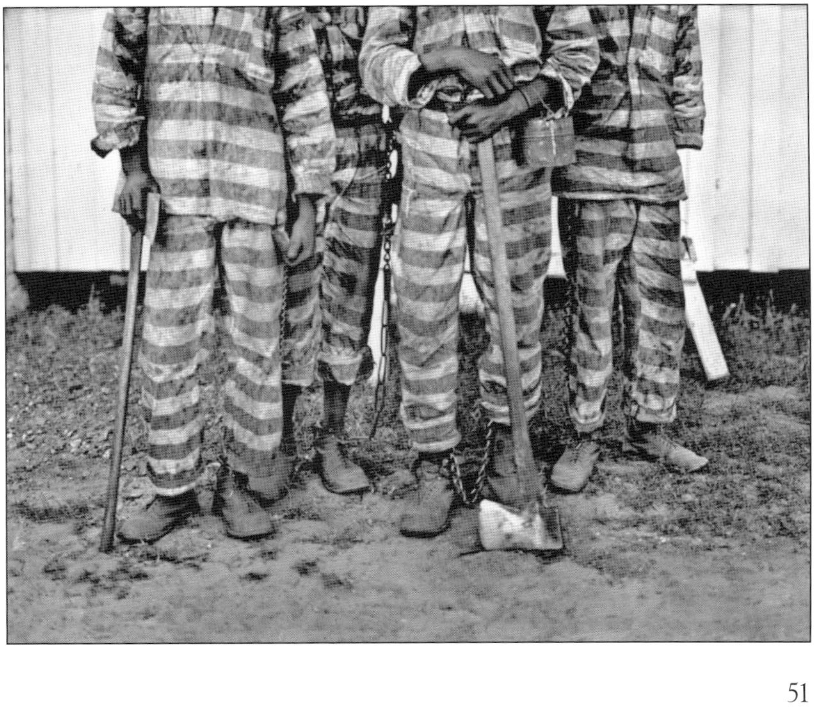

Close-up of the Stride Chain. As soon as a man arrived at a chain gang camp, he was shackled, and the chain remained in place for the duration of his sentence.

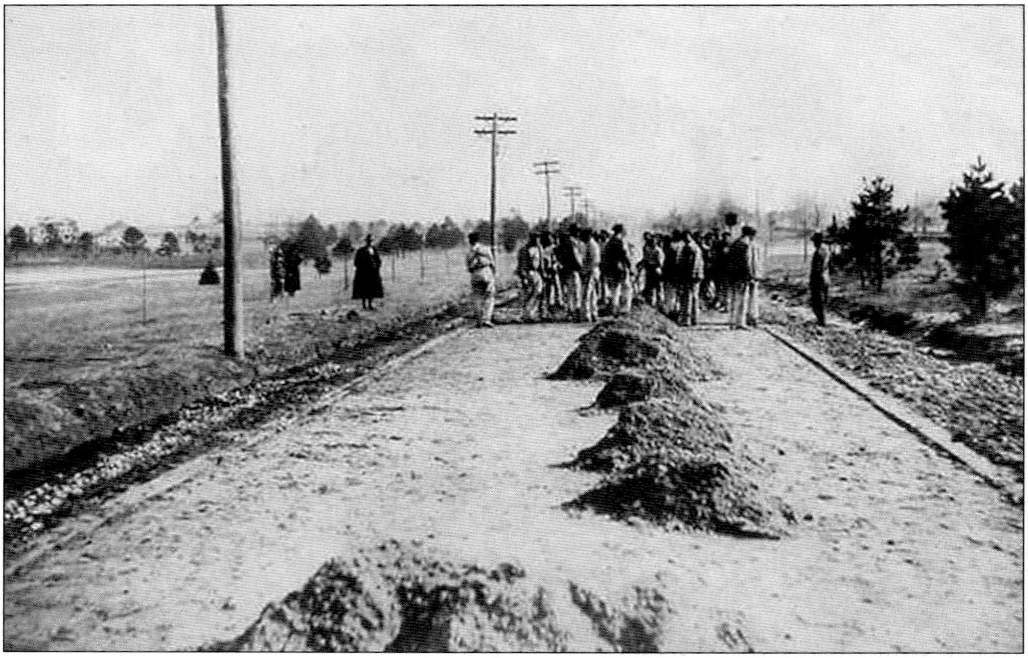

Chain Gang Road Crew in Durham County, 1919. To prevent the stride chain from dragging the ground and interfering with the work of the prisoner, another chain was affixed to its middle section. Known as the upright chain, it was topped with an iron ring, which attached to the inmate's belt and lifted the stride chain off the ground.

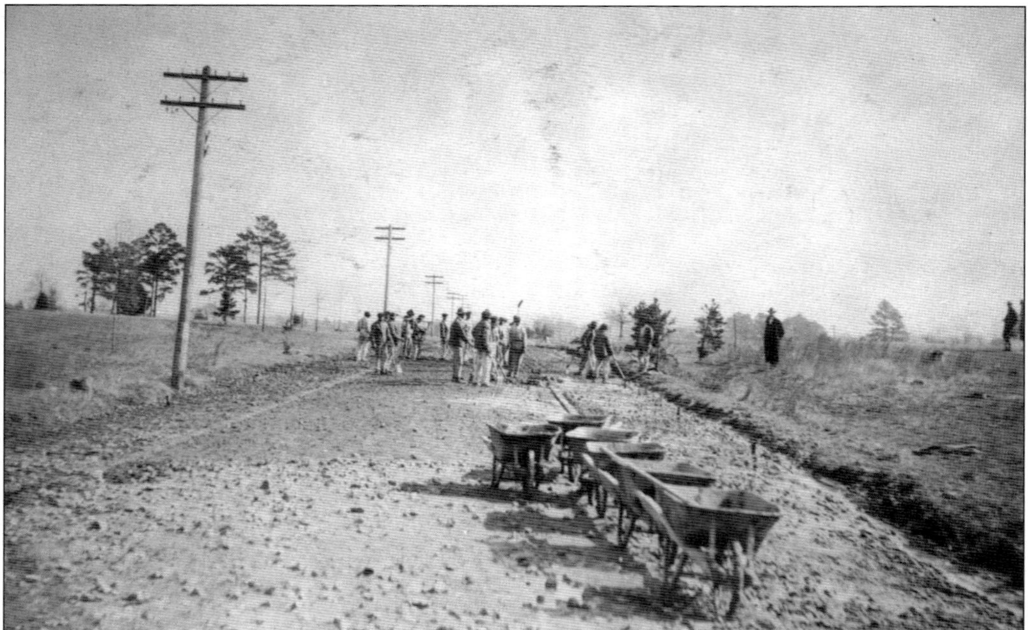

Durham County, 1919. All together, each inmate's chains weighed about 20 pounds. The upright chain also allowed the custody officers to chain the men together at night. A guard ran a chain through each inmate's iron ring and fastened it to a lock, meaning the inmates were chained to each other while in their beds.

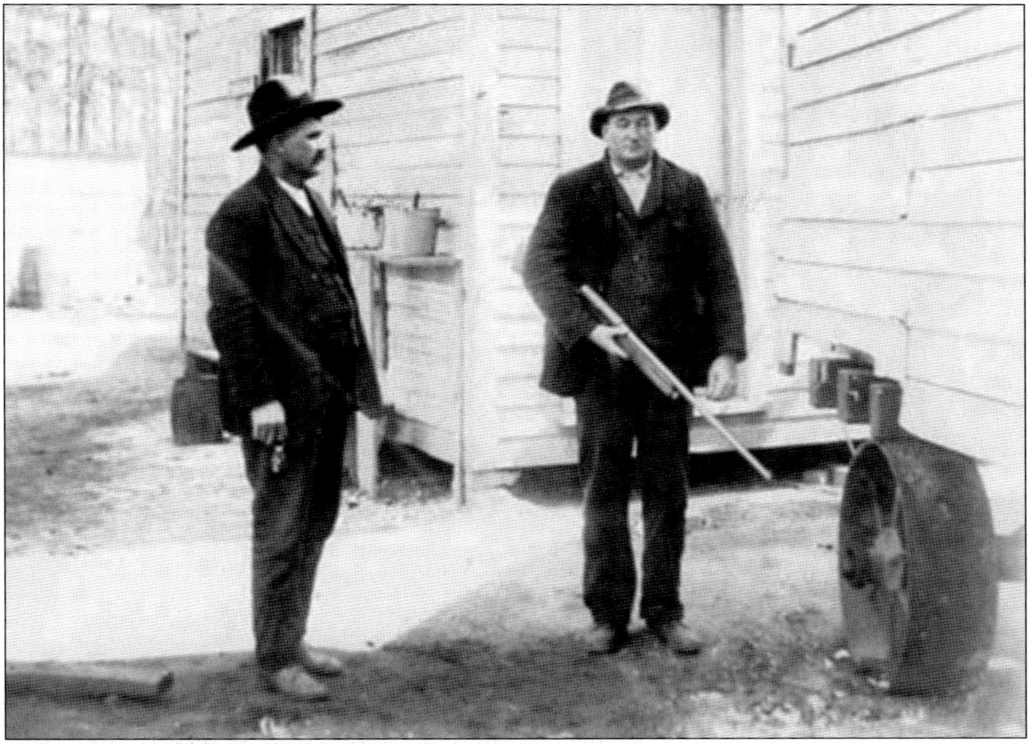

Prison Camp Custody Officer, Wake County, 1919. All of North Carolina's prison camps were under the general control of the superintendent of prisons. Individual camps were controlled by a supervisor, with the number of custody officers depending on the size of the camp.

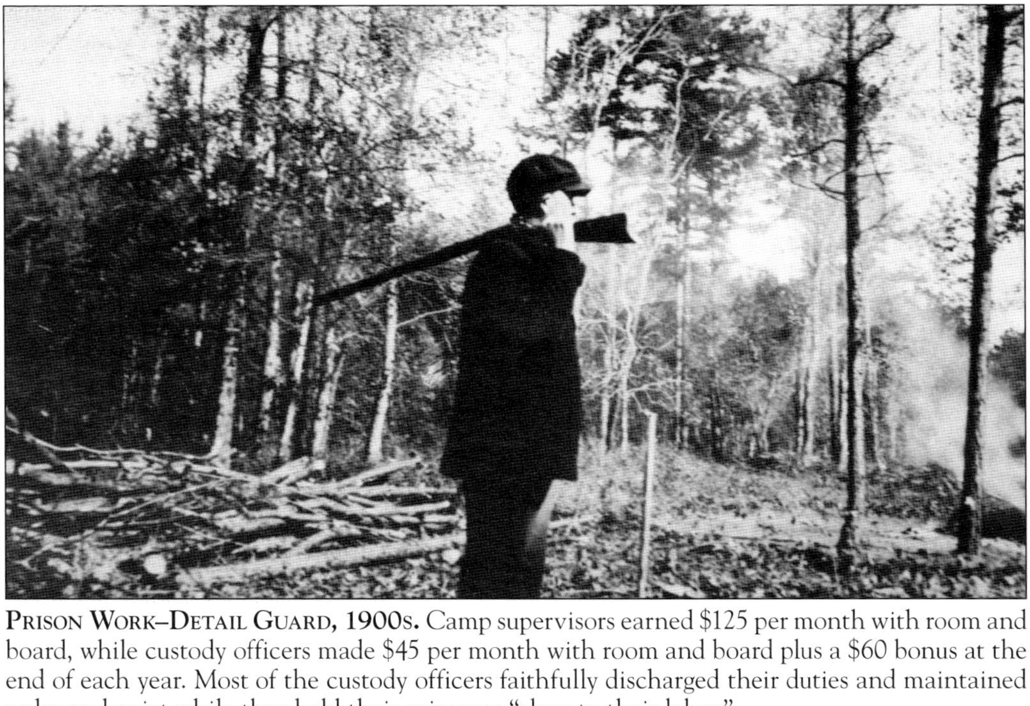

Prison Work–Detail Guard, 1900s. Camp supervisors earned $125 per month with room and board, while custody officers made $45 per month with room and board plus a $60 bonus at the end of each year. Most of the custody officers faithfully discharged their duties and maintained order and quiet while they held their prisoners "close to their labor."

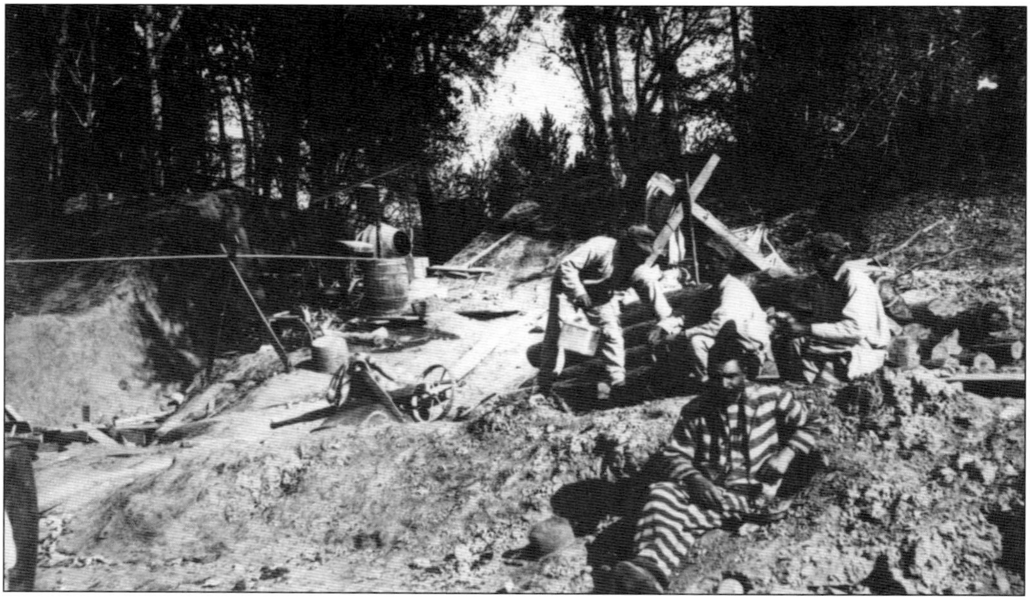

Construction of a Culvert, 1919. In certain camps, prisoners worked with free laborers, but in most, they were separated. Since the work camps were temporary, the buildings usually were simple wooden structures covered with tar paper. Some of them, considering the type of construction, were clean and well kept; others were dirty and showed a low standard of housekeeping. The kitchen, bakery, and mess hall were in one building, sleeping quarters for the inmates were in another, and the officers' quarters and offices were in a third.

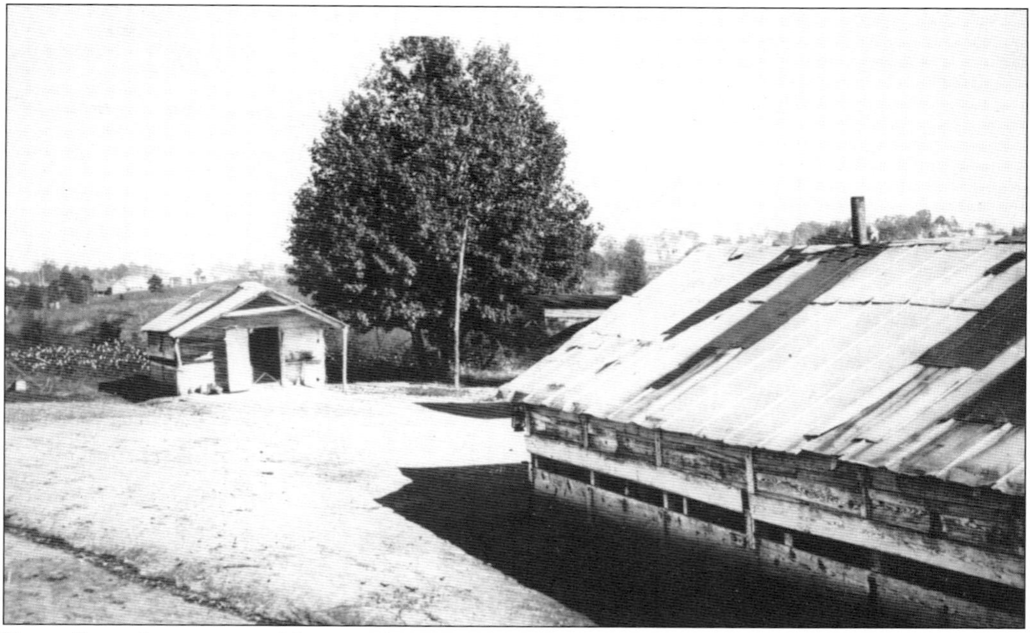

Road Camp Stockade in Monroe County, Early 1900s. The buildings pictured here housed 23 prisoners. In most camps, the space and time available for entertainment was slight. Consequently, aside from playing catch, boxing, and table games, there was little amusement and few diversions. A few camps had radios or record players. There was no educational work in the camps; religious services were conducted only occasionally.

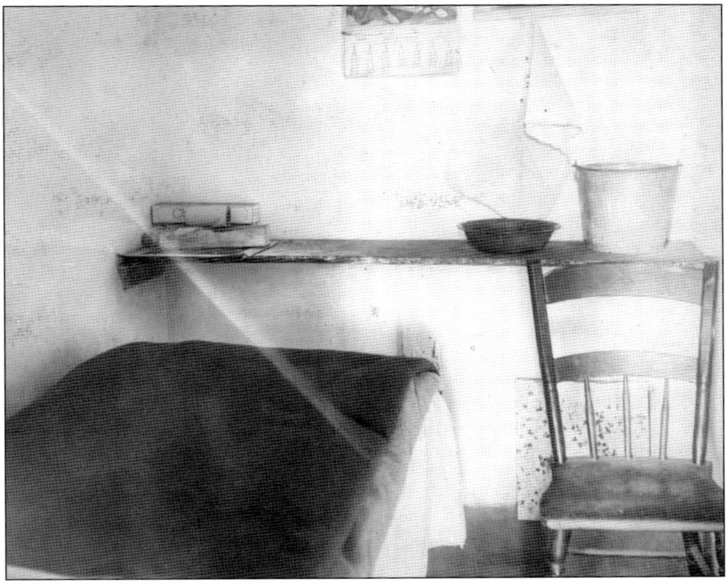

ROAD CAMP LIVING QUARTERS, 1919. The sleeping arrangements varied. While some camps provided individual beds, chairs, and desks, most were sparsely furnished. Double-decked bunks were common, and the beds were equipped with a mattress, mattress cover, sheets, blankets, and a pillowcase. Night clothes were provided as well. Some camps had electric lighting, while others had kerosene lamps.

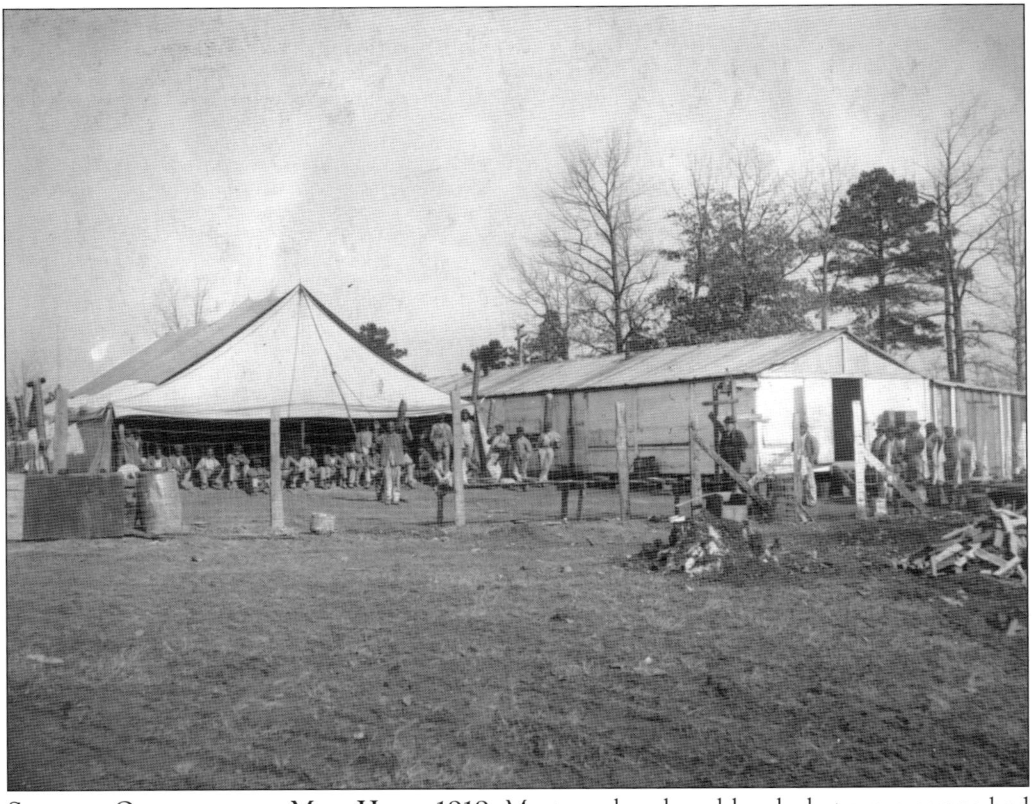

SLEEPING QUARTERS AND MESS HALL, 1919. Most employed washbowls, but some camps had galvanized iron pipes with holes a foot or two apart in which the men washed as water flowed from the holes. The toilet facilities were usually in an outhouse, the contents of which were taken away daily and burned or buried. Only two camps had showers, so most inmates bathed in washtubs in the yard. Practically all cooking was done on open ranges. A wire fence about 12 feet high normally surrounded the buildings, with guardhouses on the corners.

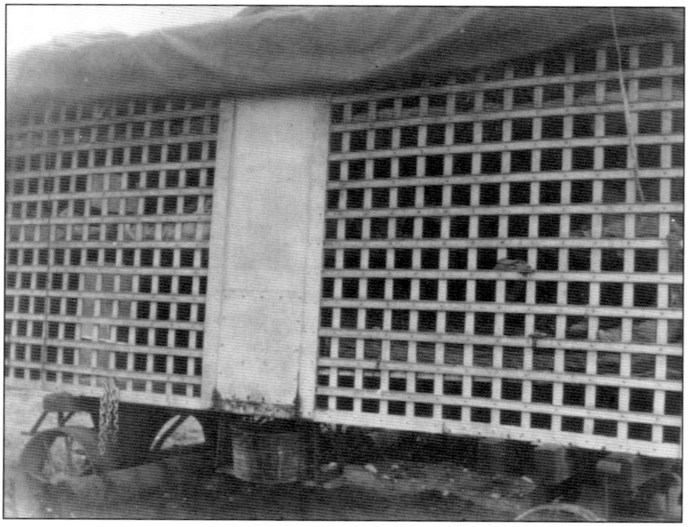

Rolling Chain Gang Car, 1900s. Not every inmate lived in a camp; many were housed in portable cars with barely enough room for the men to turn over in their bunks. The car pictured here is a 12-man car with bunks lined three deep and six to a side. The canvas curtain, which can be seen rolled up at the top, was let down at night and afforded the only protection against the elements. A slop bucket for human waste can be seen beneath the car.

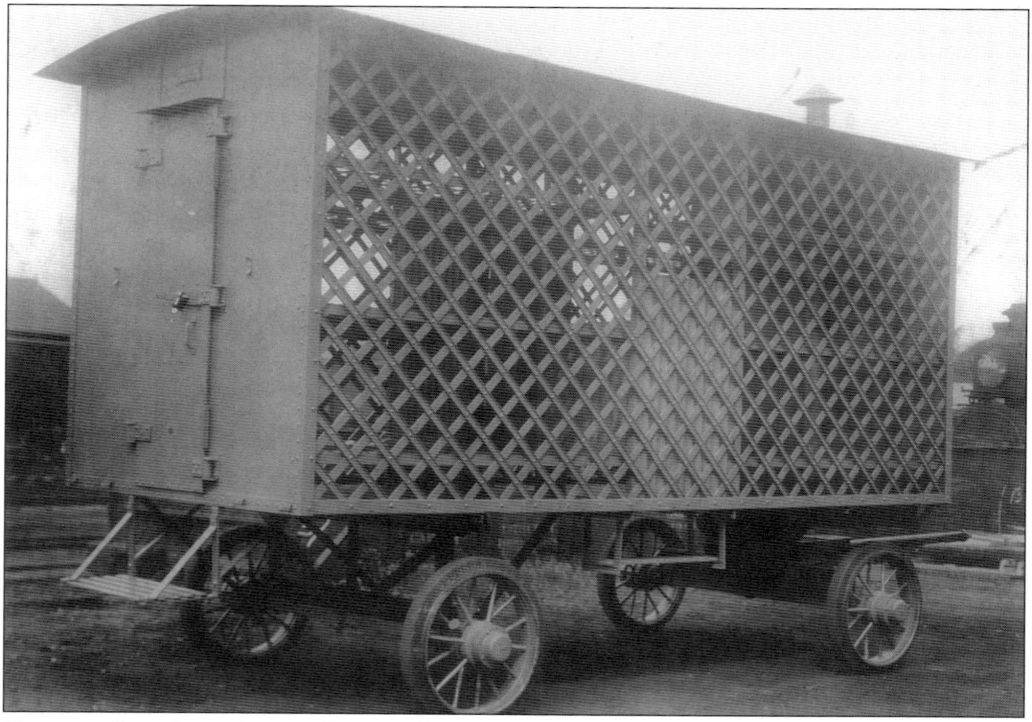

Convict Car. According to the manufacturer's 1915 advertisement, "The 12 capacity cage (7'4" x 7'4" x 15'6" net weight 4,600 lbs. 2 to 4 mules) with side curtain off. Sides made of 1 and 3/4" x 1/2" trussed channel grating riveted together on 4" mesh – plate work No. 10 and No. 12 steel jail plate reinforced with 2" stiffening angles inside and outside. All corner angles 2 and 1/2" securely riveted to gratings and plate work with 3/8" and 5/16" rivets on 3" centers. Cage mounted on 1,300 pound truck of heavy 5th wheel construction with 30" wheels, 8" tires and steel axles. Each cage fitted with heater and with an odorless, enameled iron Philadelphia prison toilet with tight fitting lid and removable galvanized soil bucket on outside." (Courtesy of Judson Manly.)

EARLY CONVICT CAR MANUFACTURED BY MANLY JAIL WORKS. The cars were not popular with the inmates, as blowing wind, rain, and cold easily penetrated makeshift protections, while the metal roof made the cars insufferably hot on sunny days. On Sundays, holidays, and days when the weather prevented labor, inmates often were confined to the cars for the entirety.

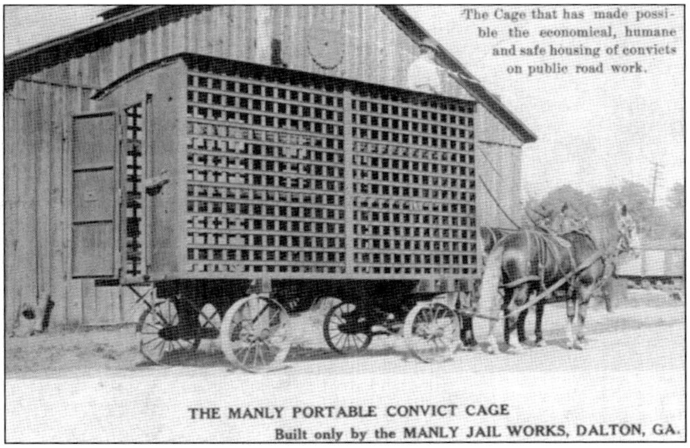

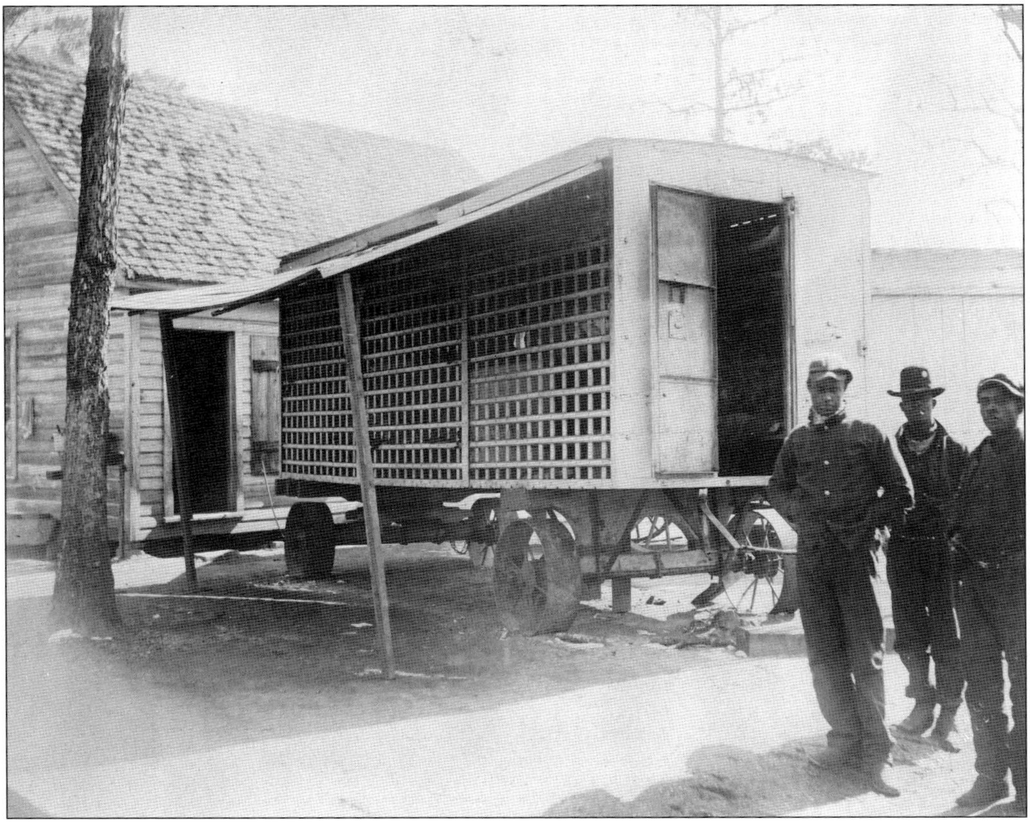

CHAIN GANG CAR, WAKE COUNTY ROAD CAMP, 1919. The cars were very small, stood on wheels, and ranged from 7 by 16 feet to 9 by 20 feet. There were usually about 18 beds. There were nine beds on each side of the car—three beds lengthwise and three high, one above the other. The 18-man convict car pictured here was sold to Wake County on November 13, 1913, from Manly Jail Works in Dalton, Georgia. Equipped with 10-inch wheels and end-flap curtains, it went to Wake County Convict Camp No. 3. The price was $567, including a heating system underneath. This photograph shows wooden covers apparently replacing the fabric curtains (that came from the manufacturer with the cars) for protection from the elements.

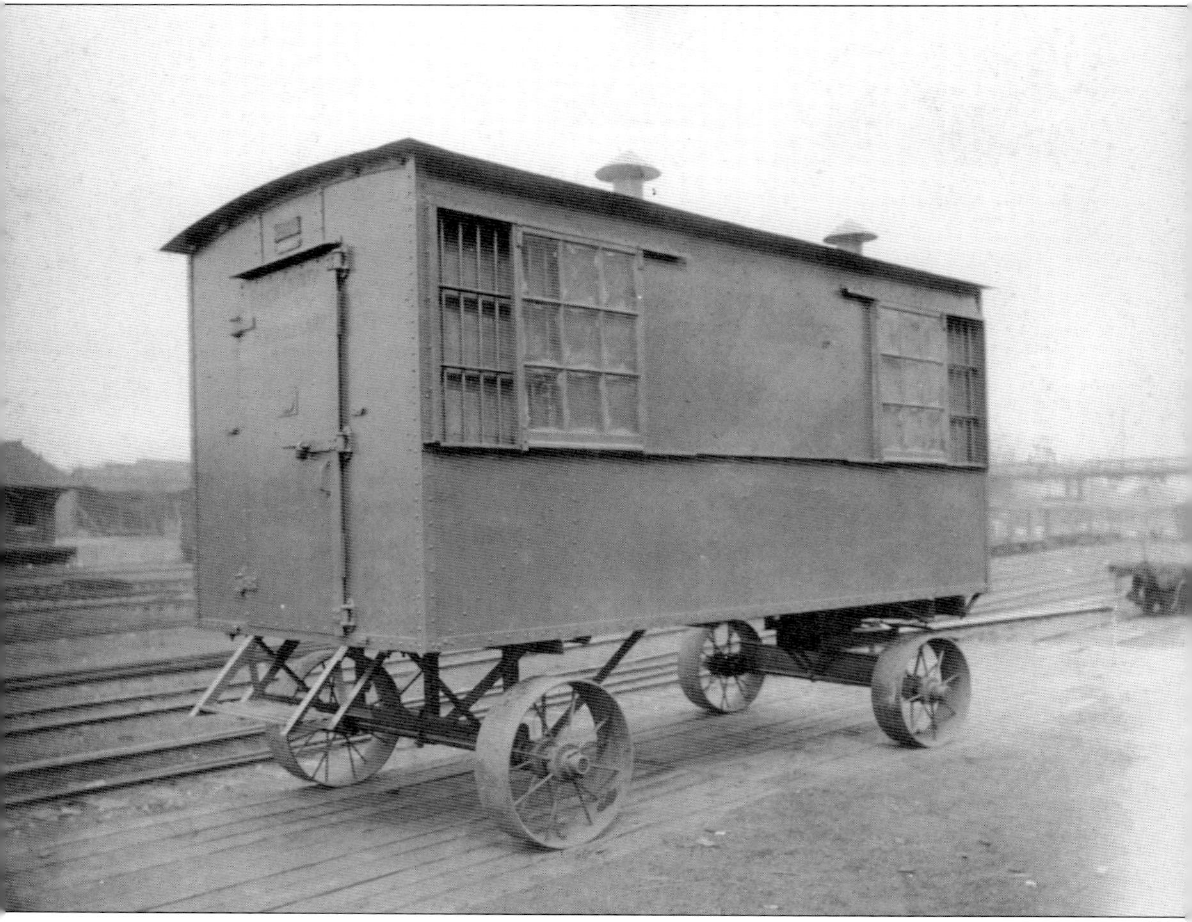

Kitchen Car Built by Manly Jail Works. Although the convict cars proved useful, the mobility of the camps caused difficulties. Custody officers had to move all the camp supplies, as well as the inmates, whenever they moved to a new worksite. To make life a little easier, these kitchen cars contained all the cooking facilities utilized by inmates and staff and ensured that wherever they camped, they had access to hot meals.

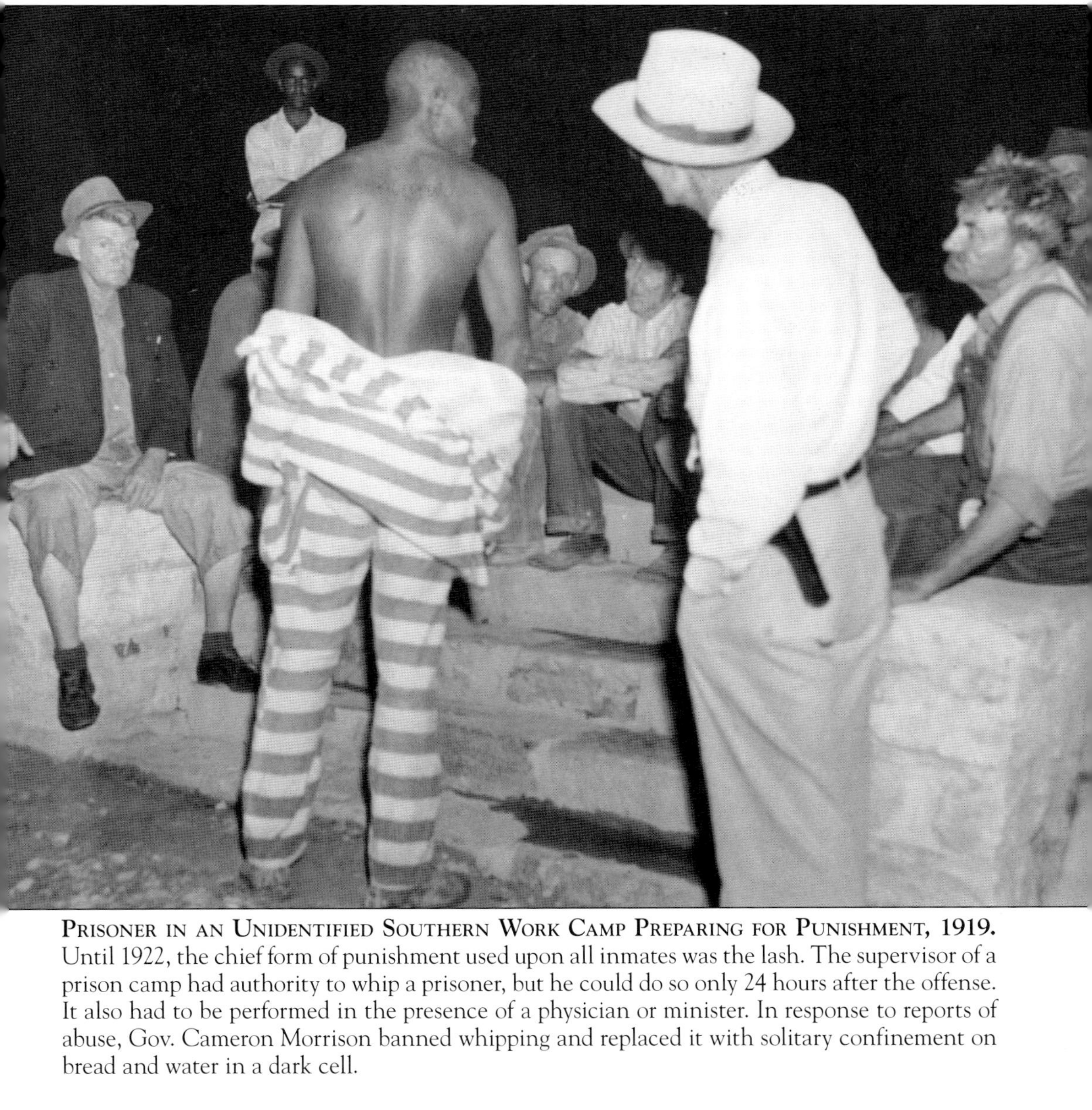

Prisoner in an Unidentified Southern Work Camp Preparing for Punishment, 1919. Until 1922, the chief form of punishment used upon all inmates was the lash. The supervisor of a prison camp had authority to whip a prisoner, but he could do so only 24 hours after the offense. It also had to be performed in the presence of a physician or minister. In response to reports of abuse, Gov. Cameron Morrison banned whipping and replaced it with solitary confinement on bread and water in a dark cell.

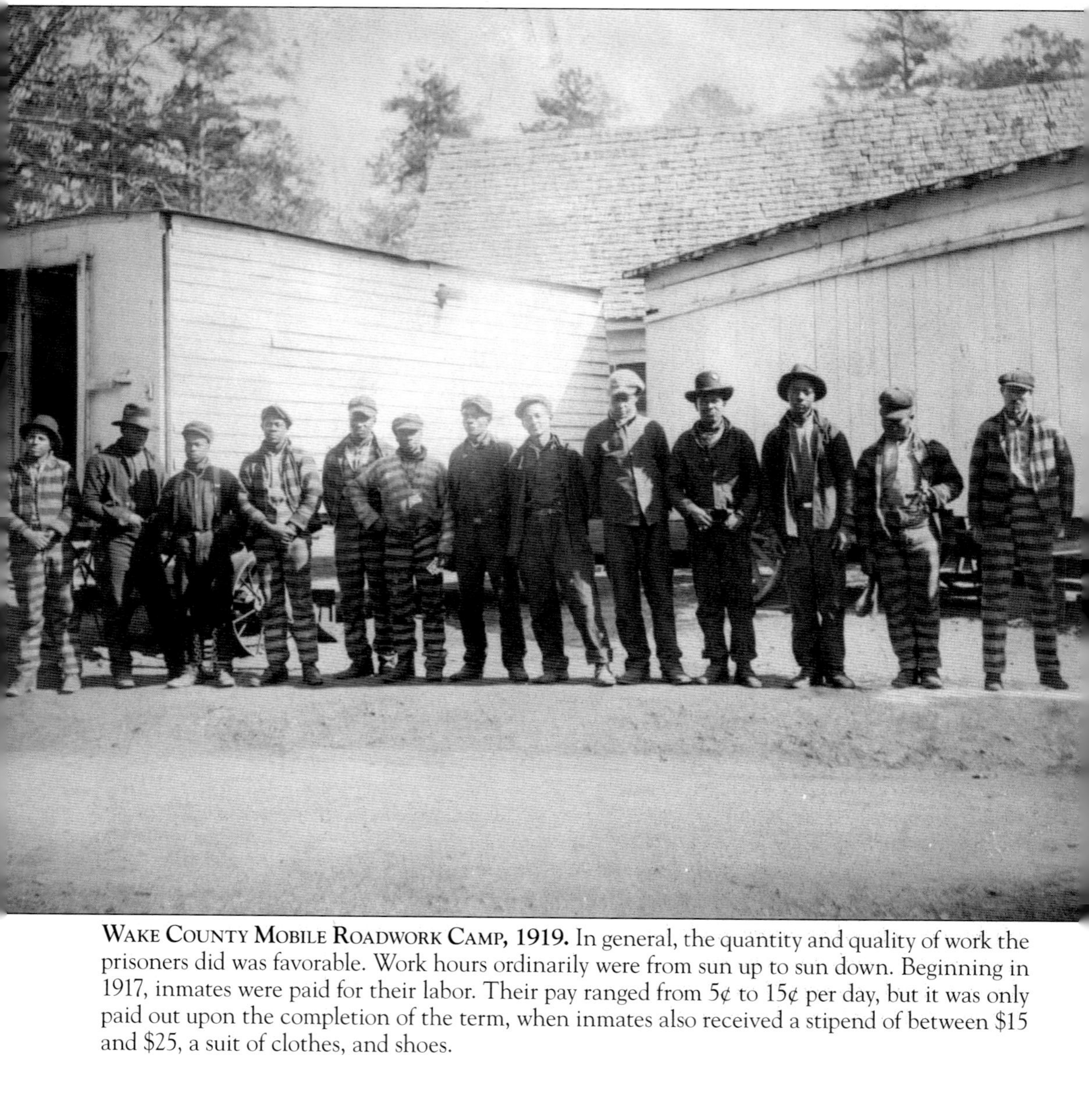

Wake County Mobile Roadwork Camp, 1919. In general, the quantity and quality of work the prisoners did was favorable. Work hours ordinarily were from sun up to sun down. Beginning in 1917, inmates were paid for their labor. Their pay ranged from 5¢ to 15¢ per day, but it was only paid out upon the completion of the term, when inmates also received a stipend of between $15 and $25, a suit of clothes, and shoes.

Five

Prison Industries

Despite the relative success of the chain gangs and work camps, by 1876, the penitentiary's board of directors reported, "In view of the large number of old and infirm convicts now in the prison, we think it would be good policy to purchase a small farm to work these decrepit prisoners on, where they would be enabled to support themselves." In 1881, the state acted on this suggestion and began to employ inmates on rented farmland neighboring the penitentiary. The success of the farming endeavor was evident from an 1892 productivity statement. Inmate farmers produced 1,022 bales of cotton worth $127,750; 3,800 bushels of peanuts worth $5,700; 29,500 bushels of cottonseed worth $30,975; 40,000 pounds of corn shucks worth $3,000; and 40,000 pounds of wheat straw worth $3,000. The total value of inmate-produced farm labor in 1892 was $171,425. By 1894, when railroad work was no longer a viable option, 80 percent of the penitentiary population was employed on the farms. Although farming produced fewer direct financial gains for the state, the offset costs created by the reduced expenditures led the administration to declare, "The farming operations . . . have accomplished good results."

Not all inmates worked on the farms, and penitentiary officials sought other industries that would keep the prisoners housed on the penitentiary grounds. Work in the laundry room, the mattress-making shop, and the tag shop, where inmates produced license plates, were common forms of on-site prison labor. Although inmates were paid for such labor, in keeping with traditional theories of penology, inmates working these jobs labored without gaining any real skills. The penitentiary created several other industries, however, that did offer inmates the opportunity to develop potentially useful skill sets, and many prisoners who learned a trade found employment upon release. Regardless of the ulterior benefits of inmate employment, administrators were determined to put as many inmates as possible to work in order to raise revenue and punish inmates for their transgressions.

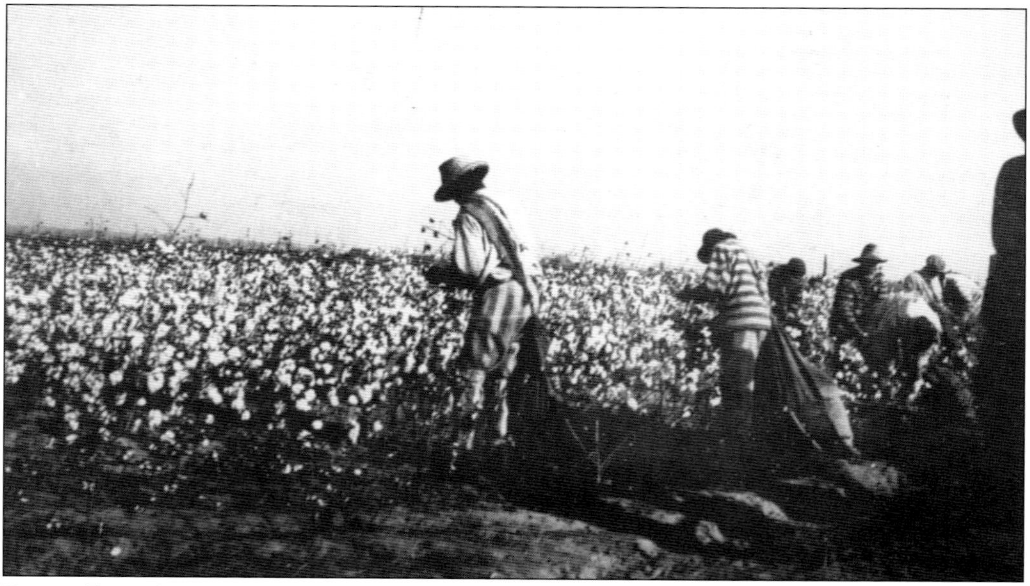

PRISON FARM COTTON FIELDS, 1918. In 1899, the state purchased the 6,500-acre Caledonia Farm in Halifax County for $61,000, and in 1920 it bought the 2,860-acre Cary Farm near Raleigh for $282,000. The state eventually had more than 13,000 acres of land under cultivation by inmate labor. Despite the occasional flood, drought, or infestation, inmate farmers annually produced tons of food that helped feed the prisoners and save the penitentiary money.

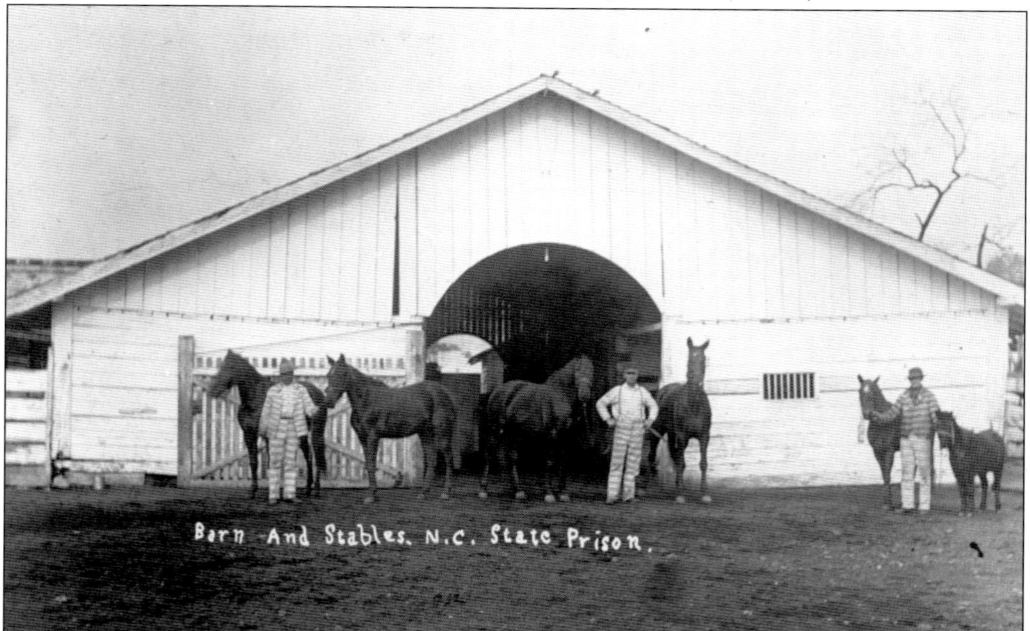

PRISONERS POSE WITH HORSES AT BARN AND STABLES, 1910. In 1910, penitentiary administrators proudly announced that the farms had earned double any previous period. Despite that, the farms faced increased expenditures as a result of the condition of much of their stock and buildings. The 1910 biennial report explained that "half of the stock was old and worn out" and needed to be replaced. While farming proved a useful and productive enterprise, like the chain gang, it was not without its collateral costs.

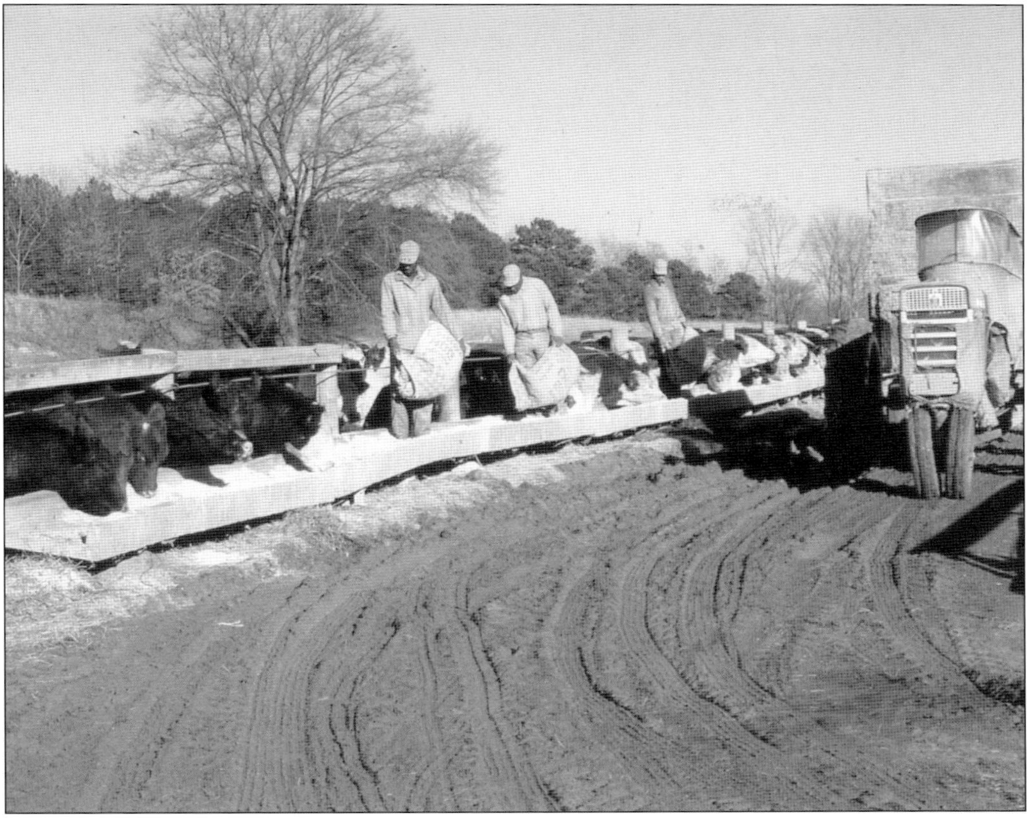

Feeding Livestock, 1930s. The state eventually replaced the worn-out farm supplies with modern technology. The expenditures paid dividends, and in the biennial report for 1910, Supt. T.P. Sale concluded, "We have now on hand a fine lot of livestock and the farm is equipped with most improved kinds of agricultural implements. By putting in these improved farming implements we have saved during the actual cultivating season, at least $100.00 per day."

Industrial Laundry Operation, 1969. Farming was not the only moneymaking industry the penitentiary employed. In 1898, John S. Hillabrant carried on a shirt-making and laundry business with the prison. He commenced operation in February 1898 and employed an average of 70 convicts at 24¢ per dozen for making shirts and 25¢ per dozen for laundering. The enterprise was not profitable to the penitentiary, because the returns paid by Hillabrant were too low.

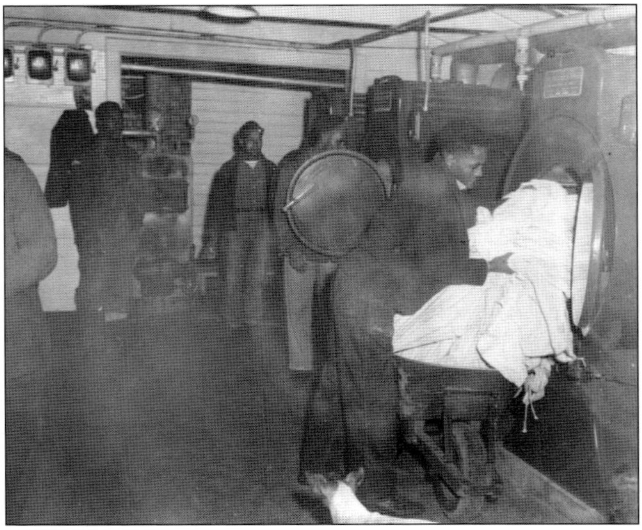

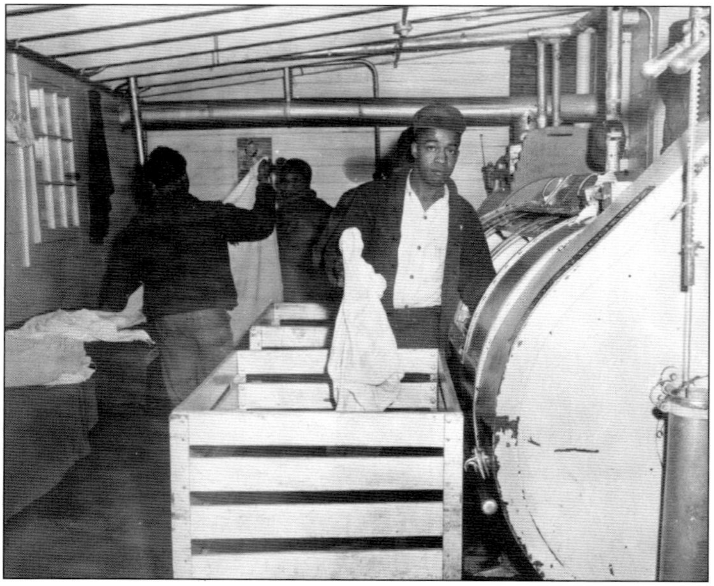

Laundry Worker, September 1969. By 1928, the industrial distribution of the prison population was chair shop, 151; laundry, 9; construction, 39; hospital, 21; mattress factory, 11; maintenance, 92; printing, 10; outside, 6; and tailor shop (women), 21.

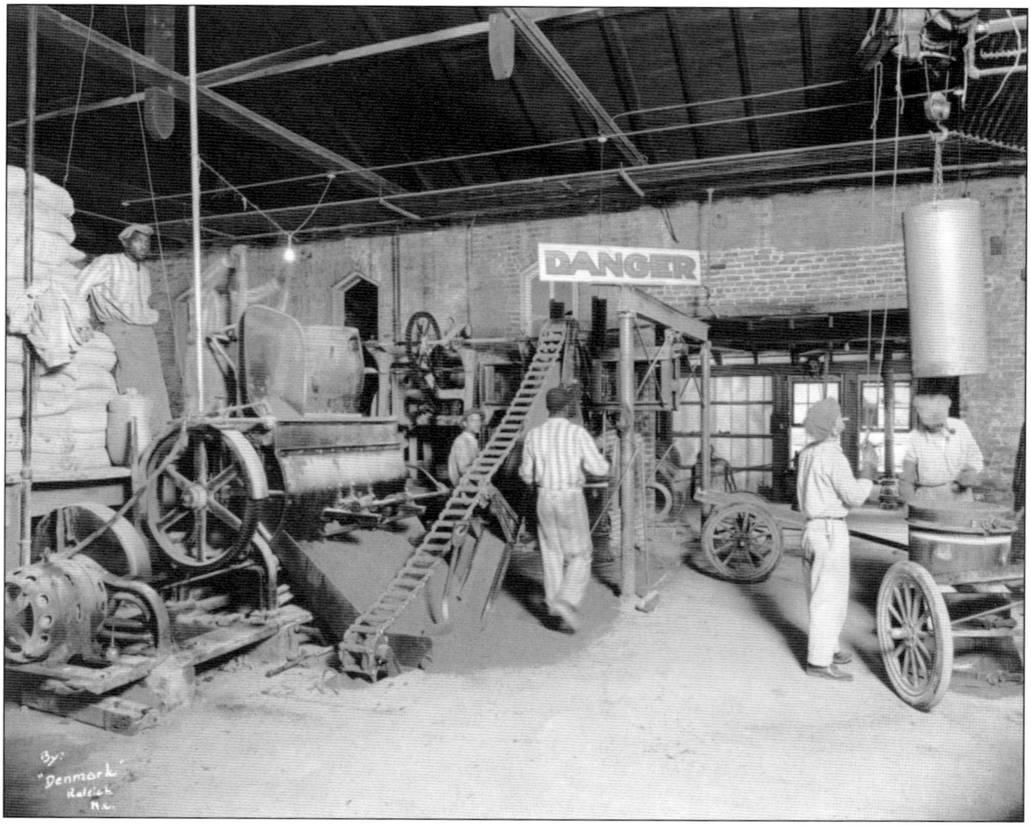

Concrete Culvert Plant, 1926. In 1926, the prison opened an on-site reinforced-concrete culvert plant. Prisoners produced culverts for sale to the state highway commission, with any surplus offered for sale to counties and towns. The commission, counties, and towns enjoyed substantial savings as a result of this relationship, the penitentiary earned a tidy profit, and inmates escaped the boredom of prison life, earned some money, and potentially gained marketable skills.

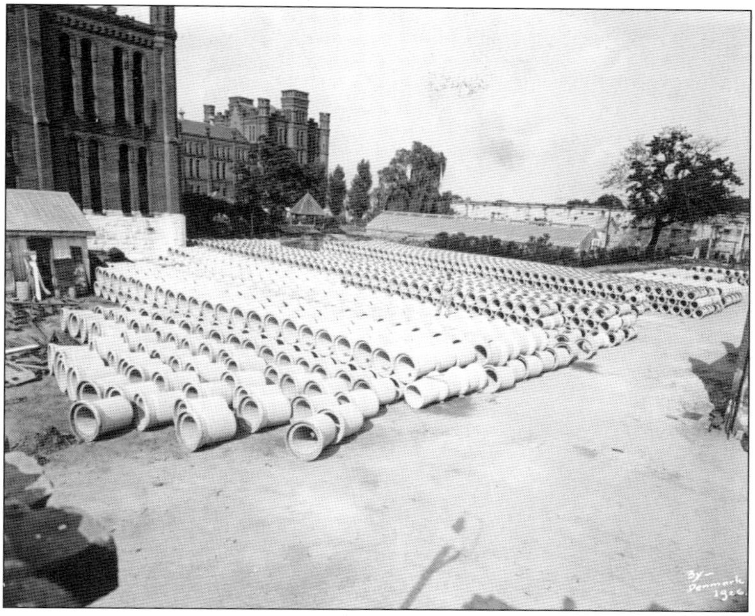

CONCRETE CULVERT STORED FOR CURING, 1926. The culvert plant operated for more than a decade, and evidence of its productivity can be seen here. In 1936, however, federal highway funding restrictions put an end to the industry. As a result, inmates were diverted to other developing on-site industries or were employed in the basic maintenance and upkeep of the penitentiary.

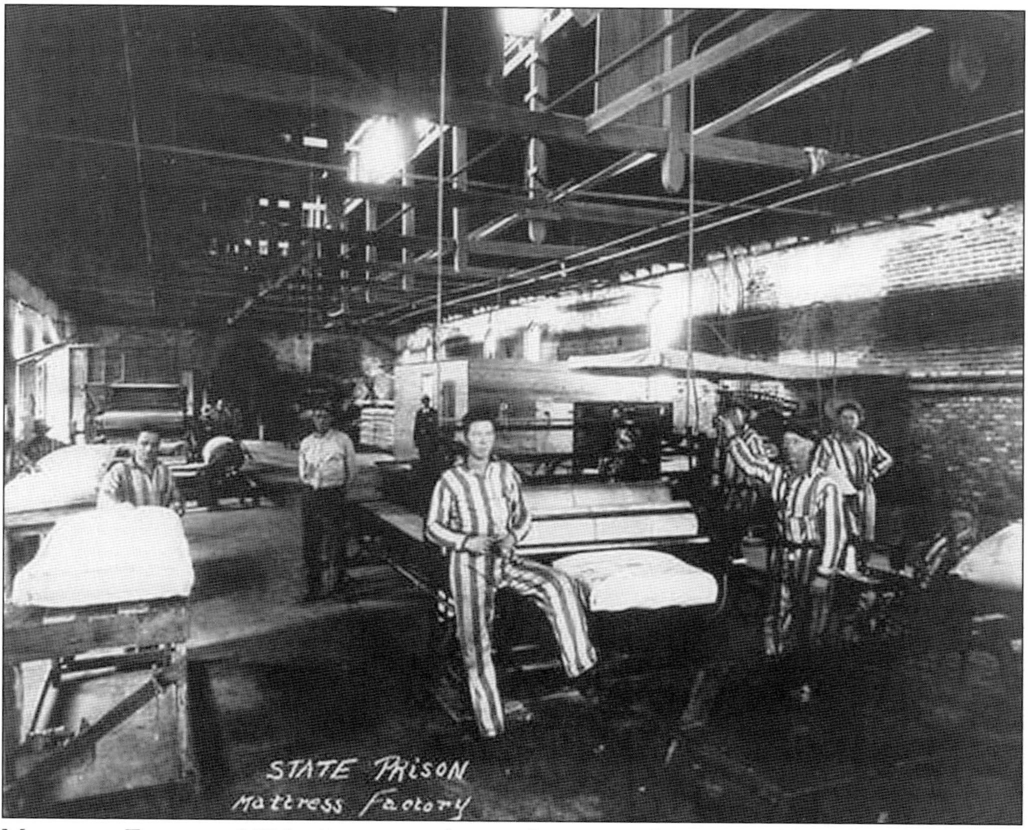

MATTRESS FACTORY, 1928. A mattress factory first opened in 1899, although mattresses for prisoner use alone were made as early as 1874. The first prison-made mattresses were stuffed with straw, but shuck (corn husks) and cotton eventually were used to create more comfortable and longer-lasting products.

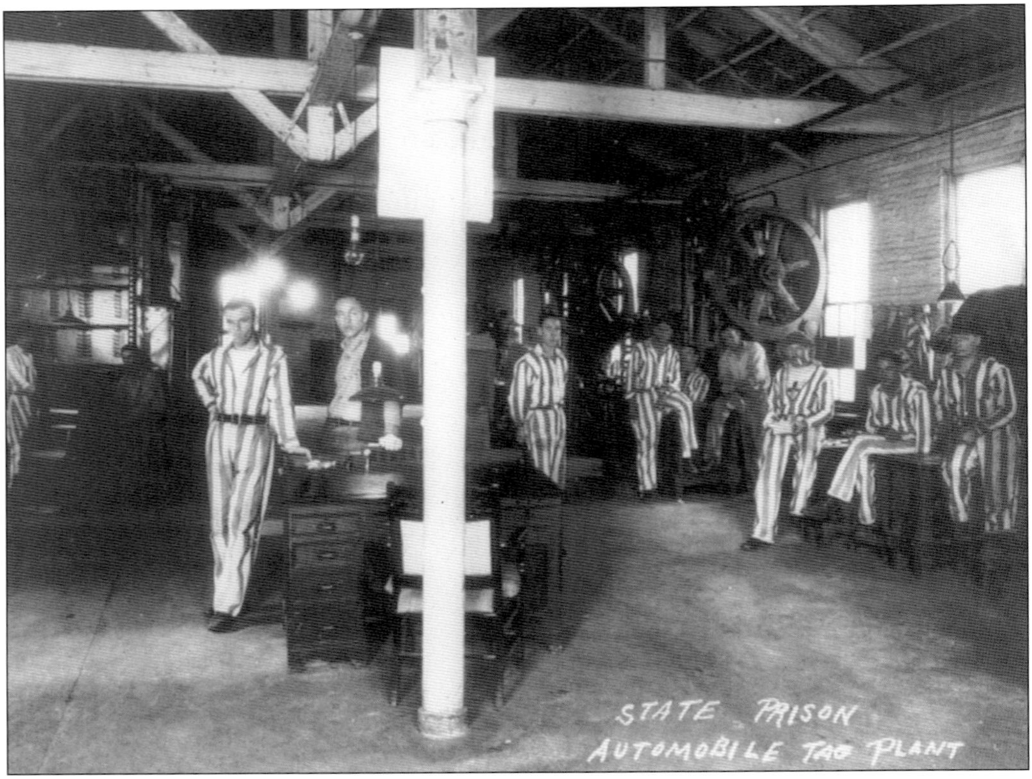

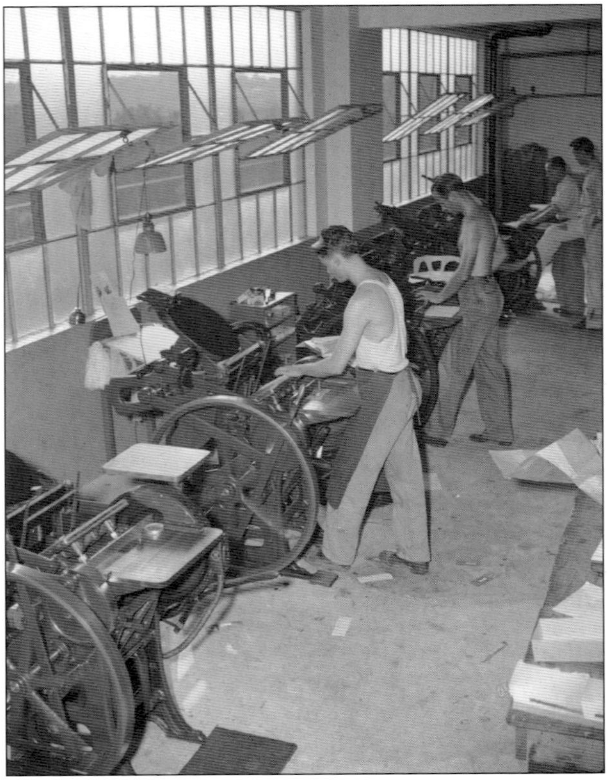

AUTOMOBILE TAG PLANT, 1928. From 1927 to 2001, inmates produced license plates. Such work was consistent with the purpose of the penitentiary; while not as difficult as breaking rocks with sledgehammers, working in the tag shop was not a skill one could easily apply outside of the penitentiary.

PRISONERS MAKING LICENSE PLATES, SEPTEMBER 1, 1940. The penitentiary continuously updated the machinery of the tag plant, and by 1935, the 20 inmates employed there produced 500,000 tags annually.

Tag Shop, 1940s. In the 1940s, the tag plant moved to a new industrial building. This image from the new facility shows some of the new machinery as well as the changing attire of the inmates. In 1928, they wore striped uniforms, but by the 1940s, they donned denim uniforms.

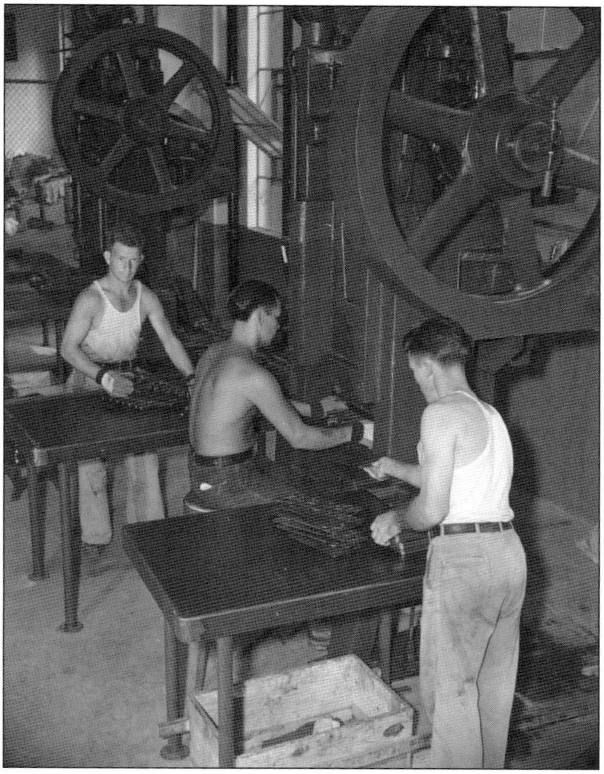

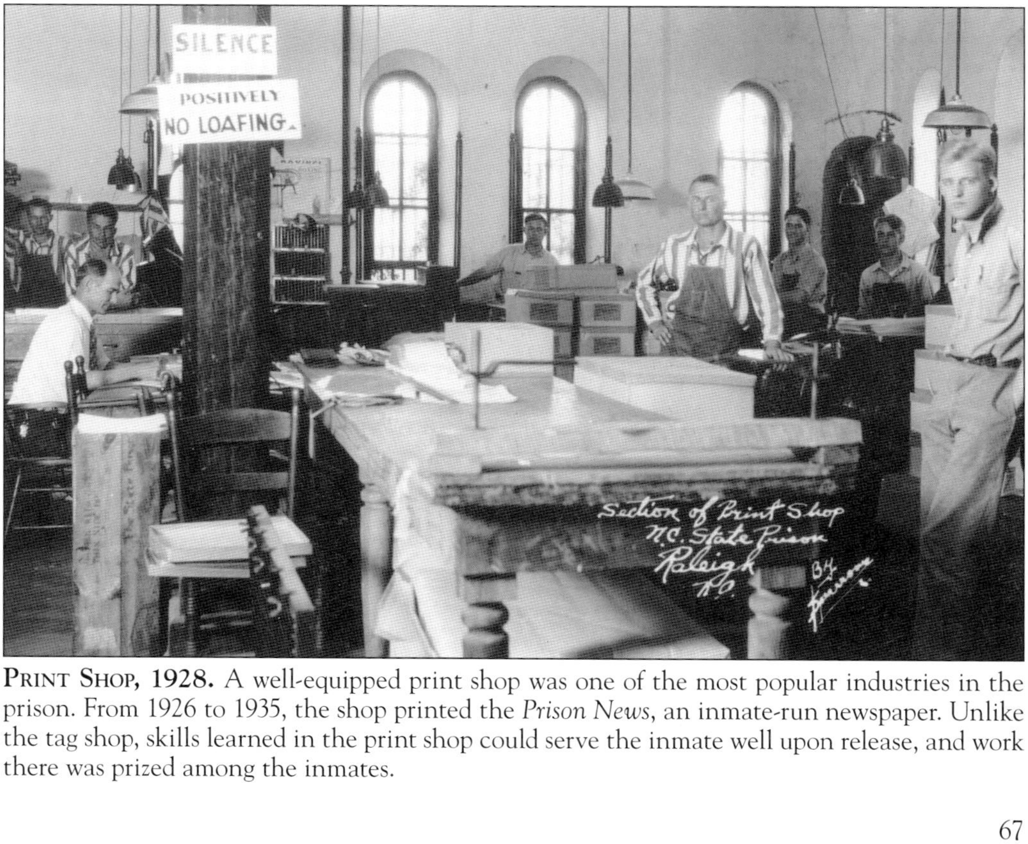

Print Shop, 1928. A well-equipped print shop was one of the most popular industries in the prison. From 1926 to 1935, the shop printed the *Prison News*, an inmate-run newspaper. Unlike the tag shop, skills learned in the print shop could serve the inmate well upon release, and work there was prized among the inmates.

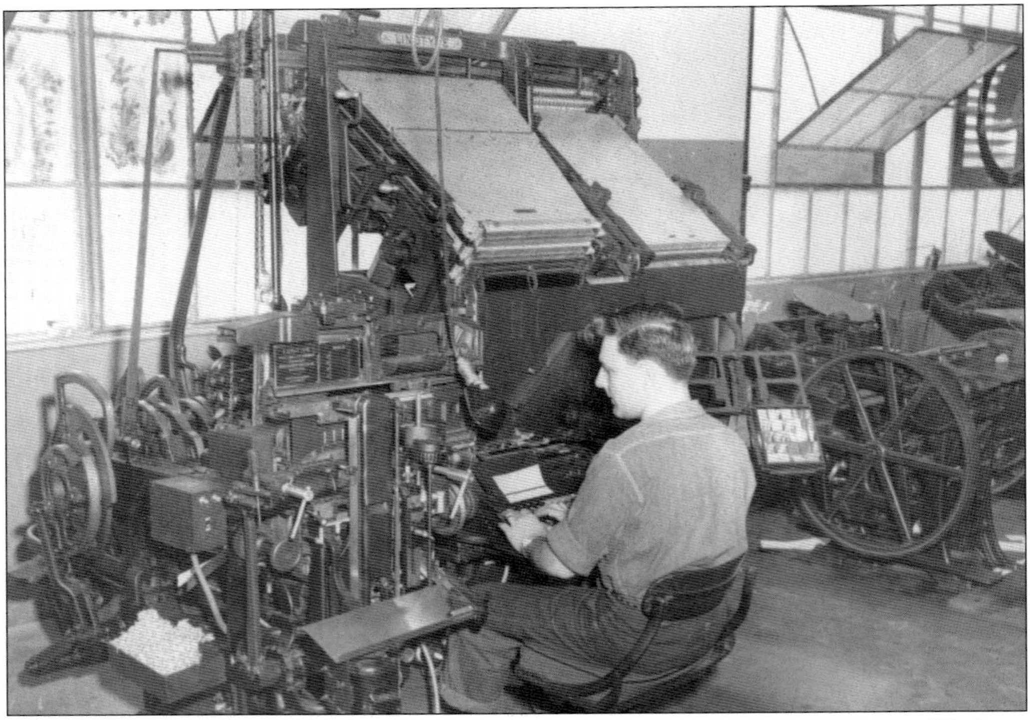

INMATE AT LINOTYPE, 1940S. Workers in the print shop produced postcards, brochures, business cards, booklets, posters, government forms, and other printable formats. They also produced copies of fingerprint records for distribution should an inmate escape.

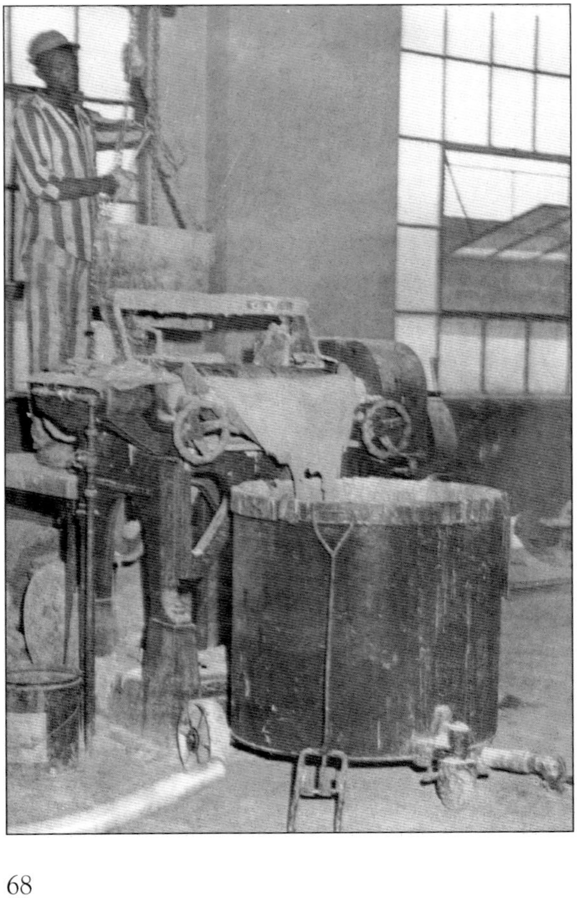

PAINT SHOP, 1952. Inmates in the paint shop produced large quantities of paint for sale to state, county, and local governments.

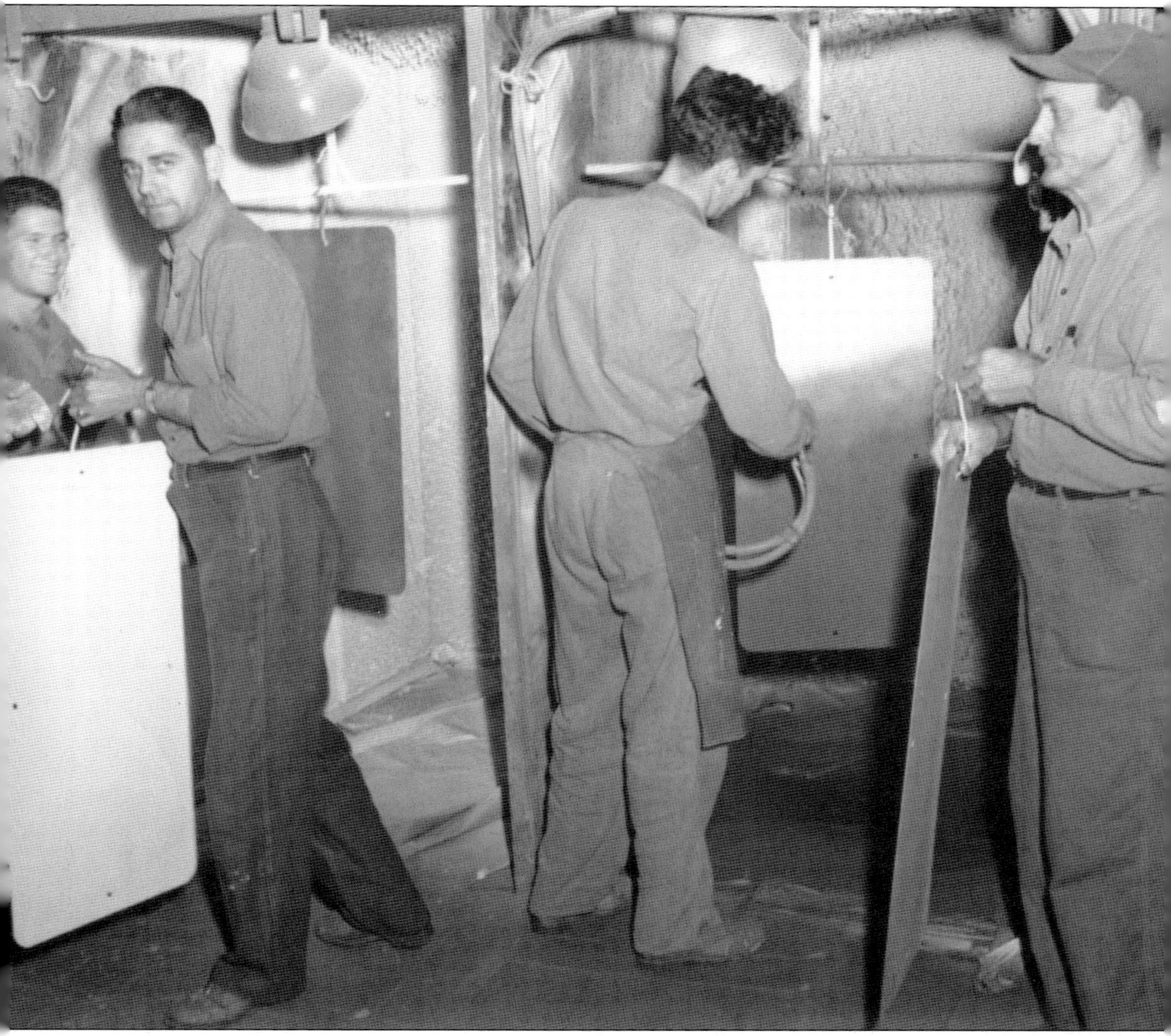

Painting Road Signs in the Paint Shop, 1952. The production of paint and painting signs provided skills that could benefit the inmate upon release.

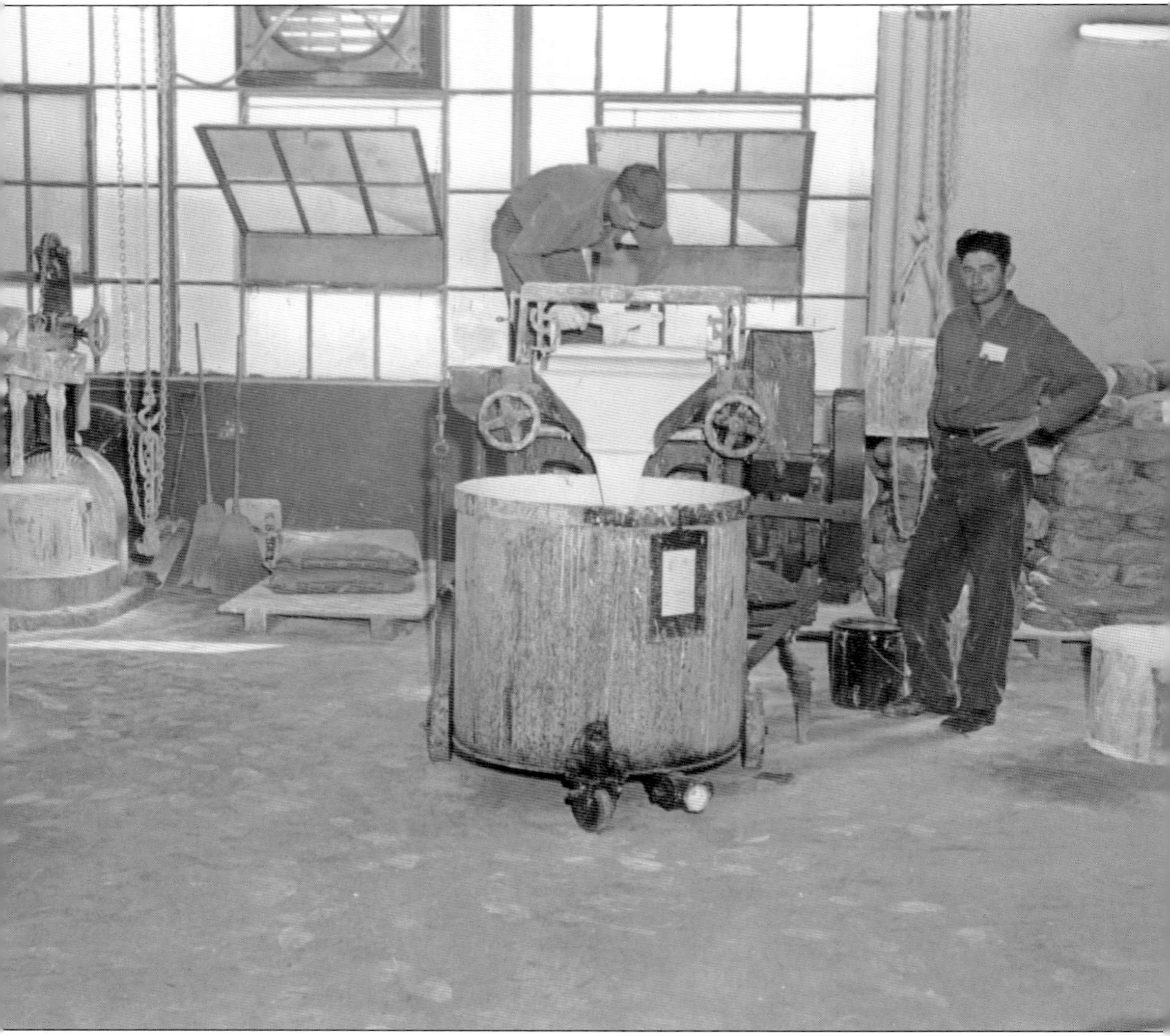

Paint Shop Worker. Those inmates who learned a trade while in prison often found employment on the outside. Such a circumstance was beneficial to all involved, as the employed ex-convict stood a better chance of setting aside a life of crime and becoming an asset to the state, rather than a continuing liability.

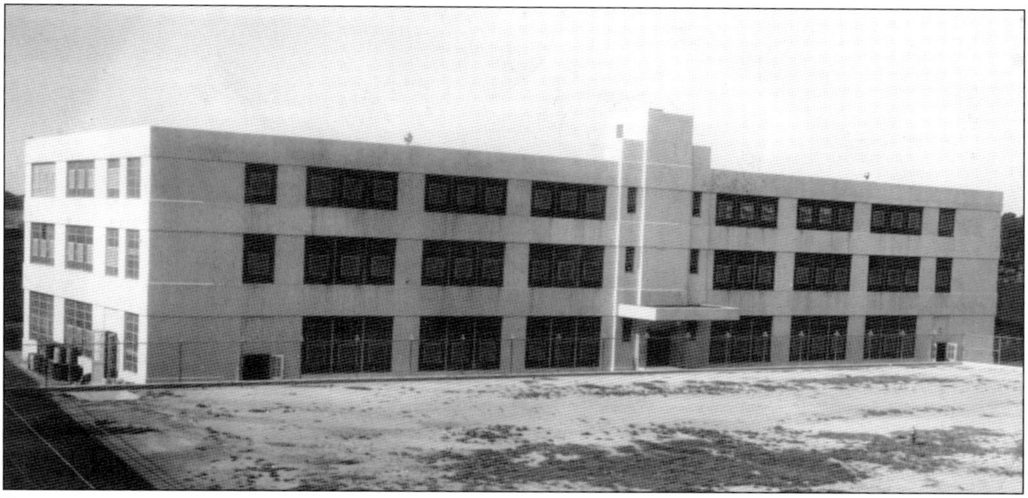

INDUSTRIAL BUILDING, 1949. By 1952, most on-site industrial jobs were performed in the industries building pictured here. Among the trades inmates could learn were welding, masonry, electrical work, carpentry, concrete work, tailoring, cooking, milling accountancy, tractor and truck driving, cabinet making, blacksmithing, dairying, plumbing, and upholstering.

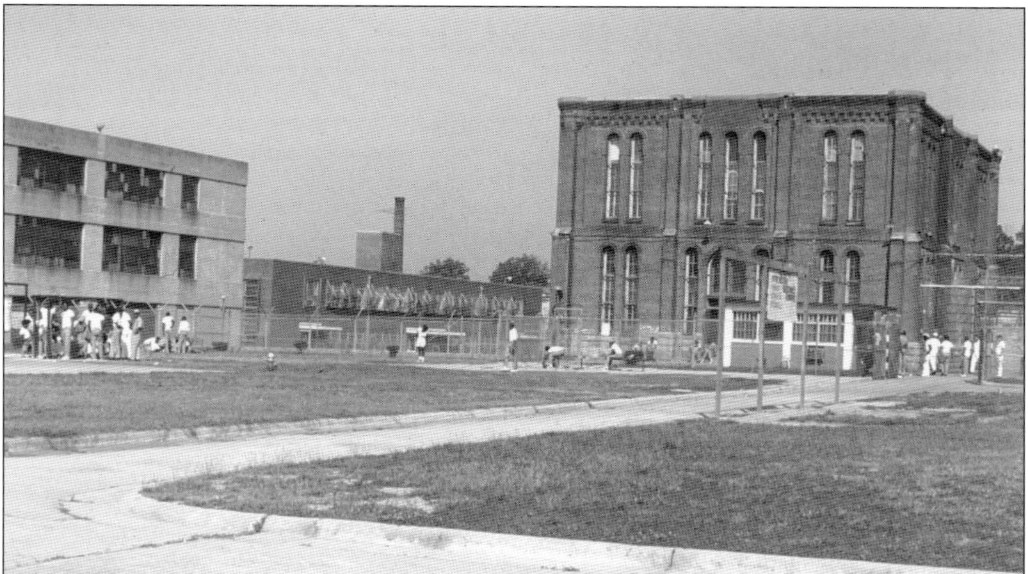

INMATES AT RECREATION, INDUSTRIAL COURTYARD, 1970S. The industrial building is the concrete structure to the left, K-Dormitory is the shorter two-story building in the center, and the truncated women's building is the taller brick structure to the right. The recreation area is in the foreground.

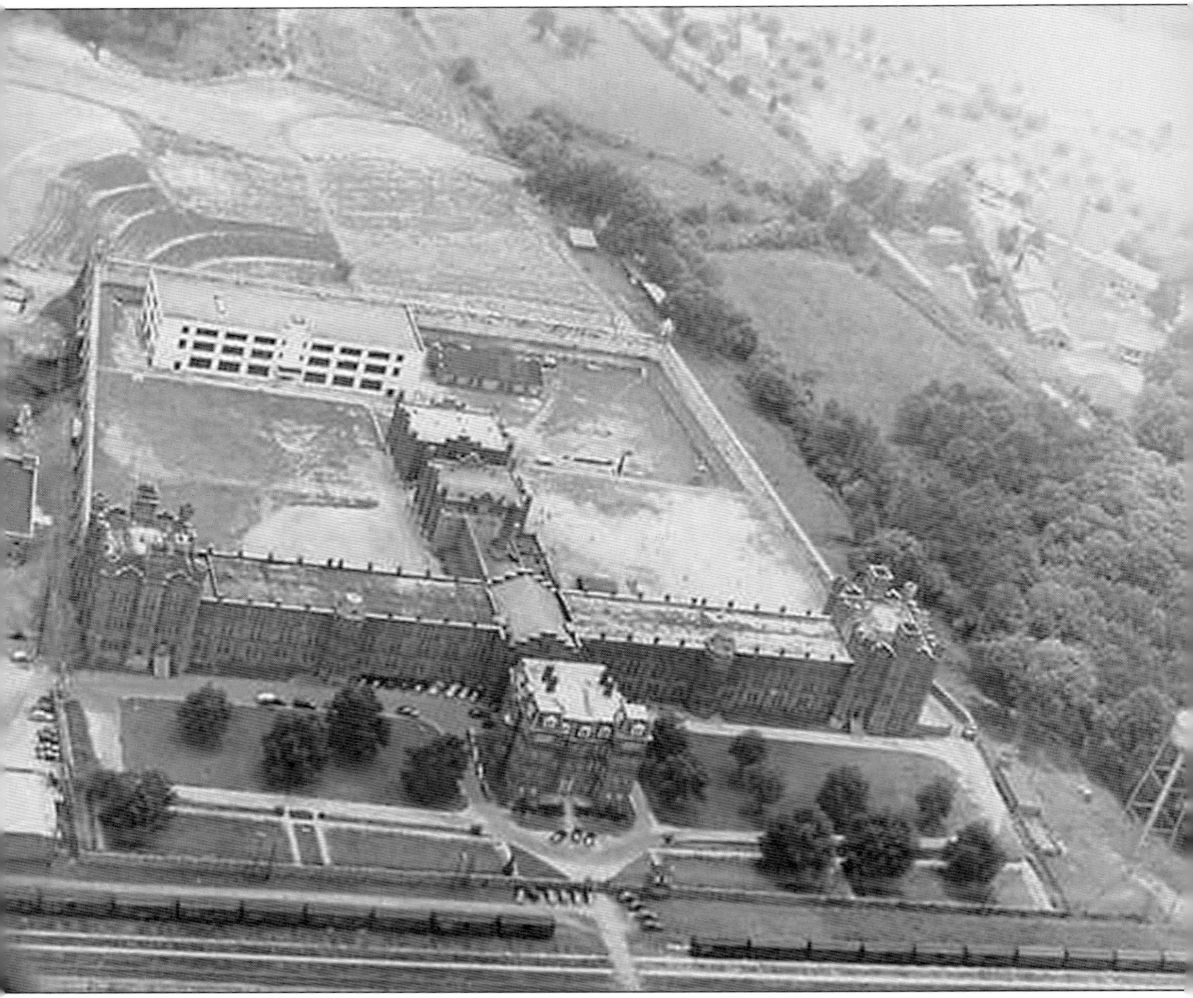

Aerial View, 1949. This photograph shows the relative location of the industrial building, in the upper left of the penitentiary complex. North of the building is the industrial courtyard and recreation area, and to the west is K-Dormitory.

Six

Institutional Work Assignments

Not all inmate workers produced profit for the penitentiary. In many cases, inmates simply maintained the penitentiary facility and met the immediate demands of the prisoners and staff. Inmates raised chickens, cooked, butchered meat, and baked bread. Some sewed and laundered clothes or cobbled shoes, while others maintained the grounds, raised flowers, and attended to the prison's tools and animals. While these inmates did not produce direct financial benefits for the state, by producing many of the necessities of life they reduced expenditures and helped keep down costs. An 1874 study determined that the state saved $101,000 by relying on goods produced from inmate labor. In 1911, inmates working six acres of land adjacent to the penitentiary provided additional cost savings when they raised crops that enabled them to can 7,000 quarts of tomatoes, 1,000 quarts of chow-chow (a pickled relish), 1,000 quarts of beets, five barrels of cucumbers, four barrels of pepper, and a substantial amount of ketchup.

Such labor also provided yet another avenue to distract inmates from the stressful realities of prison life, and many prisoners found the jobs calming. Work in the penitentiary greenhouse was especially popular, as it provided a quiet, colorful, and controlled setting in which inmates could participate in life-affirming work.

Additionally, some of these service jobs taught skills inmates could apply upon release. Work as cooks, bakers, butchers, tailors, and landscape workers may not have offered the road to riches, but it provided the possibility of honest labor. In a similar vein, such work also taught life lessons and skills that potentially could help the inmate cope with an unstructured life outside the penitentiary walls. At their heart, of course, all the jobs in which the inmates were employed served as part of the constitutional mandate that prisoners suffer the penalty of hard labor.

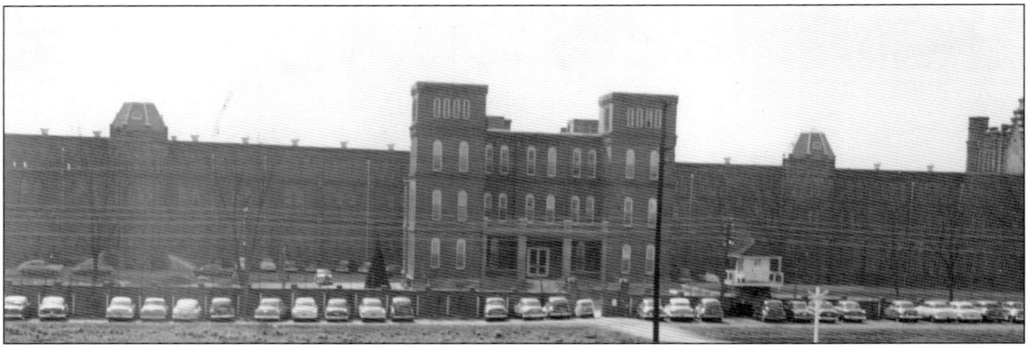

North View of Main Entrance, 1940s. Prisoners who performed institutional maintenance assignments not only served the needs of the prison community and enjoyed the potential to learn a skill, but they also learned a work ethic. Appreciating a job well done and learning to overcome obstacles with the goal of completing a task was not always within the psychological perspective of inmates. Beautifying the grounds, fixing broken equipment, or producing goods other inmates needed provided them with a sense of achievement.

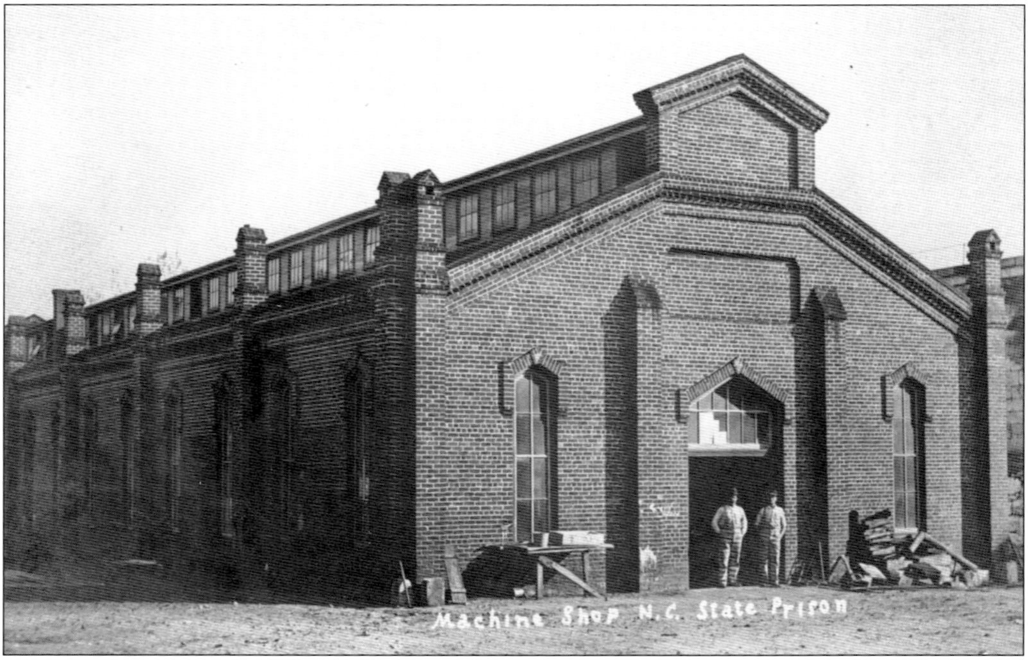

Machine Shop, 1910. One area where inmates learned a great deal was in the machine shop, where, by 1900, operations consisted mostly of repair work. Inmates worked on wagons, carts, and other equipment used at Central Prison, on the farms, and on the roads. Some inmates produced new products, including horse-drawn wagons, wheelbarrows, and all the penitentiary's iron bedsteads.

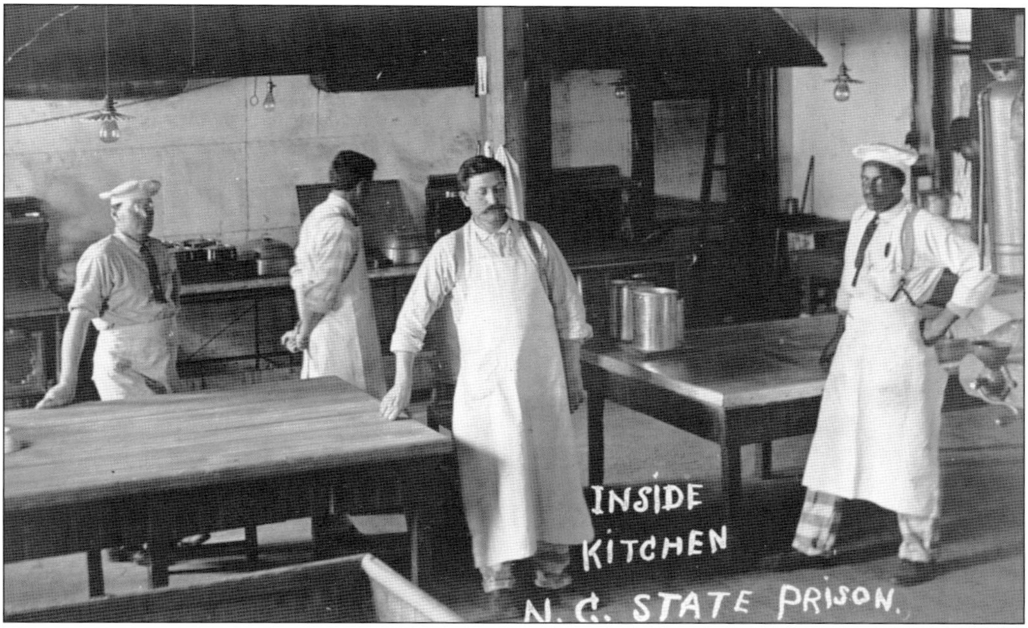

The Kitchen, 1910. According to the 1911–1912 biennial report, "The food at Central Prison was carefully prepared and properly served; it was wholesome, nourishing and plentiful. It was varied and consisted of beef, fresh fish, salt fish, bacon, and pork as meats. One vegetable and sometimes two were served every day; wheat bread for breakfast and supper, corn bread for dinner; coffee with sugar twice a day; dessert twice a week."

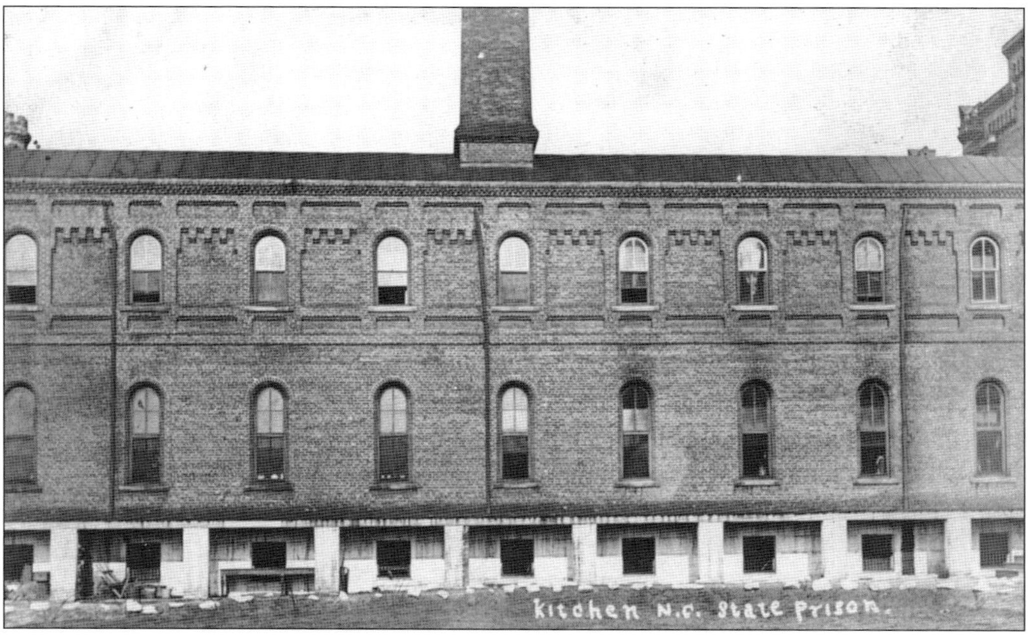

Exterior View of the Kitchen, 1910. Holiday dinners were served on Easter, the Fourth of July, Thanksgiving, and Christmas, and prisoners received a present of apples, oranges, cakes, candy, mixed nuts, and raisins on Christmas Eve. These gifts were well received, as fresh fruit rarely was served as a part of the regular meal. Inmates, wearing aprons over their prison clothes, were responsible for these very popular meals.

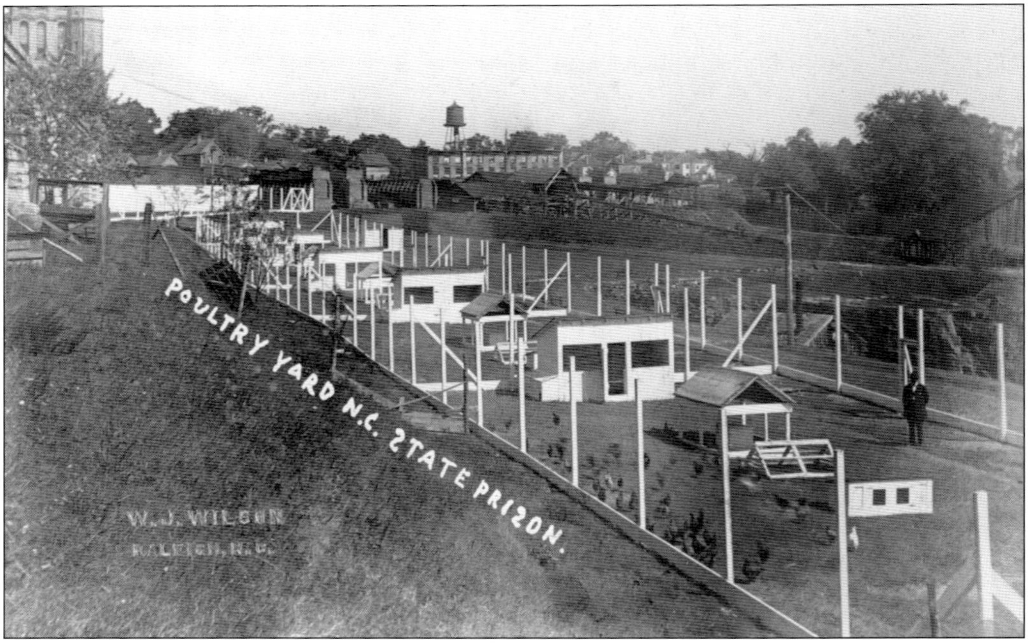

Poultry Yard, 1913. The prison dairy supplied all the milk inmates consumed, while the poultry yard furnished the chickens and eggs.

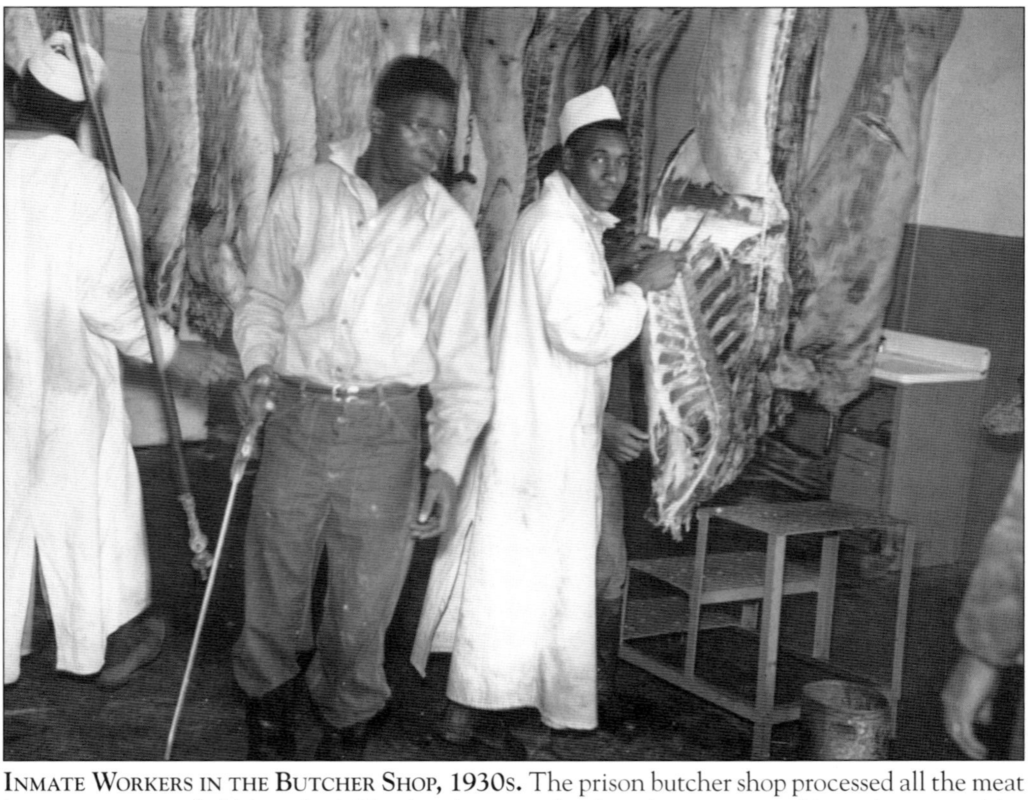

Inmate Workers in the Butcher Shop, 1930s. The prison butcher shop processed all the meat inmates consumed. Although civilian butchers ran the shop, inmates served in various capacities and learned the skills of the trade.

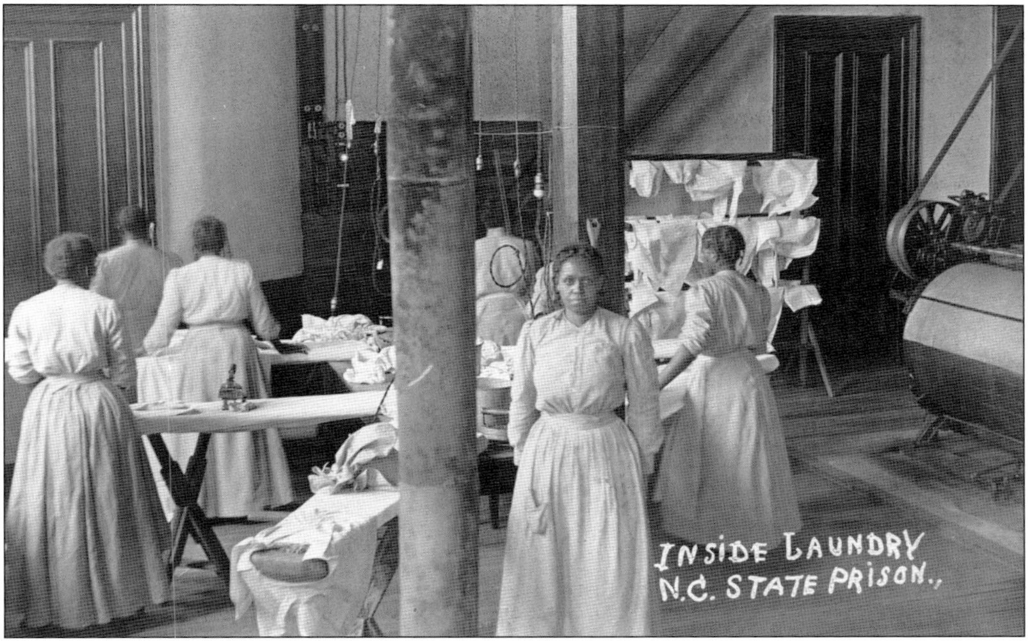

LAUNDRY SHOWING FEMALE PRISON WORKERS, 1910. The labor women performed at Central Prison was quite valuable, as they made clothes for the entire population and did much of the laundry for inmates and employees. In addition to the penitentiary's laundry, women did the laundry for the Confederate veterans' home.

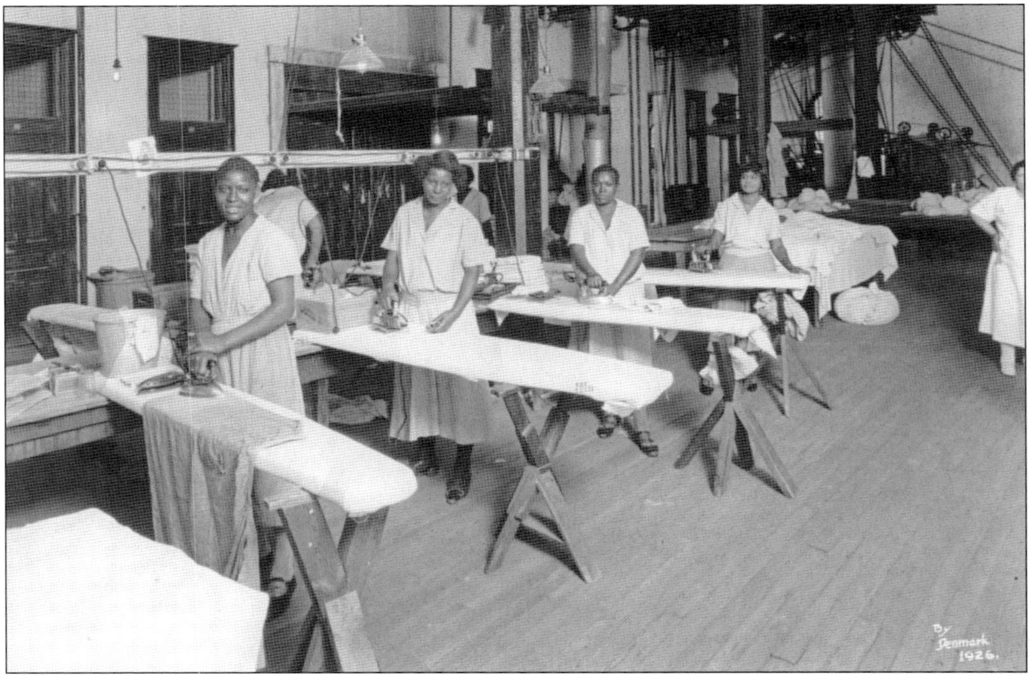

FEMALE PRISONERS IRONING, 1910. The laundry and sewing machines were operated by electrical motors, which enabled efficient cleaning, mending, and sewing. According to the 1909–1910 biennial report, female inmates employed in the laundry were "kind and obliging to prisoners as well as officers" and maintained "good discipline."

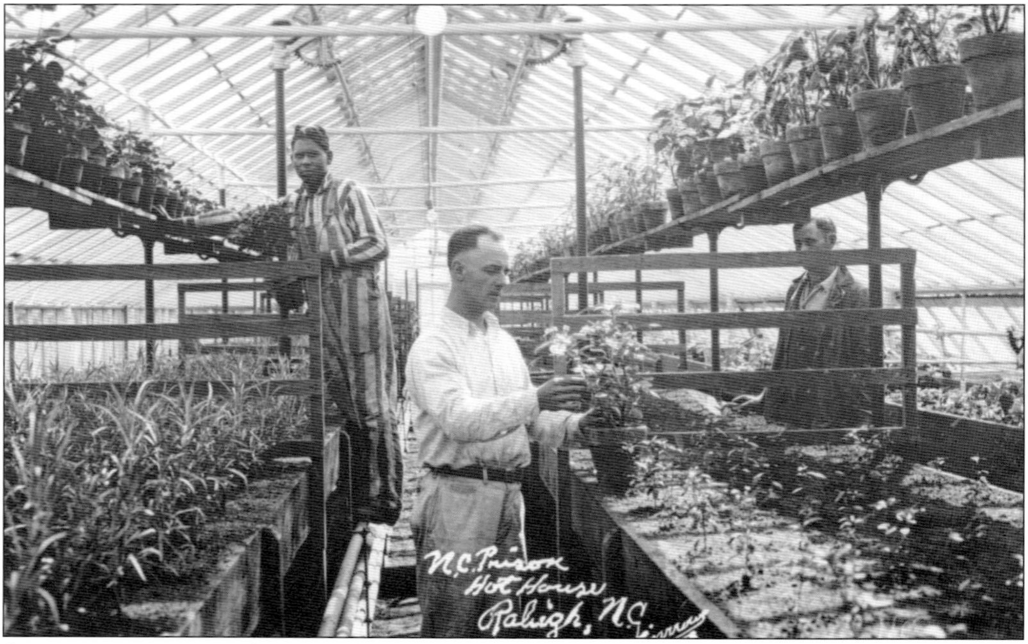

GREENHOUSE, 1930s. Flowers and plants were raised by prisoners for sale to florists. Although not considered as such at the time, this type of activity could have been quite therapeutic for inmates, as it was quiet, required focus, provided direct interaction with bright and colorful flowers, and offered the opportunity to cultivate life.

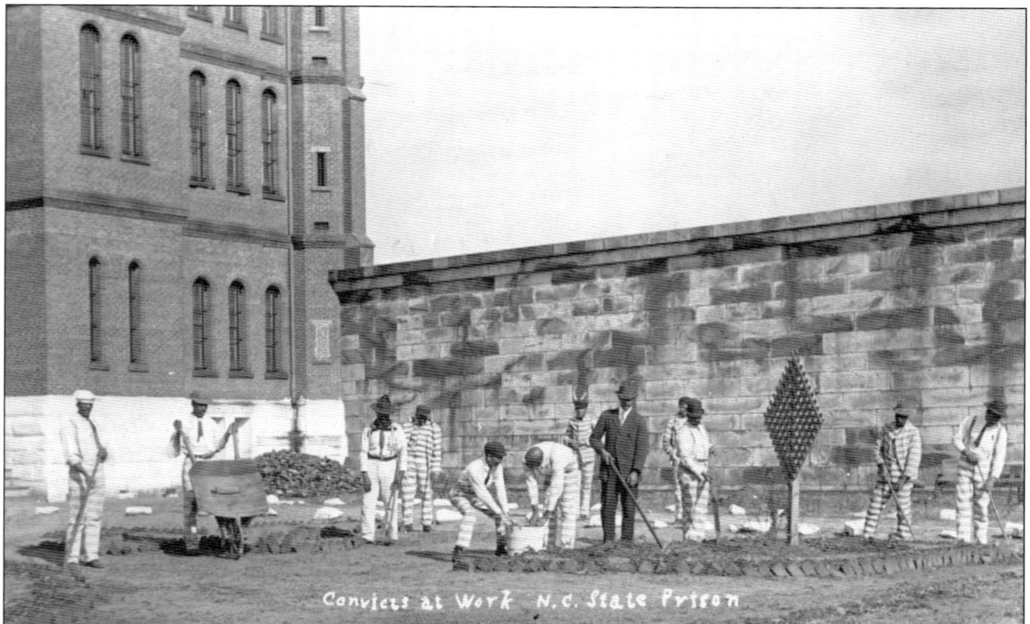

CONVICTS AT WORK IN THE YARD, 1910. Inmates also tended the prison grounds. Although the buildings and wall cast a foreboding pall over the prison, thanks to inmate labor, the grounds themselves were colorful and lush.

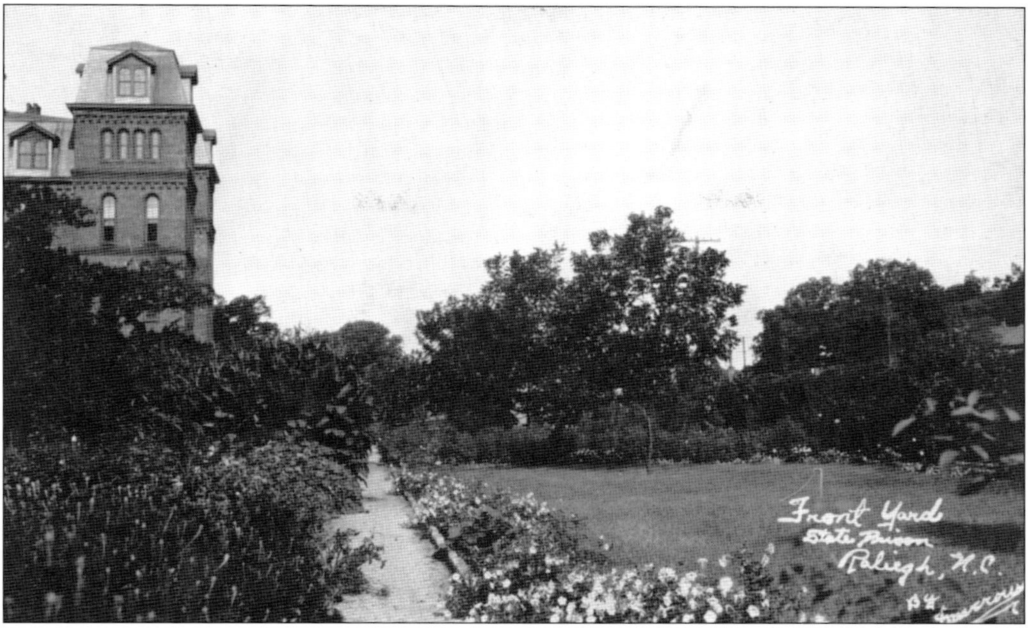

FRONT ENTRANCE, 1910. As early as 1874, with the prison still a decade away from completion, the board of directors noted the extensive labor employed in grading the grounds in their report for the same year. They applauded the fact that a beginning had been made to lay out and beautify the grounds about the intended administration building and facing on the line of the railroads.

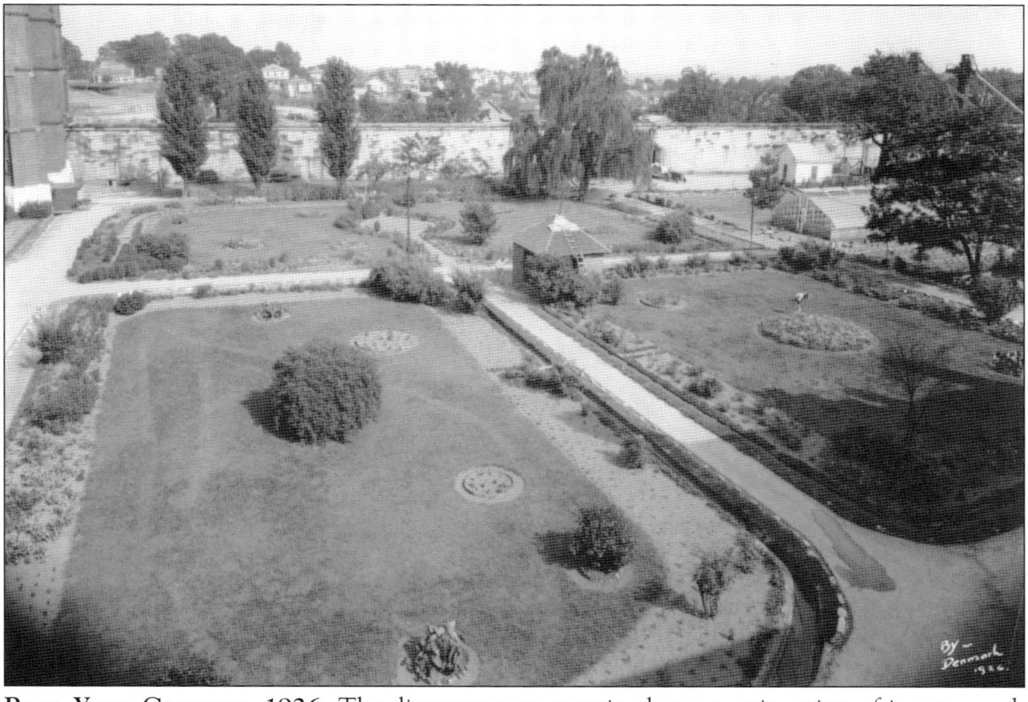

REAR YARD GROUNDS, 1926. The directors were certain that a continuation of inmate work would ensure that "by the time the permanent offices are ready for occupancy; these grounds will relieve the dull and gloomy appearance of the solid masonry so common to prison buildings." These images make clear that the directors' hopes were fulfilled.

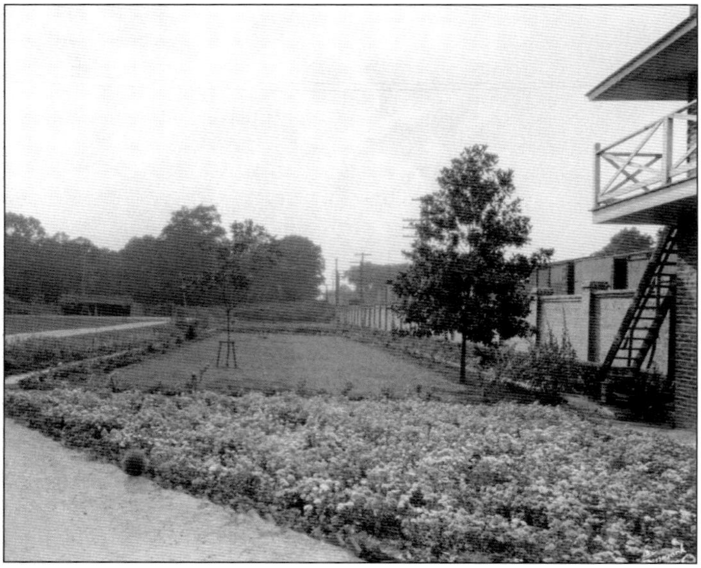

FRONT YARD GROUNDS, 1926. Beautification efforts continued throughout the penitentiary's existence. In 1910, warden T.P. Sale reported, "The entire prison has undergone a vast change in the past two years. It was our purpose from the beginning to renovate from top to bottom. This has been done and the prison as it is today shows everything to be in a neat, clean, sanitary condition, and there seems to be no cause for complaint from any source."

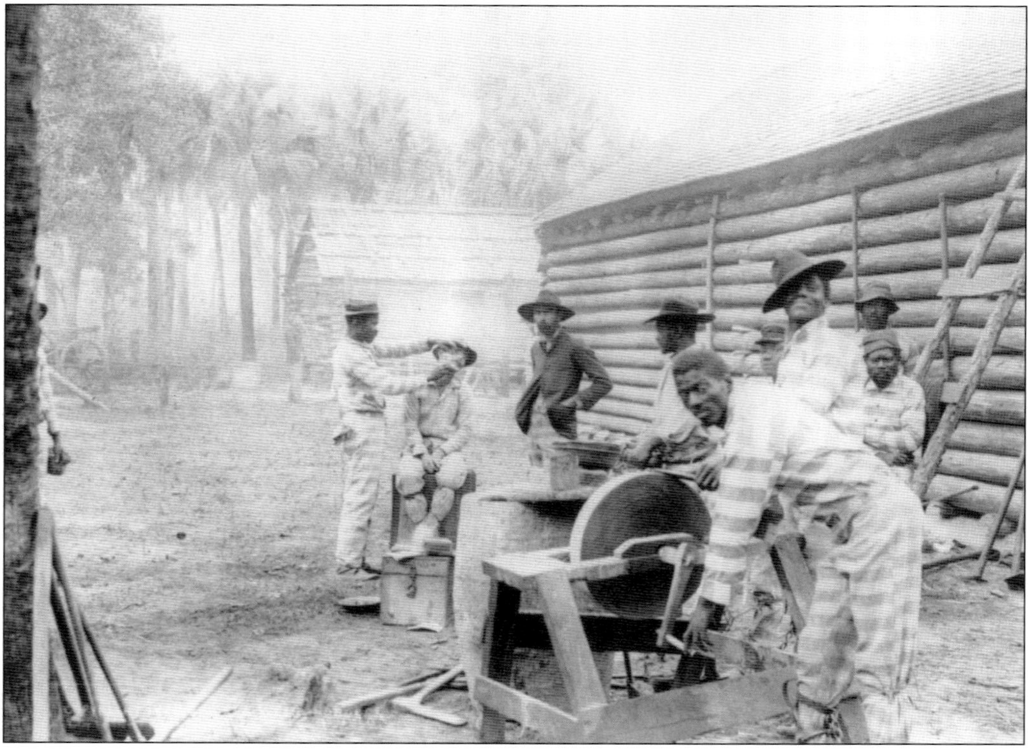

OLD TEMPORARY STRUCTURES, PRISON GROUNDS WORK CREW IN LEG IRONS. "Indeed," Warden Sale continued, "we feel that we have cause to congratulate ourselves upon the clean, healthful, sanitary conditions that now exist, and the methods used in bringing about these results. Dr. W. S. Rankin, the efficient Secretary to the State Board of Health, said, while making an official visit to the prison some time ago, that it was the cleanest institution of its kind he had ever visited."

Seven

INMATE CLASSIFICATIONS

When Central Prison first opened, inmates were classified according to risk. As inmates came to be known to custody officers, the more dependable could earn trustee status, which gave them relative freedom and limited oversight. In 1901, the state senate ended the practice after learning that inmates serving lengthy sentences and convicted of violent crimes had gained trustee designation. In 1917, the legislature revised the inmate classification system. All prisoners were classified as Grade A, B, or C. Grade A was the honor status, and Grade C consisted of incorrigibles with behavioral or disciplinary issues. The classifications were based on the crime the individual committed as well as their conduct in prison. In 1925, Supt. George Pou called for additional reforms. In 1927, the state enacted several of Pou's requests, including changing the inmate dress code and implementing indeterminate sentencing, by which inmates received time off for good behavior. Grade A inmates were assigned khaki clothing and were eligible for 8.5 days reduced sentence per month for good conduct, Grade B inmates wore vertical stripes and were eligible for 6.5 days reduced sentence per month, and Grade C inmates wore horizontal stripes and were eligible for 4.5 days reduced sentence per month.

In the 1930s, the privileges were altered yet again. Grade A inmates donned blue denim uniforms, gained yard privileges all day on Sunday and holidays, could write letters every Sunday, and received 9 days per month for good behavior and 30 days at the end of each year served. Grade B inmates wore brown khaki uniforms, had yard privileges only on holidays, could write letters twice a month, and received 7 days per month for good behavior. Grade C inmates received horizontally striped uniforms and could write letters only once a month. The uniforms allowed corrections officers an easily identifiable indicator of an inmate's likely behavior, while the classification system and privileges served as the carrot and stick to entice inmates toward good behavior.

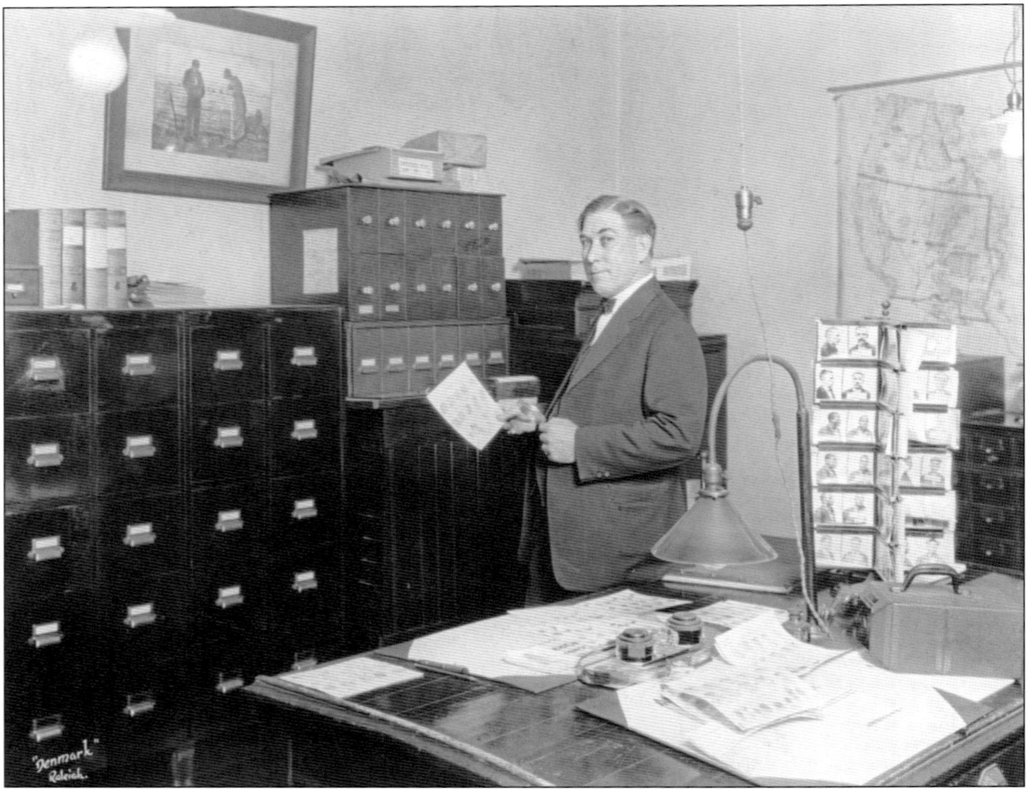

STATE BUREAU OF INVESTIGATION OFFICE, 1926. The State Bureau of Investigation was established in 1923. According to H.H. Honeycutt, then the deputy warden and director of the bureau, when prisoners arrived at the penitentiary they were given a haircut, shaved, and bathed. The deputy warden then produced a full physical description of the inmate; recorded the serial number, crime, and sentence; gathered personal information about nearest kin; and made two copies of the prisoner's fingerprints.

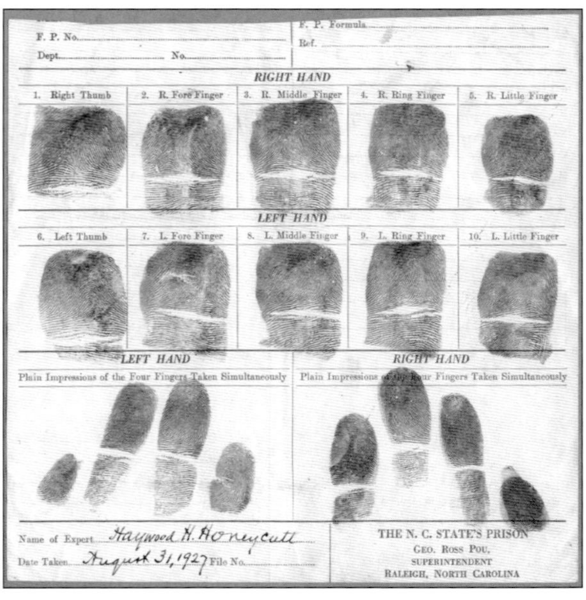
F. P. No.
Dept. No.
F. P. Formula
Ref.

RIGHT HAND

1. Right Thumb | 2. R. Fore Finger | 3. R. Middle Finger | 4. R. Ring Finger | 5. R. Little Finger

LEFT HAND

6. Left Thumb | 7. L. Fore Finger | 8. L. Middle Finger | 9. L. Ring Finger | 10. L. Little Finger

LEFT HAND
Plain Impressions of the Four Fingers Taken Simultaneously

RIGHT HAND
Plain Impressions of the Four Fingers Taken Simultaneously

Name of Expert Haywood H. Honeycutt
Date Taken August 31, 1927 File No.

THE N. C. STATE'S PRISON
GEO. ROSS POU,
SUPERINTENDENT
RALEIGH, NORTH CAROLINA

FINGERPRINT, 1927. Fingerprinting served two purposes. First, the Department of Justice used prints to notify prisons if a new arrival had escaped previously from another prison. This allowed the administration to place the inmate under conditions of heightened security. Second, it facilitated the recapture of escaped inmates. Of the 143 escapees from Central Prison, recaptured by 1928, fingerprints were used to identify 102 of them.

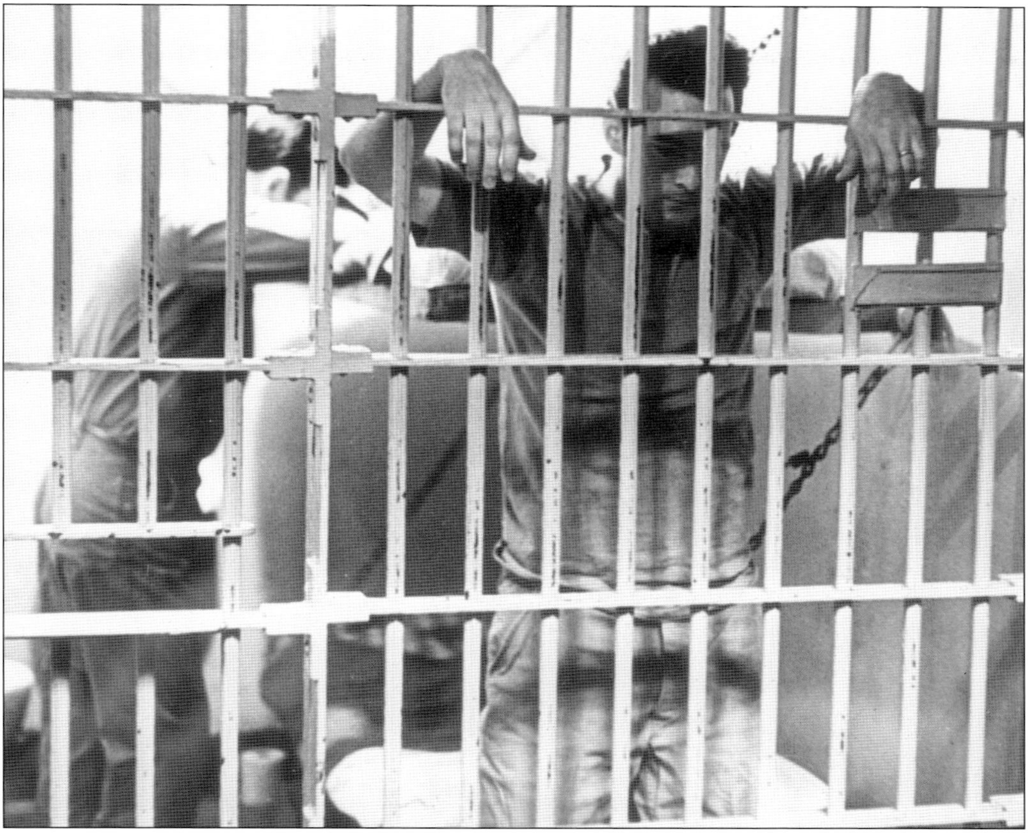

Prisoners in Their Cell, 1950s. The improved record keeping offered penitentiary officials a better understanding of the crimes for which prisoners were sentenced. Records from the late 1920s indicate that the most common offenses were manslaughter, murder, larceny, and breaking and entering.

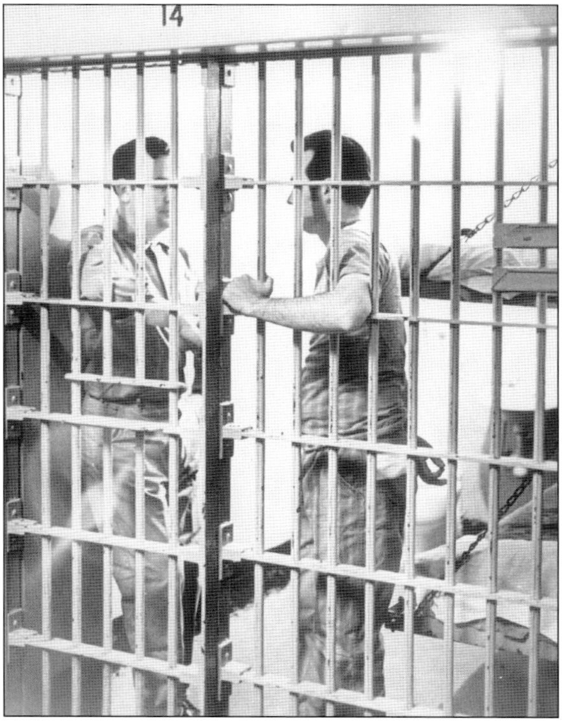

Prisoners Talking in Their Cell, 1950s. Other common crimes included arson, assault, robbery, forgery, and producing alcohol. Those same records also note some rather uncommon crimes, including bigamy, "seduction," "elopement," and "operating a smoke screen." In all, 2,323 inmates convicted of more than 50 different crimes passed through Central Prison between 1928 and 1930.

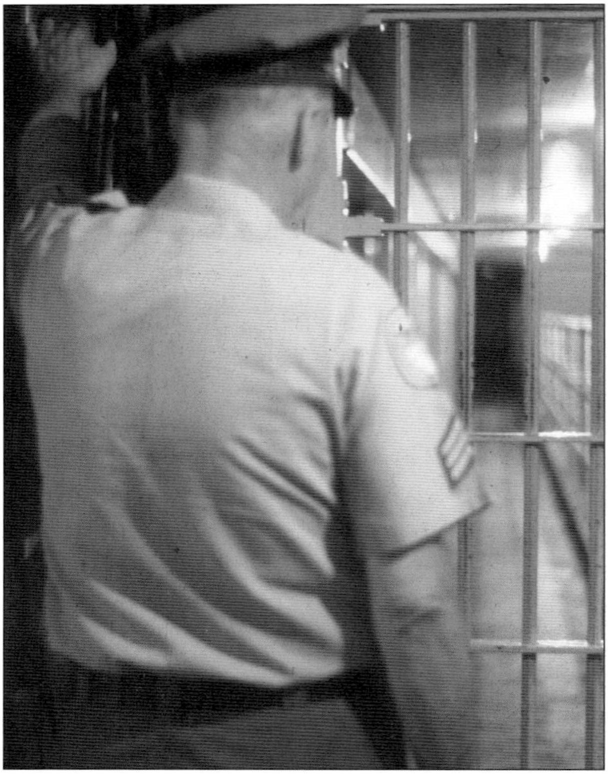

GUARD IN CELL BLOCK, 1960S. In 1932, Honeycutt, who became warden in 1929, simplified the rulebook. Many prisoners claimed ignorance when citied for misbehavior, so Honeycutt reduced the number of prison rules to 11 and had them printed in pamphlet form. Additionally, all prison employees received a pamphlet containing rules for the treatment of prisoners under their care. Such precautions proved effective in reducing disciplinary problems.

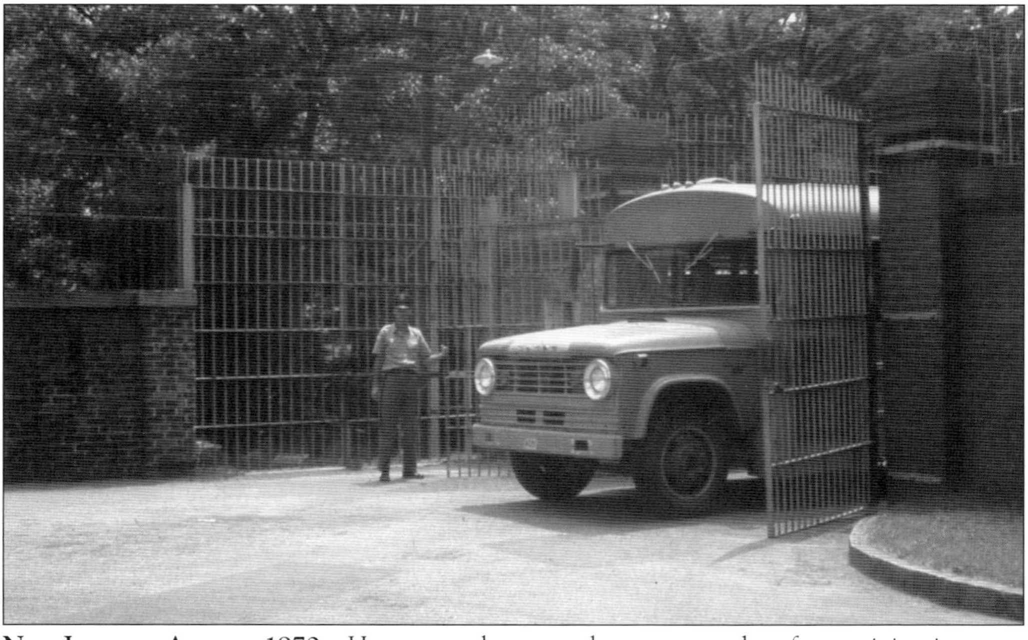

NEW INMATES ARRIVE, 1970S. Honeycutt also created a new procedure for receiving inmates. When a prisoner arrived, he was bathed and disinfected. All his street clothing was burned or shipped home, and he was issued a penitentiary uniform. Once dressed, the new inmate was taken to the warden's office, where he was presented the penitentiary rules, which also were explained to him. He then was fingerprinted.

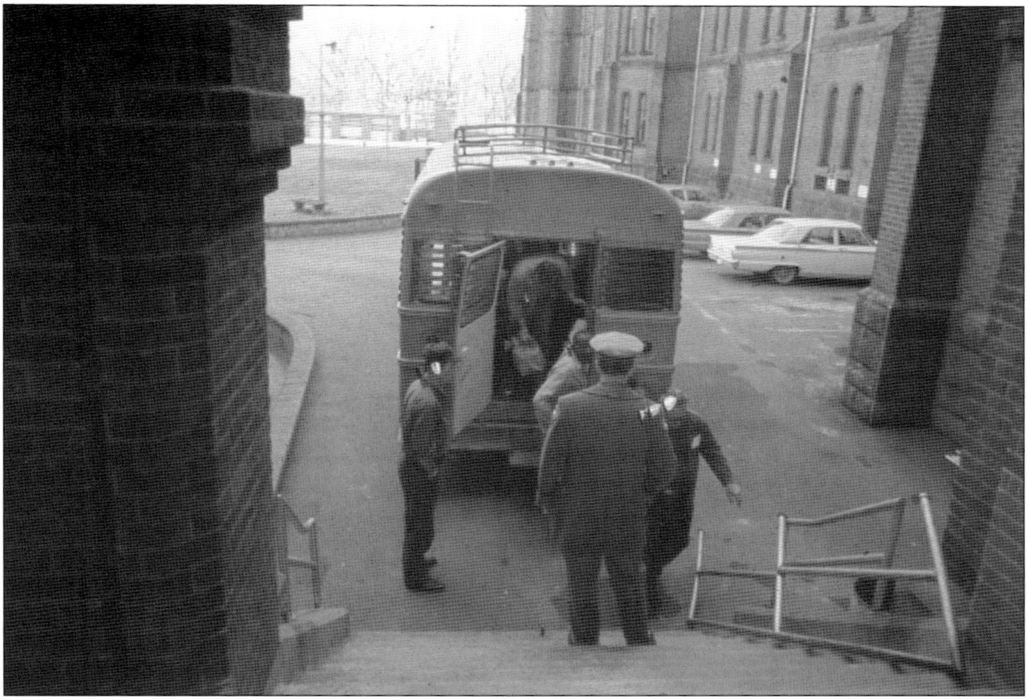

New Arrivals, 1970s. After the inmate was fingerprinted, he was photographed face on and in profile. Officials then recorded his physical description and history. Once his information was recorded, he was examined by a physician, a dentist, and a surgeon, and then physically classified. With his physical classification complete, he reported to the warden's office, where he was assigned work duty based on previous experience and mental and physical capacities.

Inmates Sharing a Cell, 1950s. The reforms continued with improved health standards. Upon arrival, all inmates were vaccinated against smallpox and typhoid fever and given a Wassermann test for syphilis along with any necessary treatment. The penitentiary also created a separate facility for tubercular inmates and began to abide by the sanitary requirements set by the board of health. With inmates living in close proximity, these reforms helped create a healthier institution.

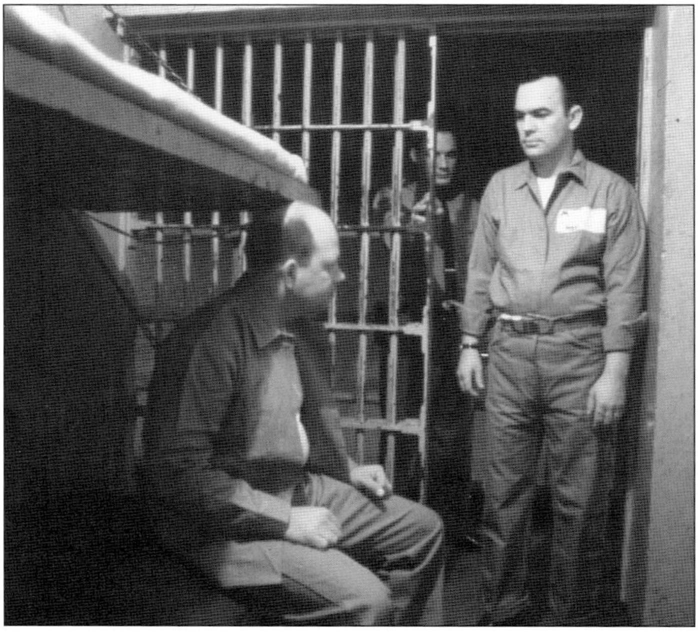

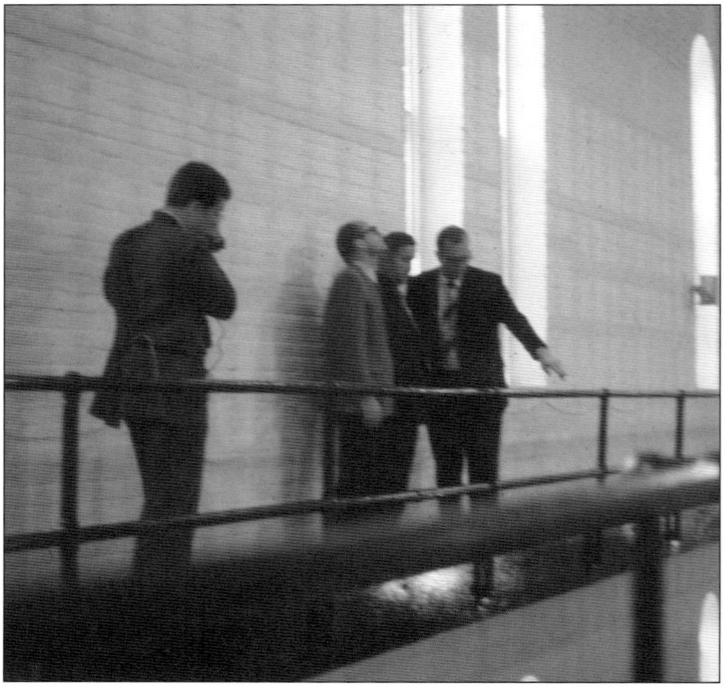

PRISON OFFICIALS INSPECT CELL BLOCK, 1970s. Administrative elements of the penitentiary also were reformed. New physical equipment was installed, modern systems of bookkeeping and accounting were introduced, and a new ranking system of the physical and mental condition of inmates was adopted. These reforms made it easier for officials to govern the penitentiary and custody officers to regulate the inmates.

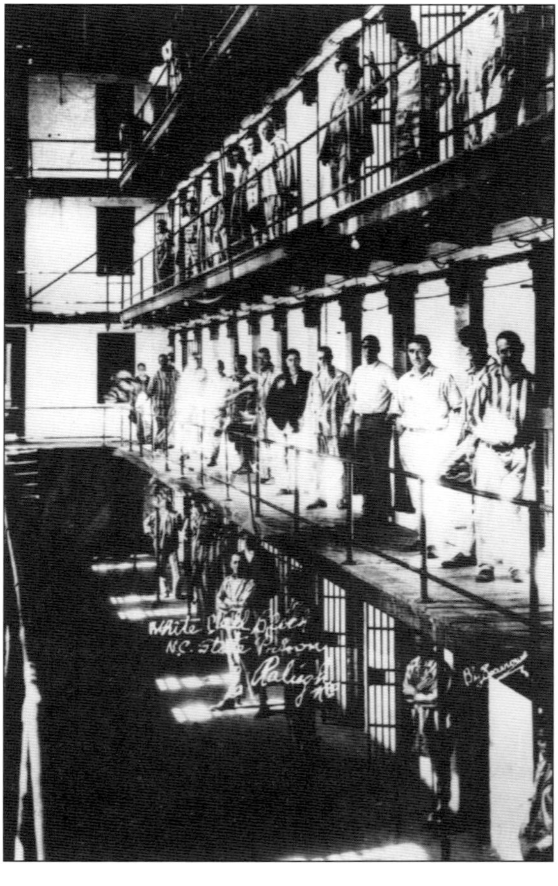

FIVE-TIERED SEGREGATED WHITE CELL BLOCK. Despite these reforms, several small riots and escape attempts upset the penitentiary's order. In 1932, racial segregation was introduced in the road camps as one means of improving discipline. At the prison itself, white and African American prisoners had always lived in separate cell houses and ate in different dining rooms or on different sides of the same room. While all female prisoners were housed in the same building, white women were employed at sewing, and African American women performed the laundry work.

ARCHWAY THROUGH WHICH NEW ARRIVALS WERE RECEIVED. Another effort to improve discipline was the partial segregation of prisoners by age. As early as 1870, penitentiary officials wrote in their annual report to the general assembly, "Perhaps no other means would so greatly aid in the discipline of the Prison and so greatly facilitate the efforts for the reformation of the convicts . . . [than] to separate the young, those yet *infants* in the eye of the law, especially if it be their first offense, from the great herd of criminals."

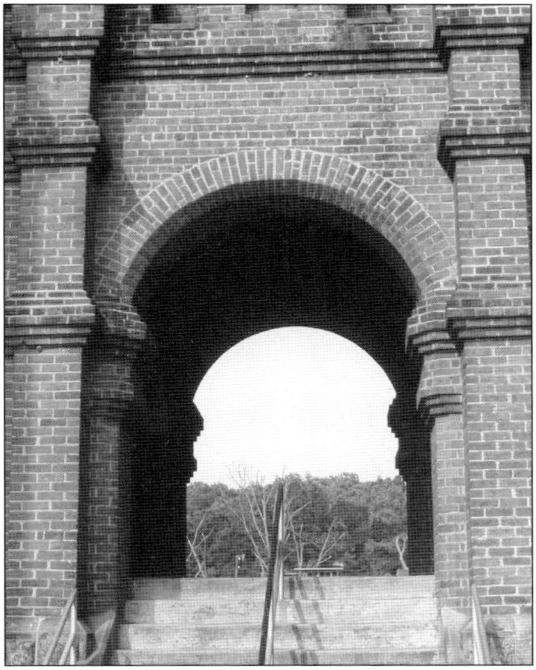

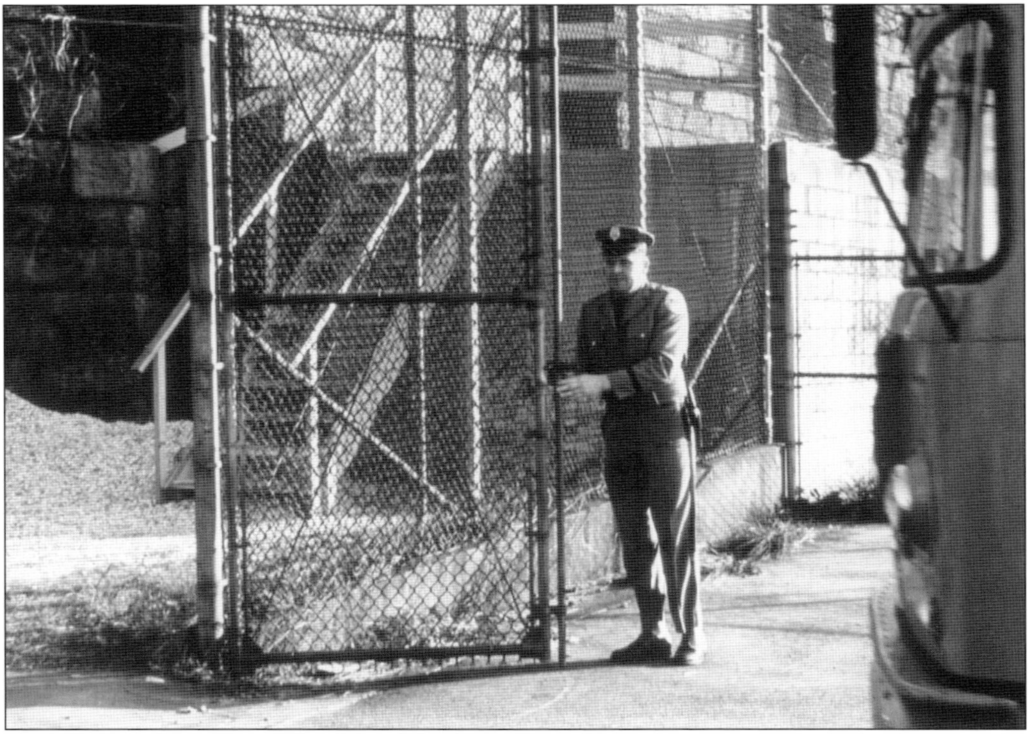

NEW PRISONERS ARRIVE BY BUS, 1970S. When the state failed to act, in 1886 warden William J. Hicks again asked for "some other means of dealing with the juvenile offenders of our state." The state still hesitated, so in his 1892 report, Hicks used numbers to justify his concerns. He noted that the prison held 41 inmates between 8 and 15 years old and 352 between 15 and 20 years old. That meant that one-third of all inmates were under 20 years of age.

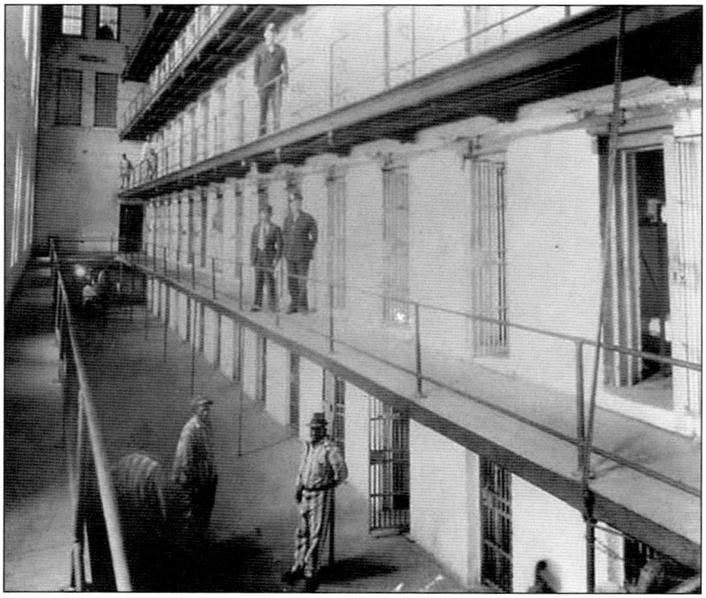

African American Cell Block, 1928. Reforms still were slow to emerge, as evidenced by the fact that of the 1,795 inmates in Central Prison on January 31, 1928, it was documented that 28 percent (501) were under 20 years of age when received, 17 percent (307) were between 20 and 24, and 27 percent (487) were between 25 and 29. Young offenders continued to predominate, and it was feared the penitentiary served as a finishing school for professional criminality.

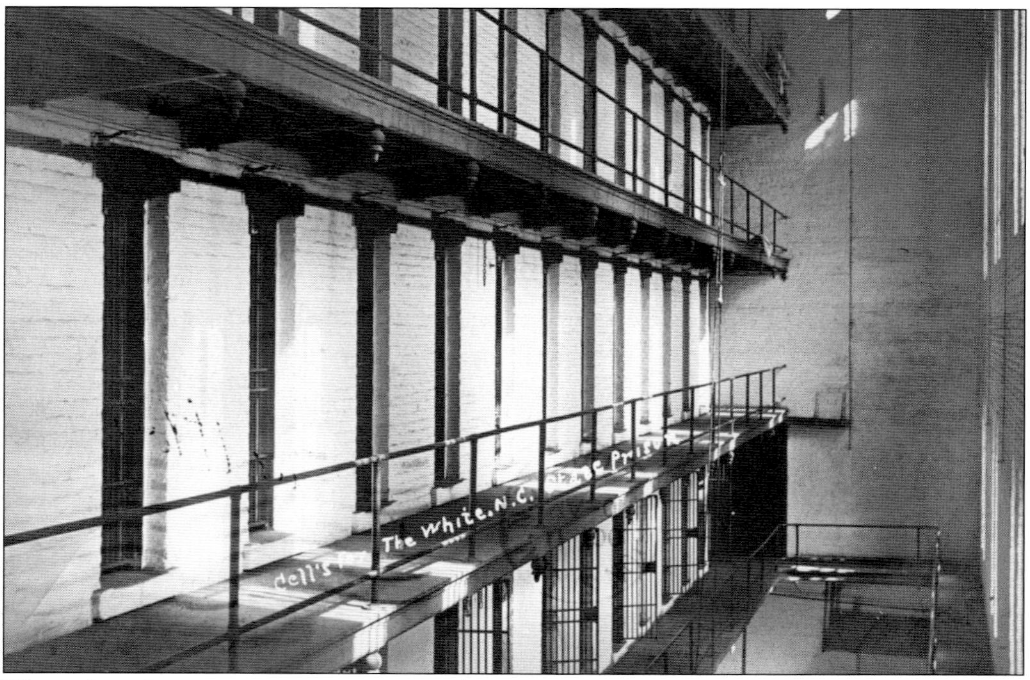

White Cell Block, 1910. In 1928, it was documented that 55 percent (992) of the inmates were African American, 40 percent (728) were white, and the remainder were Native American. Some 17 percent (302) were illiterate, while 51 percent (921) had only a grammar school education.

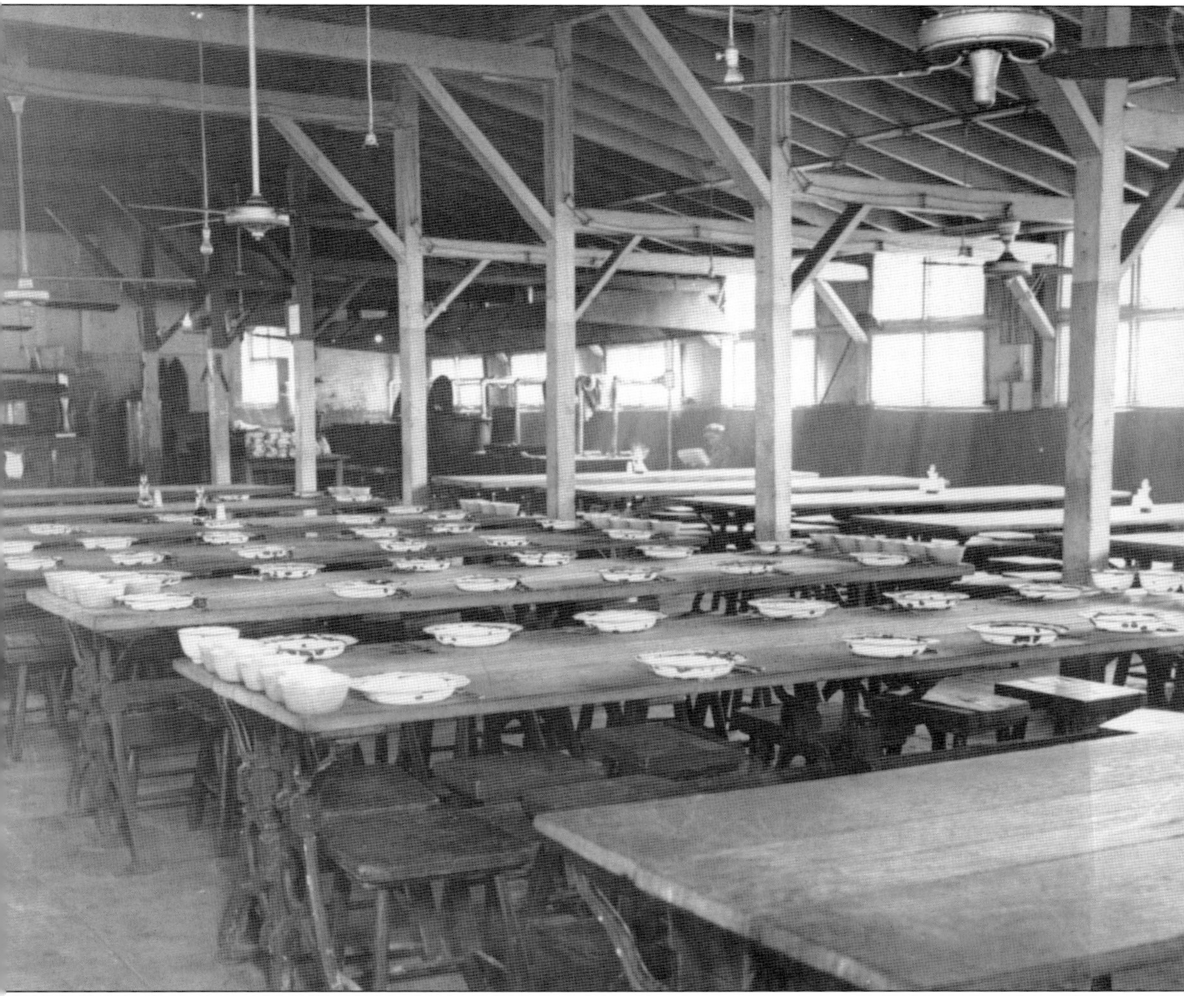

White Dining Hall, 1928. In 1928, some 48 percent (871) of the inmates were serving up to five years, 28 percent (502) were serving from 5 to 10 years, 15 percent (279) were serving from 11 to 20 years, 2 percent (41) were serving from 21 to 30 years, 1 percent (92) were serving from 31 to 40 years, and the remainder were serving terms of 40 years to life.

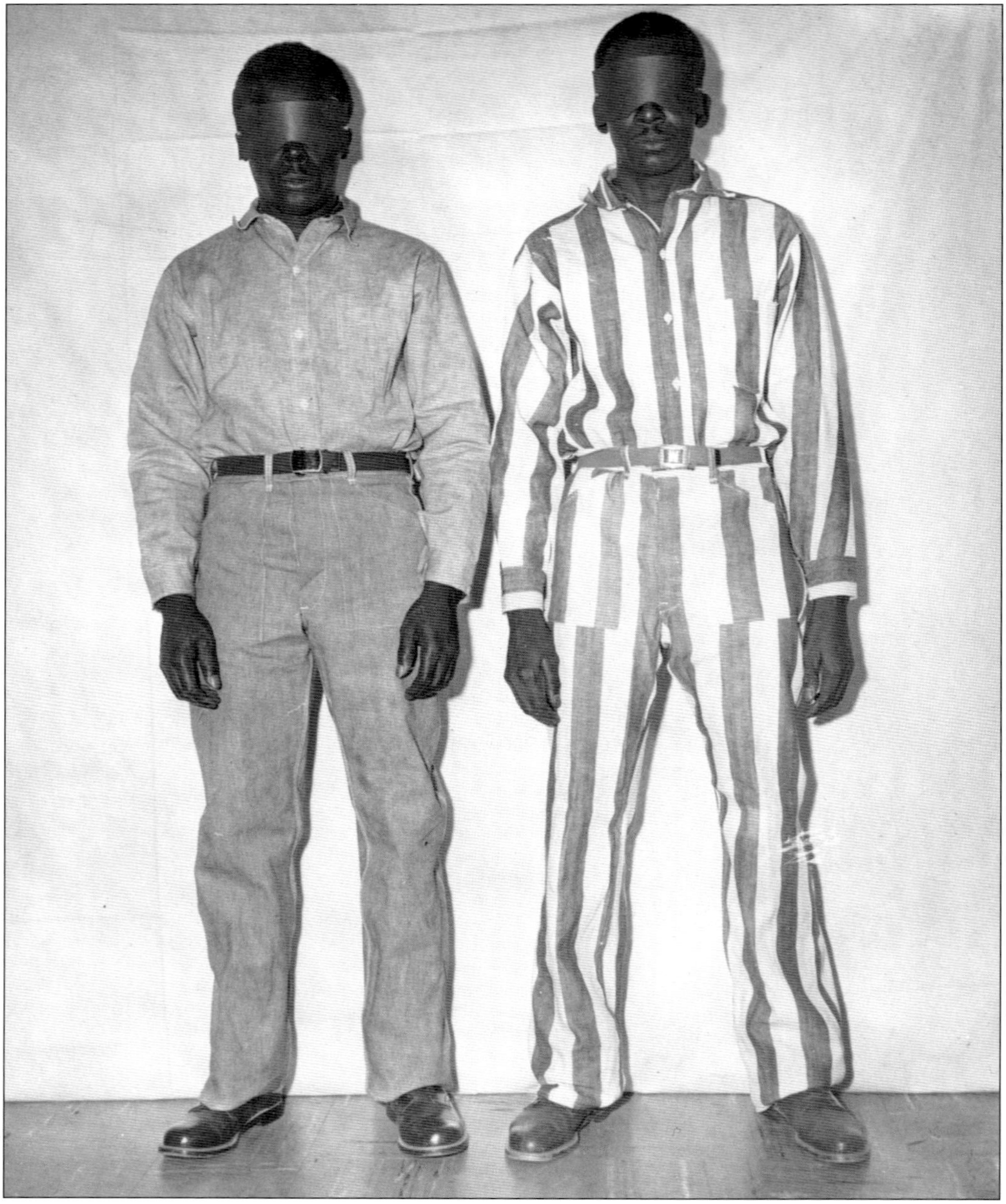

INMATE UNIFORMS, VERTICAL STRIPES AND GRAY, 1930S. Regardless of age, race, or sentence, prisoners were dressed according to their classification to make identification easier. On the left is a 1920s-era Grade A inmate dressed in khaki, while on the right, a Grade B inmate wears vertical stripes. Grade C inmates wore horizontal stripes. Inmates who were demoted in grade for various violations of institutional rules were forced to change attire. Grade C inmates, who could not be demoted, were sent to isolation cells. In 1921, the administration established seven honor grade camps—four for African American inmates and three for white inmates. Prisoners assigned to these camps worked without armed supervision, yet the number of escapes was less than in those camps where all work was done under armed guard. This was so despite the fact that 13 inmates were serving life sentences. By 1932, approximately 33.3 percent of the total prison population belonged to the honor grade group.

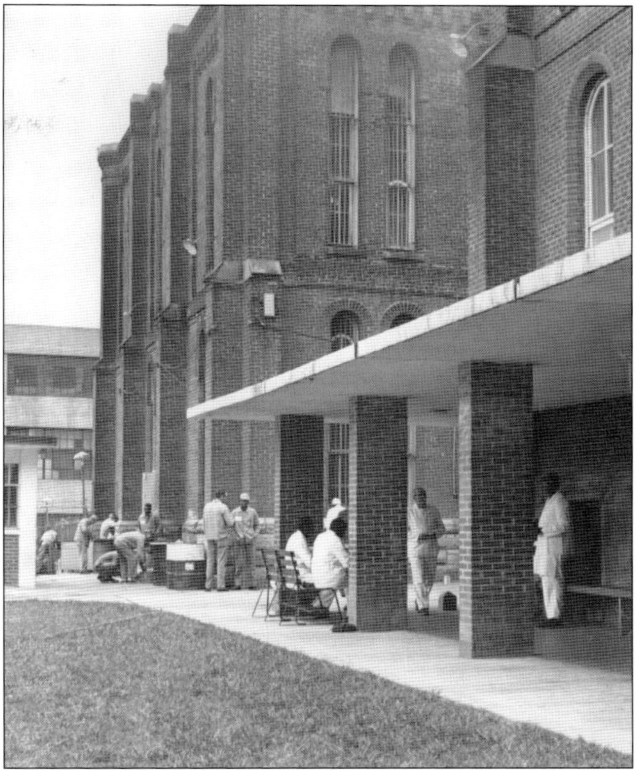

Inmates in the Industrial Courtyard, 1970s. In 1921, half of the state's prisoners were in the incorrigible Grade C. In an effort to improve that statistic, Gov. Cameron Morrison ordered that all prisoners serving definite sentences have their terms reduced to one-fourth the original length, dependent upon good behavior. The policy was applied by subsequent governors, and the percentage of prisoners in the incorrigible grade quickly fell from 50 to 20 percent.

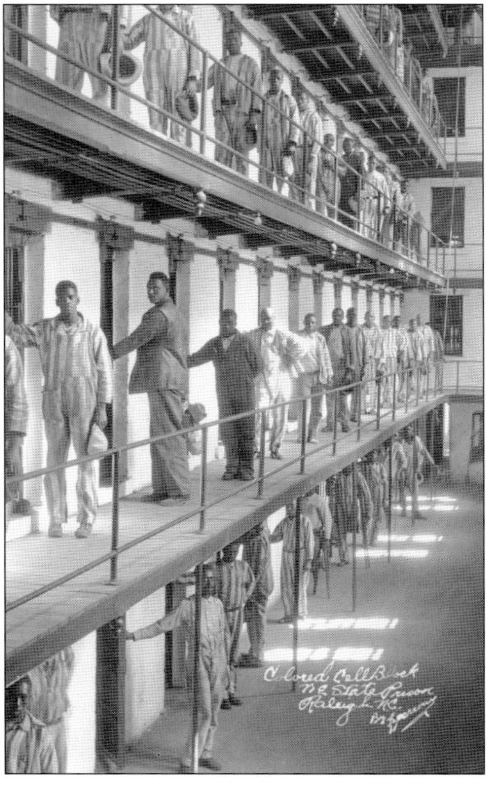

African American Cell Block, 1928. The number of incorrigibles continued to fall, and in 1928, Superintendent Pou noted that fewer than 10 percent of inmates were assigned to Grade C, while 30 percent were in Grade A, including several who were serving life terms. Further evidence that the reforms worked was his assertion that "the general morale of the prisoners is good." While he acknowledged several escape attempts and one mutiny, he found discipline improved.

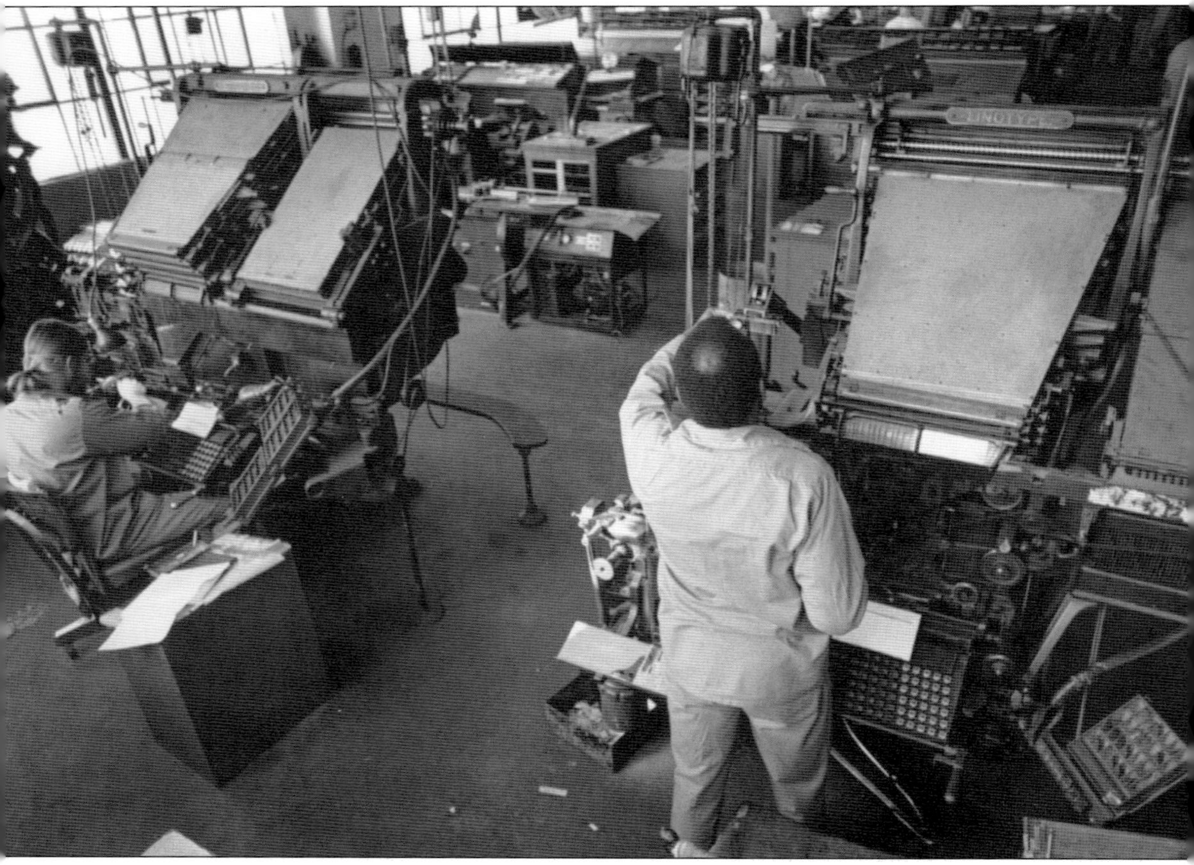

Print Shop Workers. In the 1930s, the penitentiary continued its efforts to improve discipline by making work assignments based on an inmate's "vocational [skills] and adaptability." Prison officials understood that "some men can always do a given thing not only better but more cheerfully than others," and placed inmates in jobs for which they were suited. Not only did this reform affect discipline, it demonstrates a shift in ideology from punishment to reform and rehabilitation.

Eight

Offender Treatment

From the beginning, Central Prison required inmates to undergo a regimented daily schedule that offered little opportunity for social interaction or personal regeneration. Combined with the general loss of freedom, the lack of human interaction often caused inmates to become unruly. In an effort to make the stress of prison life a little easier to bear, administrators slowly allowed inmates greater privileges. In 1890, the penitentiary opened a small library funded by a 10¢ visitor's fee. Those inmates who were unable to enjoy books due to illiteracy could attend literacy classes beginning in 1926. That same year, the penitentiary formed a softball team, which provided inmates an outlet for their athletic and competitive energies. The penitentiary also organized boxing, basketball, and football games among the inmates. By the 1940s, the Jail House Jubilee performed twice a week, a 46-piece band offered inmates musical entertainment, movies were shown on Saturday afternoons, and occasionally, a notable visitor dropped by.

The penitentiary also provided health and spiritual care. Physical care came in the form of doctors, dentists, and emergency medical services. Inmates who arrived ill were segregated from other inmates and treated until the contagion was contained. Those who became ill while serving time had access to medical staff and modern medical services. Mentally ill inmates received only limited treatment, however, and were eventually transferred to a state mental asylum. The physical health of inmates was supplemented by efforts to attend to their spiritual needs. Sunday school and chapel sessions were provided regularly for the inmates, as clergy from the Raleigh area volunteered their services.

Despite providing such opportunities, penitentiary administrators remained worried about inmate control, and in 1940, a censor was empowered to ensure all reading material entering the facility was appropriate and contained no reference to guns, sex, or crime. The censor also read all the incoming and outgoing mail. Life at Central Prison was thus a balance between security concerns and the human needs of the prisoners.

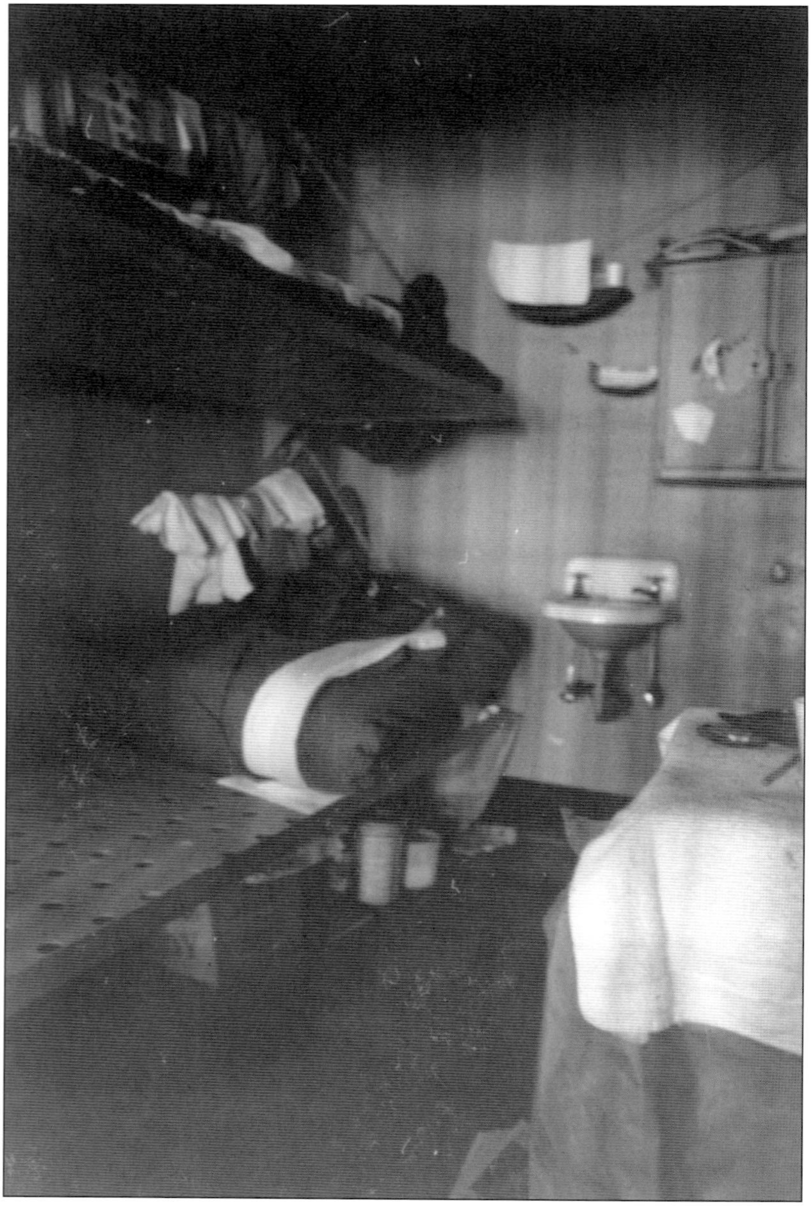

Standard Two-Man Cell, 1940s. The following enumerates the daily routine of the inmates from *Rules and By-Laws of 1869 for the Government and Discipline of the North Carolina Penitentiary during its Management by the Penitentiary Commission*: "1. The officer on duty at the Guard-Room will ring the bell at five o'clock A.M., in the summer, and at six A.M. in the winter as a signal for all the prisoners to rise, dress, wash and make up their beds, etc., and that all the overseers and guards off duty may assemble at the Guard-room. 2. After sufficient time for these purposes, the keepers will unlock the cell doors, and march the inmates to receive their rations and then back to the cells and locked up. 3. The keepers will report their convicts ready for labor. 4. At seven o'clock A.M., all the convicts will begin work and continue till 12 P.M. One hour will be given for dinner in summer and 45 minutes in winter—after which they will return to labor until sundown in the winter and seven o'clock, P.M., in summer. 5. At nine o'clock P.M., at a signal all the prisoners will be required to repair to their beds."

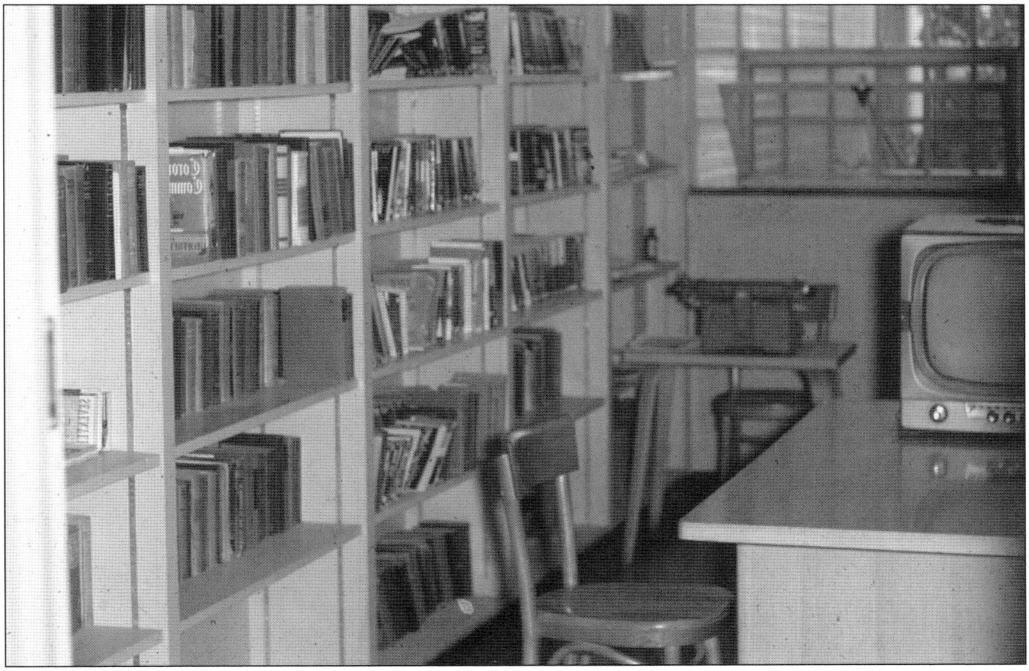

Library in K-Dormitory, 1960s. Beginning in the 1920s, prisoners were allowed to use the library for two hours on Sunday and one evening per week (white prisoners on Tuesdays and African American prisoners on Thursdays). Inmates could check out books and take them back to their cells. The reading materials were rather sparse, but books offered an emotional escape and the opportunity for intellectual edification.

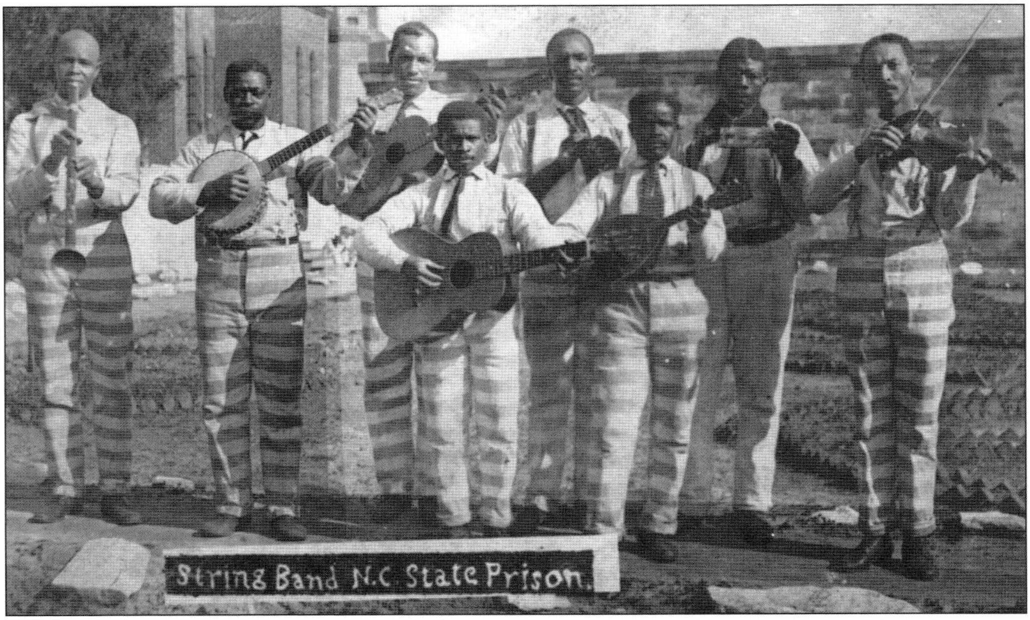

String Band, 1909. The penitentiary provided a record player with records and a piano for those inmates interested in musical entertainment. Those desiring live entertainment could enjoy the string band pictured here. An impressive collection of musical inmates provided the prisoners an array of musical stylings. A stage in the chapel served as the location for many musical events.

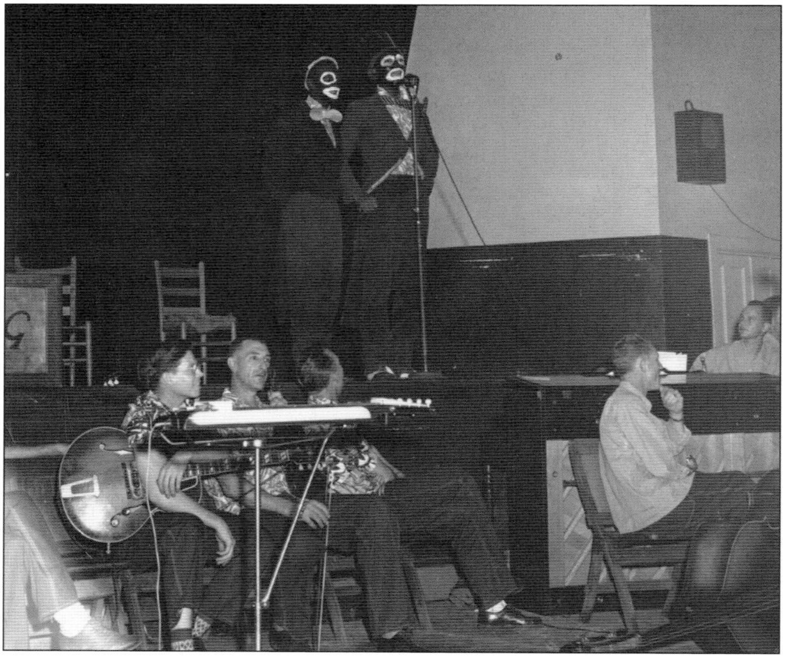

Entertainers in Blackface, 1950s. The penitentiary occasionally featured entertainment from outside the walls. Bands, choirs, and minstrel shows offered inmates a variety of escapes from the drudgery of prison life.

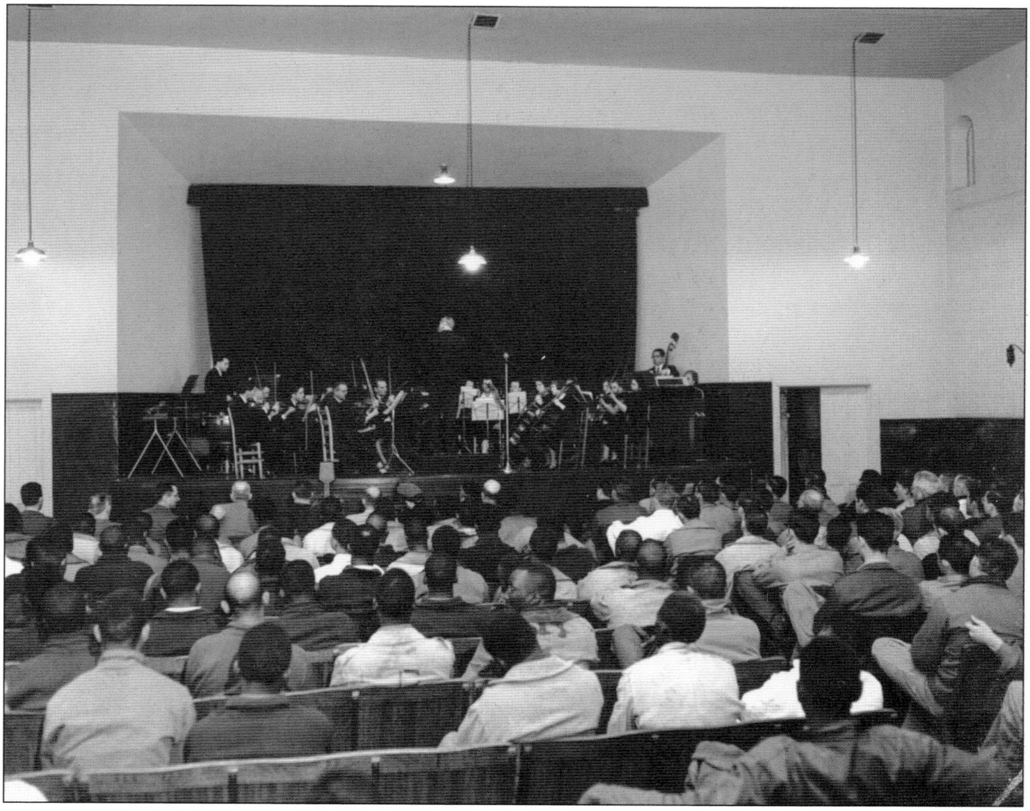

North Carolina Symphony, January 22, 1951. Churches and local colleges also staged performances, and penitentiary officials welcomed those events as "instructive and helpful."

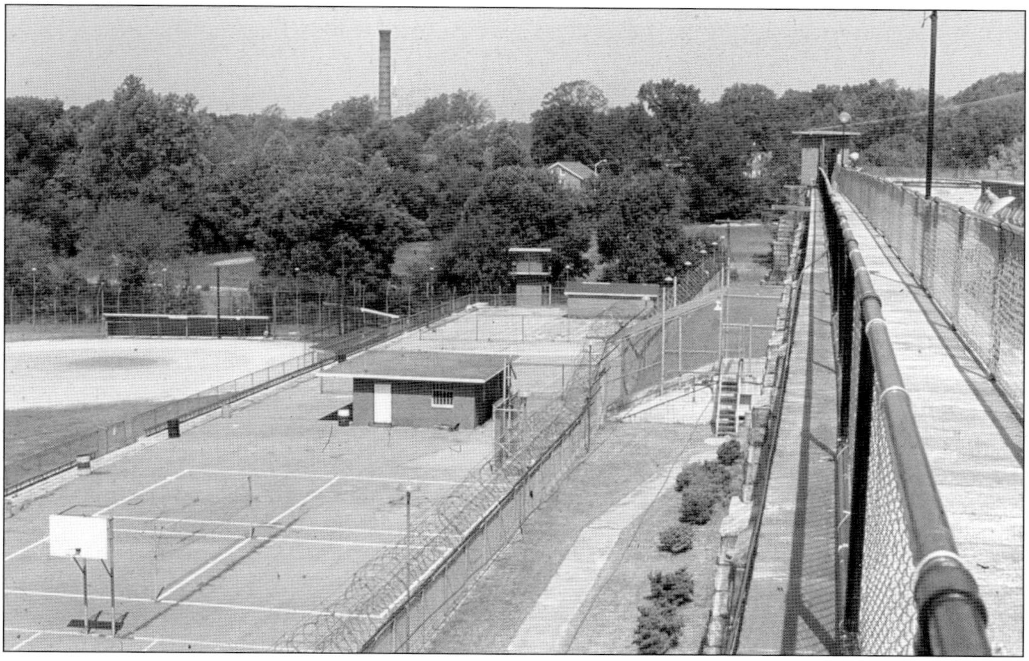

Prison Baseball Diamond. In 1926, the last of the original temporary structures in the rear of the penitentiary were torn down and the grounds made into a ballpark for the prisoners. This field was a source of pleasure for the prisoners and helped keep up their morale, especially when they joined the Raleigh City League and played civilian teams outside the penitentiary walls.

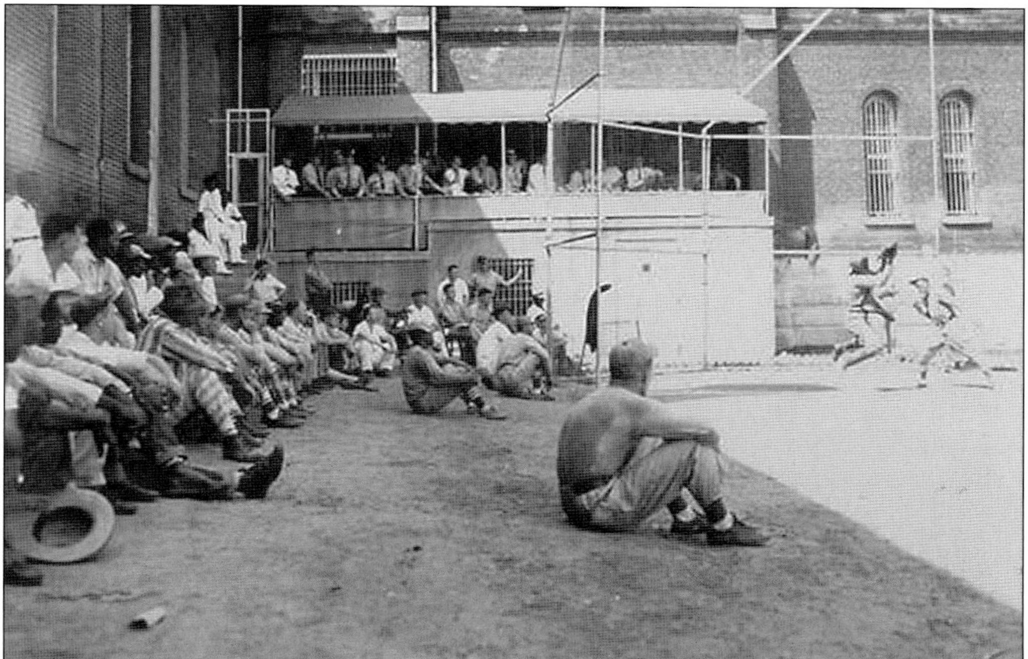

Inmates Enjoying Baseball, 1928. The men were given the yard on Saturday afternoons and all day Sunday and holidays. Baseball was a popular pastime, but inmates also could attend the movie theater or listen to individually owned radios.

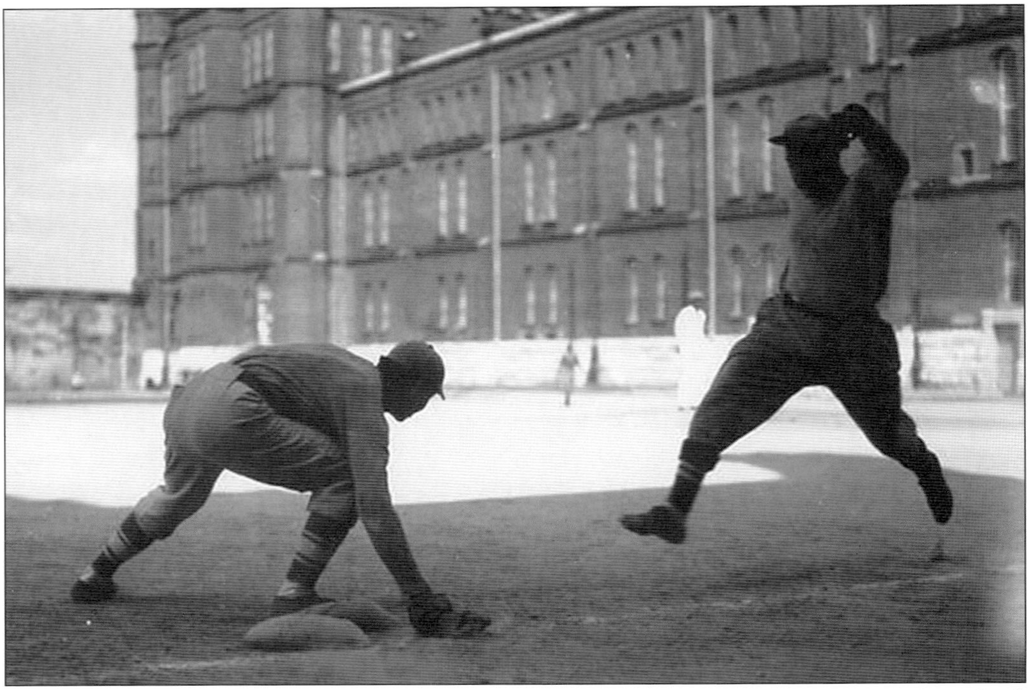

Playing Baseball, 1928. By the 1930s, the commissary gave inmates a place to purchase food, tobacco, cold drinks, candy, and toiletries. The commissary profits funded the purchase of baseball outfits, boxing gloves, and other athletic equipment. In his 1932 report, Warden Honeycutt acknowledged, "We find that the men enjoy taking part in different sports and we are glad to be able to provide for them in this way."

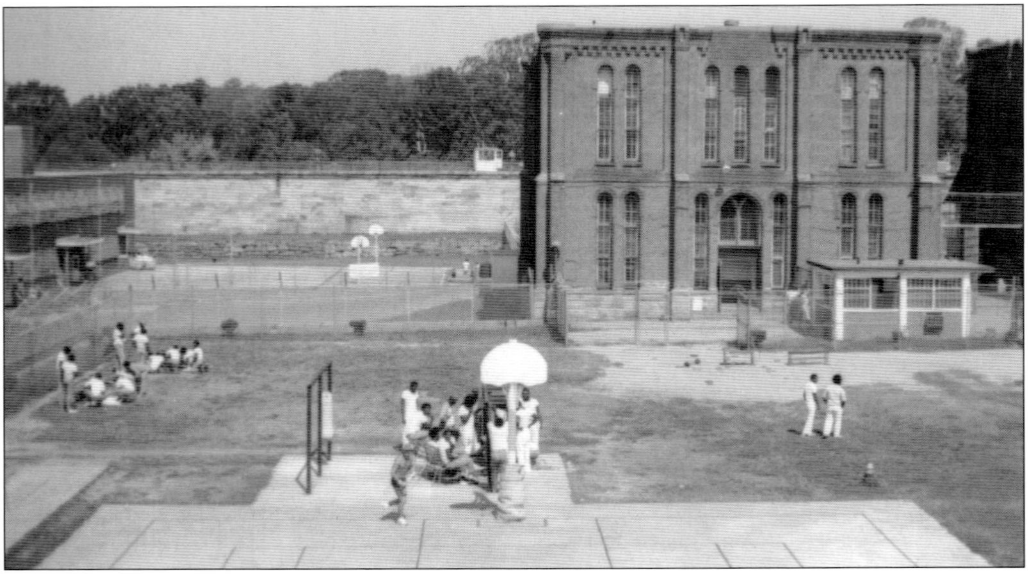

Inmate Recreation Area, Women's Prison Building in the Background, 1970s. Baseball was not the only athletic endeavor prisoners could enjoy, and the recreation yard offered the opportunity to play basketball, shuffleboard, and volleyball. Punching bags also were available for those honing their boxing skills. Those inmates not interested in exercise could simply enjoy the sunshine, fresh air, and the outdoors.

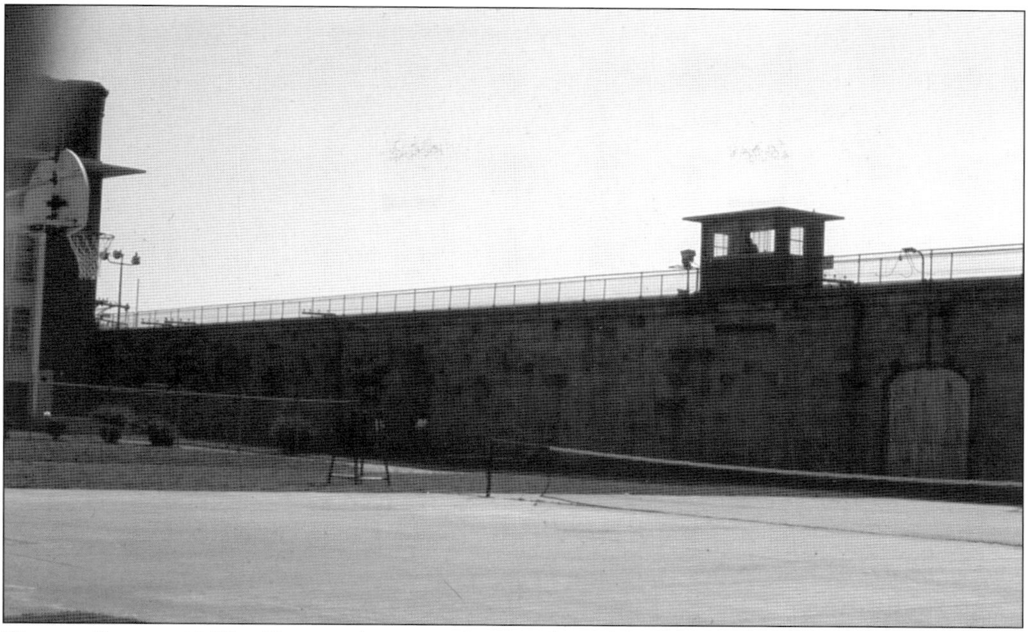

TENNIS COURT, 1970S. Tennis also proved a popular athletic pastime within the penitentiary walls. Regardless of the sport and the opportunity to enjoy the daylight, inmates were never able to escape the fact that they were behind bars, as the presence of the wall and the guard towers loomed large even on the recreation yard. On rare occasions, however, the men were treated to something really special.

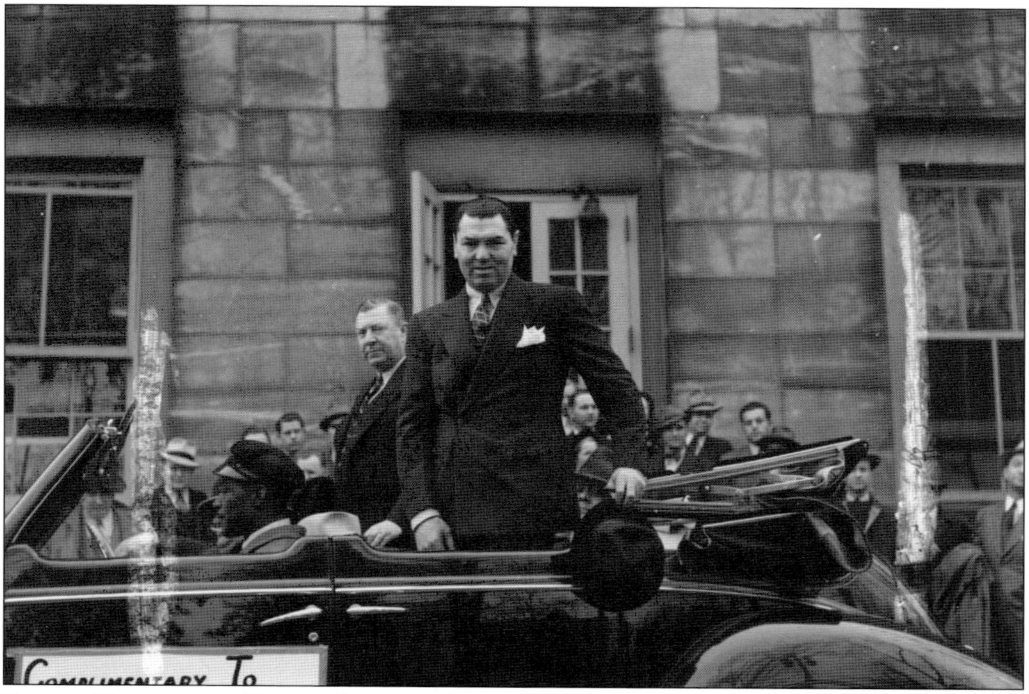

FORMER HEAVYWEIGHT BOXING CHAMPION JACK DEMPSEY VISITS CENTRAL PRISON IN 1939. Boxing champion Jack Dempsey visited the inmates on January 12, 1939. One of the most famous boxers in American history, Dempsey was one of several celebrities to offer their time to the inmates.

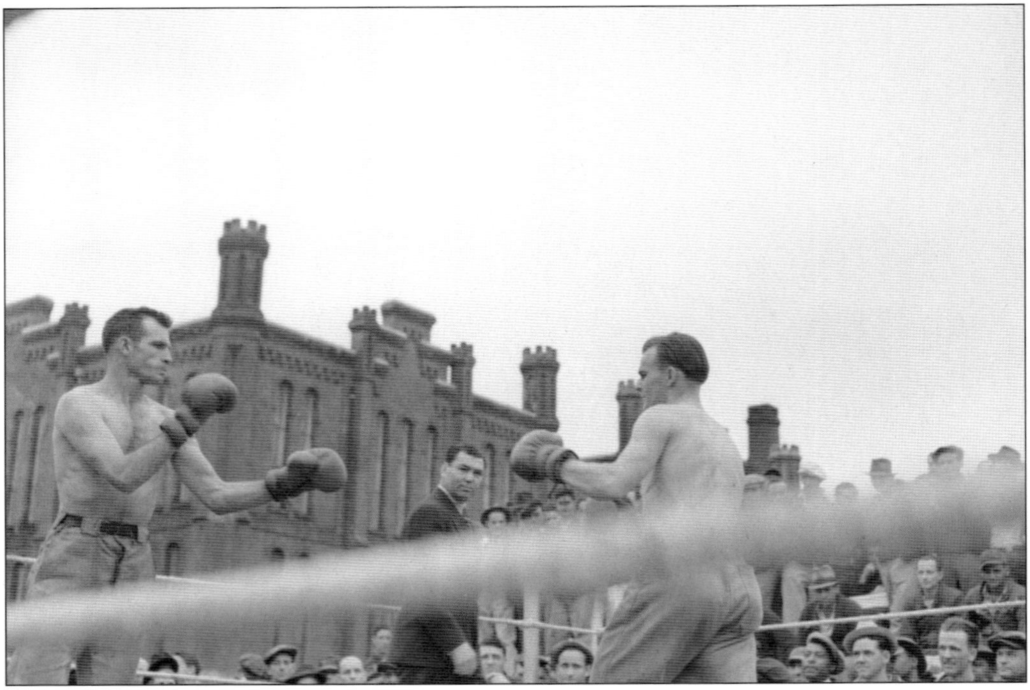

Dempsey Referees Boxing Match, 1939. During his visit, he gave boxers prefight instructions, offered a few tips on how to handle themselves in the ring, and refereed the bout between Creed Woody and Archie Safewright, two of the penitentiary's best boxers.

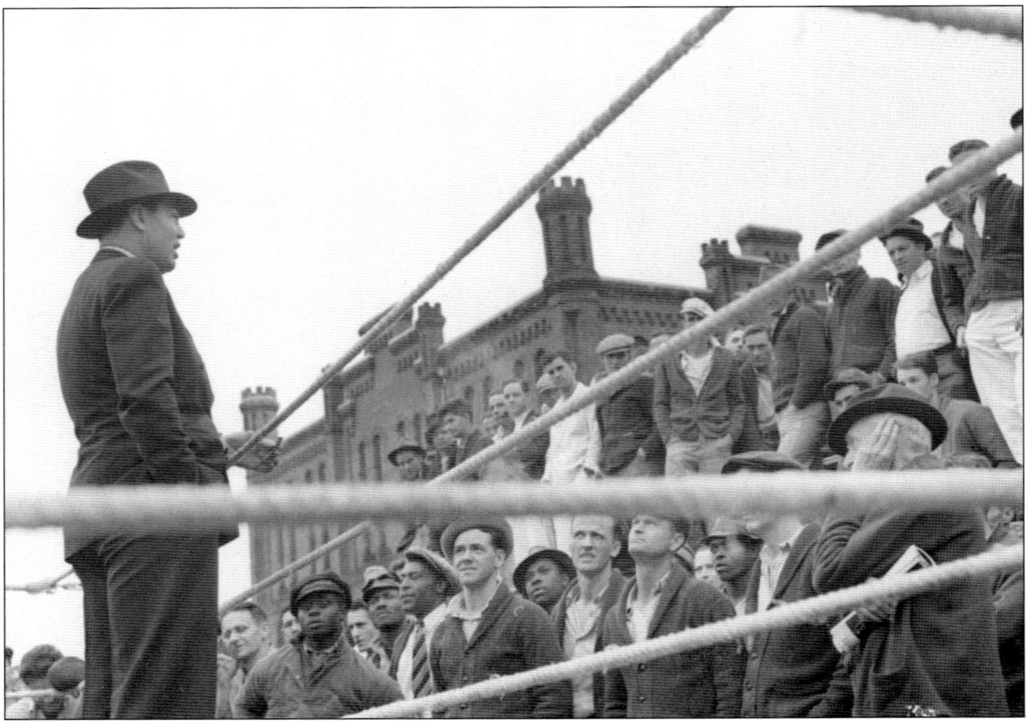

Jack Dempsey, 1939. Dempsey did more than interact with the boxers; he also spoke with the inmates and penitentiary officials after the bout.

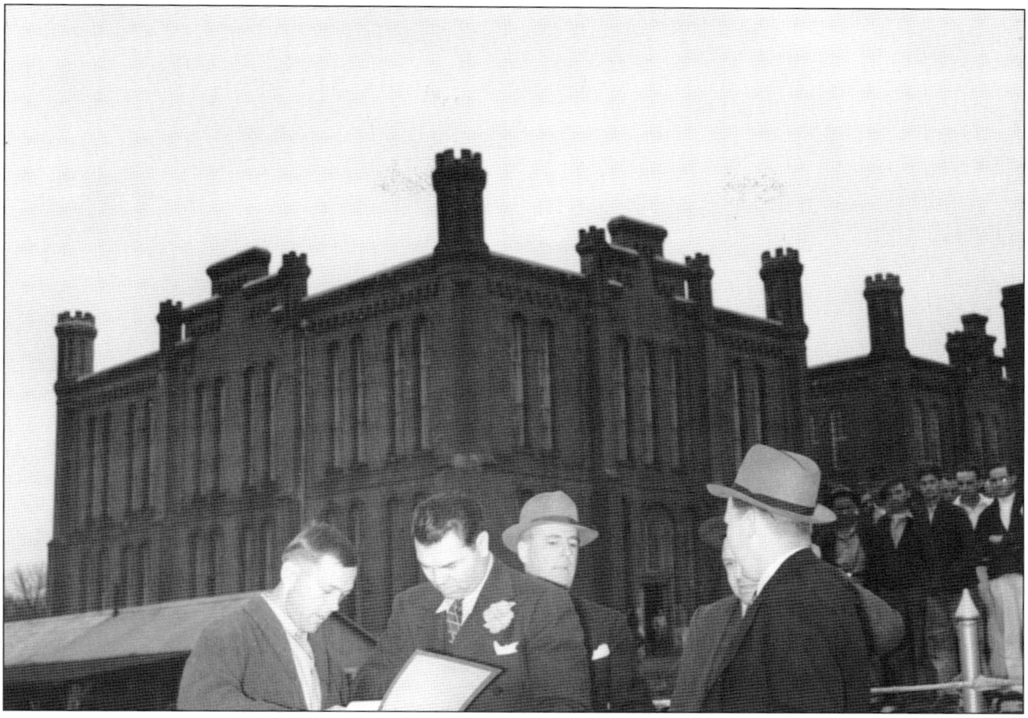

JACK DEMPSEY SIGNING AUTOGRAPHS, 1939. Dempsey offered his audience advice, insight, and his personal philosophy in the hopes that they could learn from his experiences.

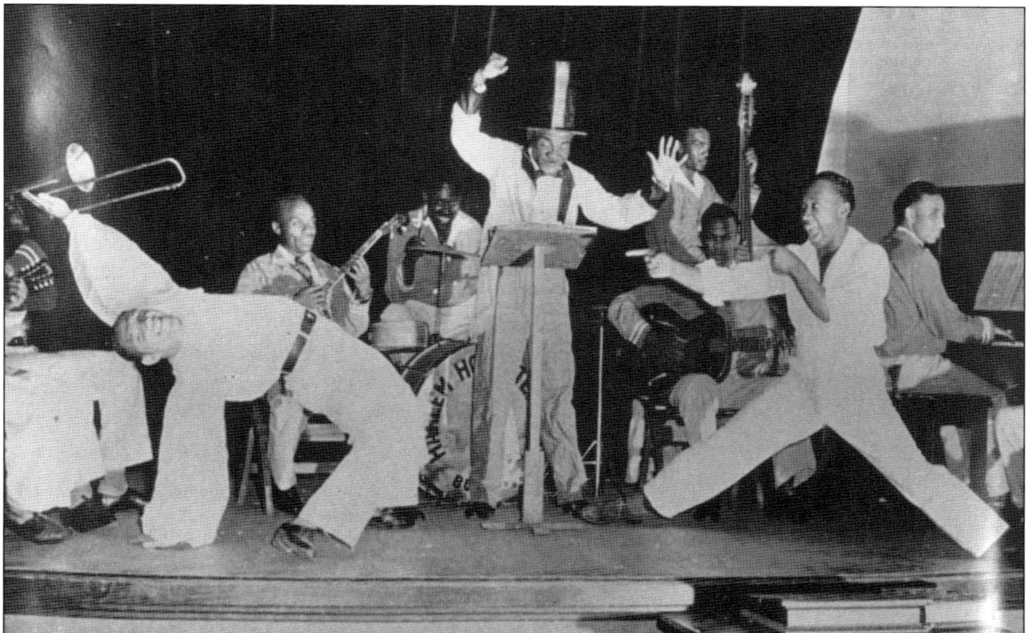

PRISONERS GIVE A BENEFIT SHOW, JUNE 1942. Although incarcerated, inmates were not totally isolated from the outside world and appreciated the needs and suffering of others. Amidst World War II, prisoners held a benefit for the British War Aid Relief Society. The 90-minute minstrel show did not charge admission, but the prison raised $91 in donations during the performance.

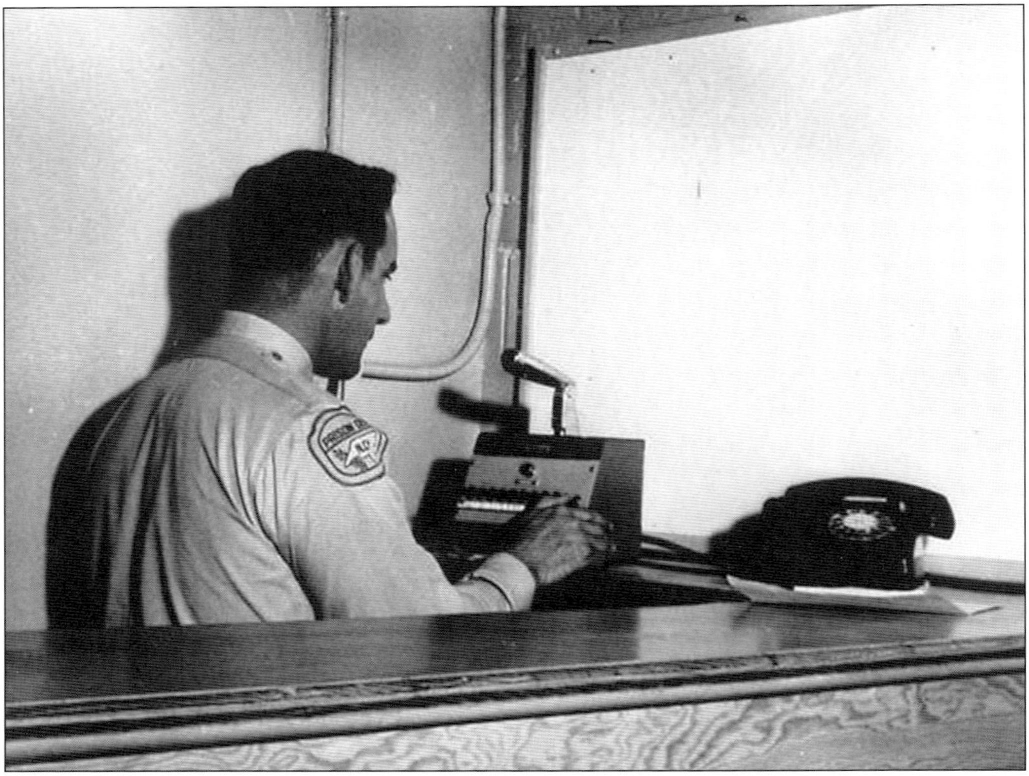

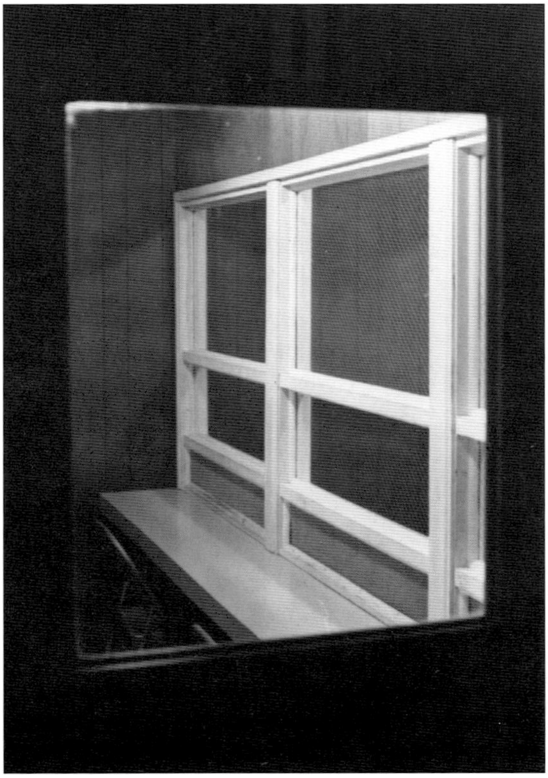

Visiting Hall Officer, 1950s. Visits from family and friends were one of the most important elements of prison life. While happy moments for the inmate and his family, the visits proved worrisome for the administration, which feared the ingress of contraband. Penitentiary custody officers vigilantly oversaw the visitation area and reprimanded those prisoners and visitors who violated the rules.

Visitor Partition, 1950s. In an effort to avoid having to issue reprimands, most inmates were prevented from making any physical contact with their visitors. Closed visits ensured that no exchange of contraband could occur, as the inmate and the visitor were separated by a wall and could only see and communicate through a reinforced-glass window.

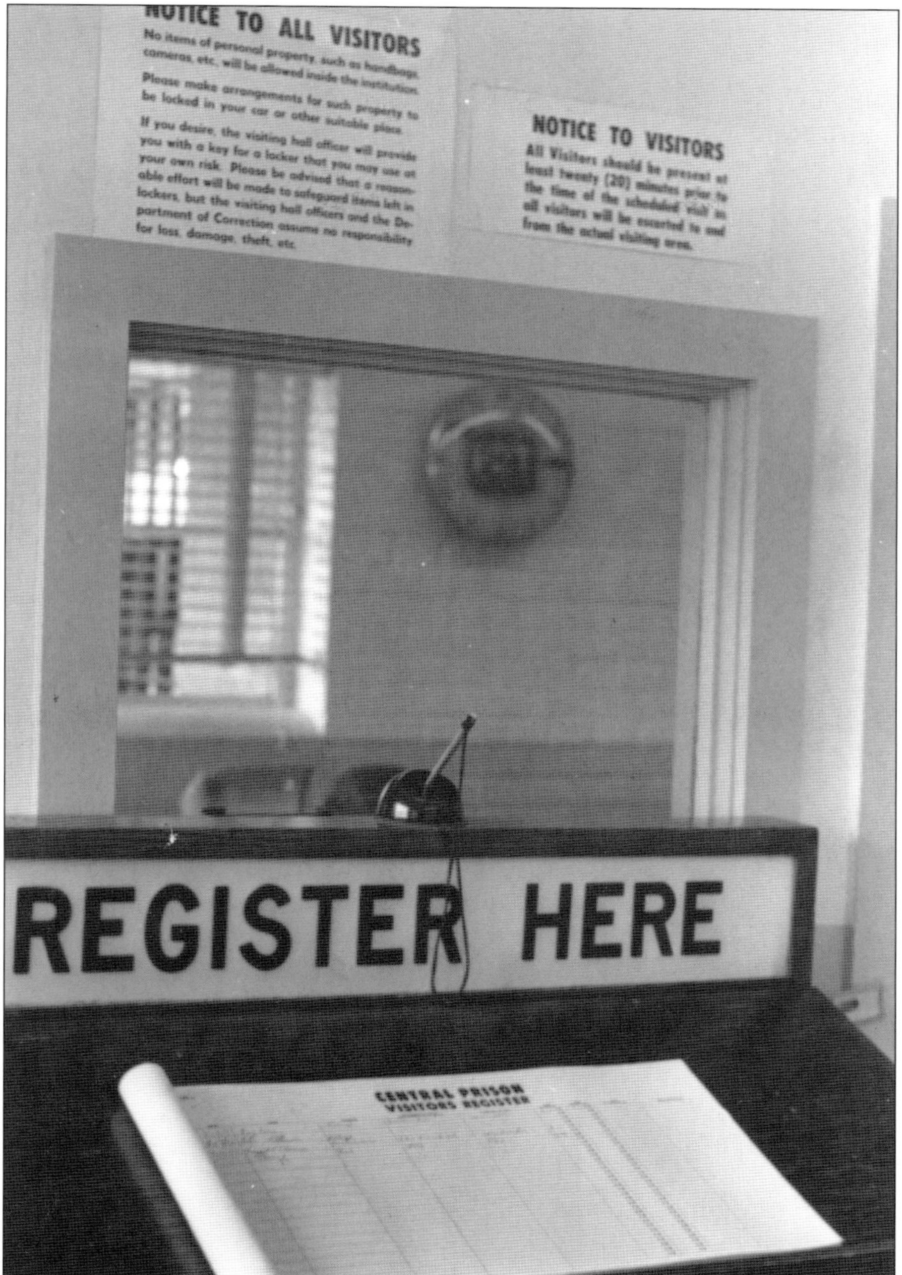

Visitor Registration Log, 1950s. All visitors to Central Prison faced the following warnings and rules: "Notice to All Visitors, No items of personal property such as handbags cameras, etc., will be allowed inside the institution; Please make arrangements for such property to be locked in your car or other suitable place; If you desire, the visiting hall officer will provide you with a key for a locker that you may use at your own risk; Please be advised that a reasonable effort will be made to safeguard items left in lockers, but the visiting hall officers and the Department of Correction assumes no responsibility for loss, damage, theft, etc.," and "Notice to Visitors, All visitors should be present at least twenty (20) minutes prior to the time of the scheduled visit as all visitors will be escorted to and from the actual visiting area."

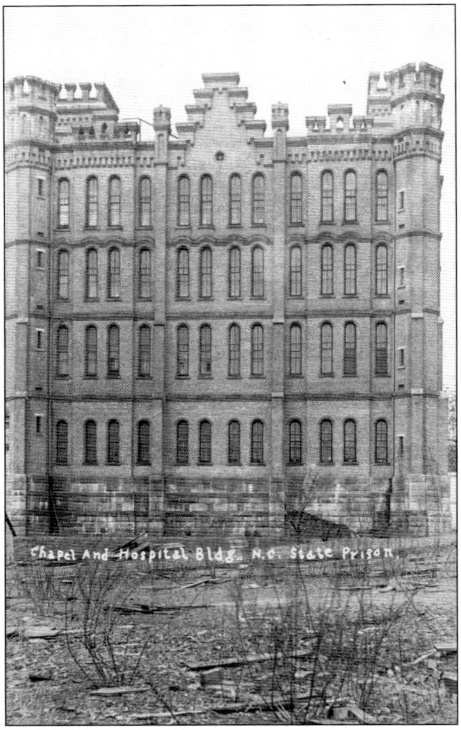

Chapel and Hospital Building, 1912. Beyond finding means to keep the inmates entertained, the penitentiary also cared for their health. The hospital was situated on the third and fourth floors of the east pavilion.

Hospital Ward, 1926. A physician was present for the reception of new inmates, and he recorded their health and determined if they were fit for labor; he also responded to any inmate requesting immediate medical attention.

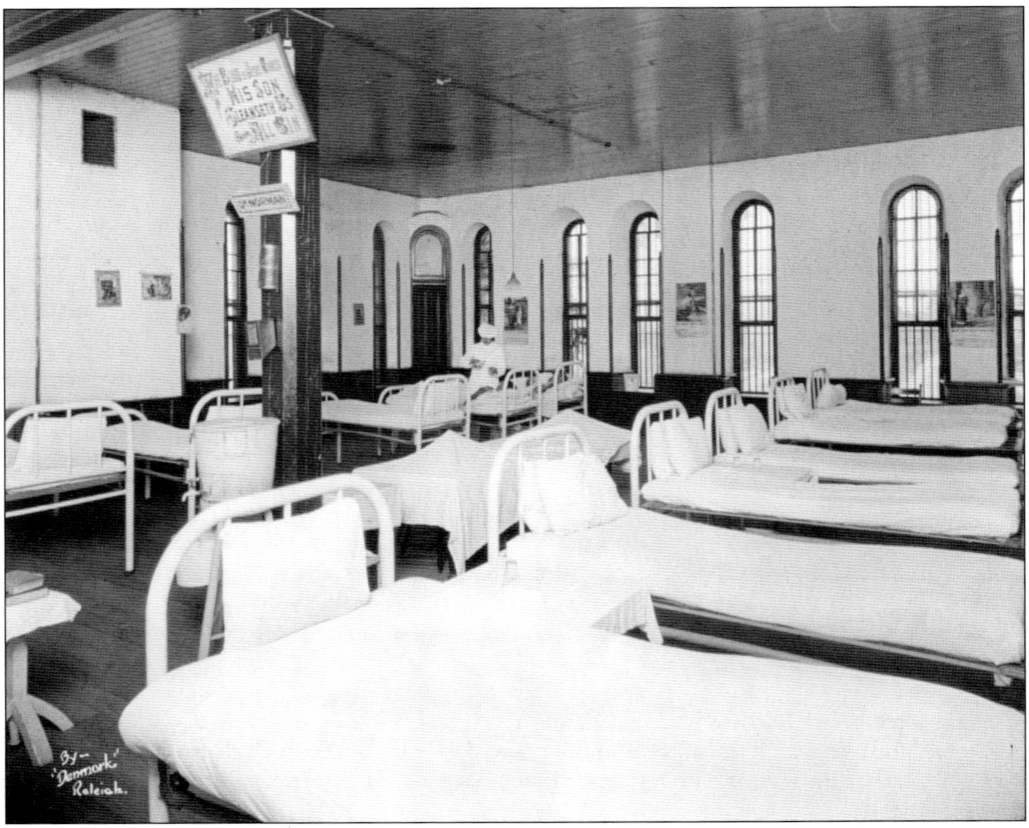

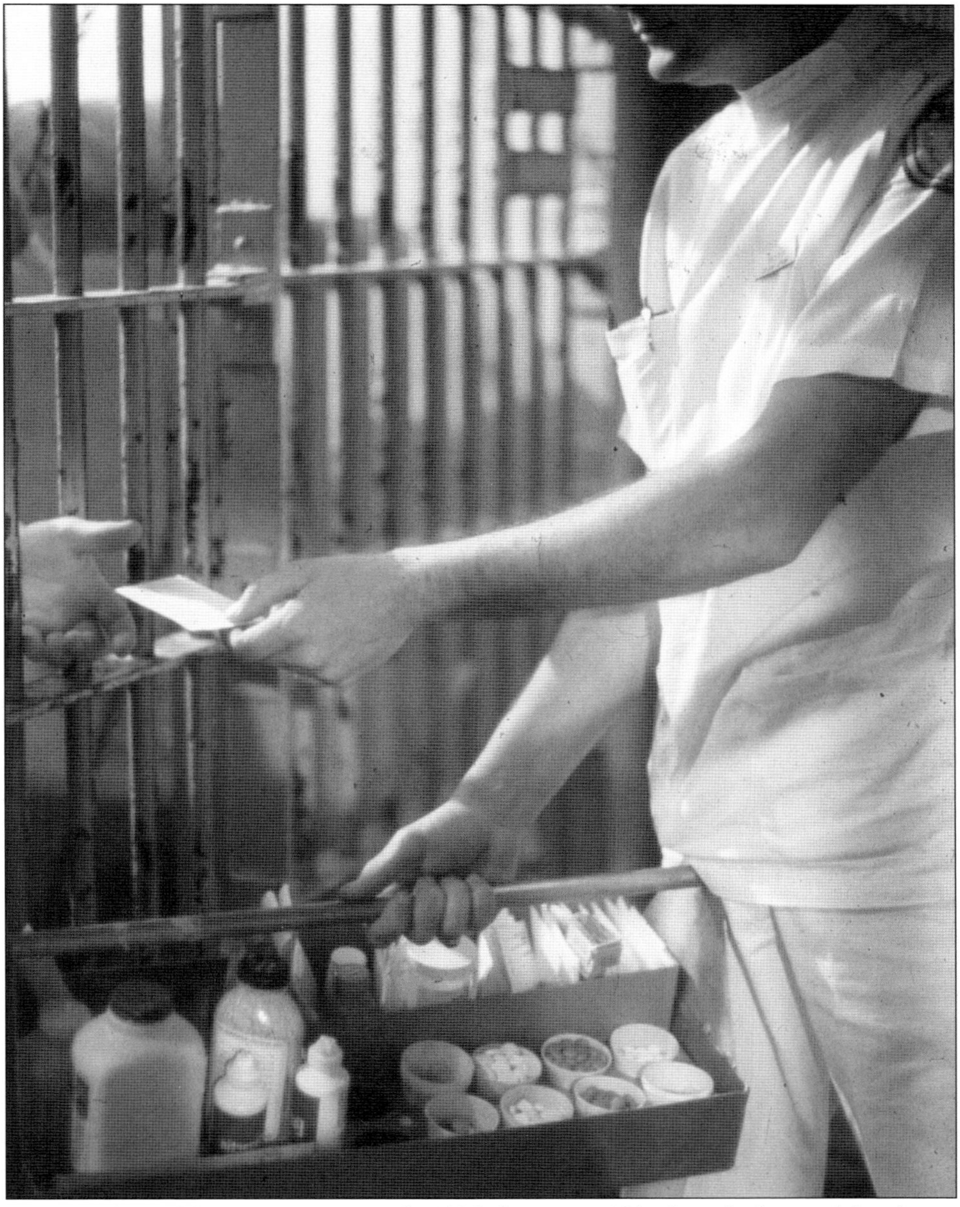

DELIVERY OF DAILY MEDICATION, 1980S. In 1926, there were 13 beds in the hospital for white men and 10 for African American men. The warden served as the physician in charge, while a dentist was available three times a week; a pharmacist, two consulting surgeons, a consulting orthopedist, and six inmates completed the medical personnel. The penitentiary doctor reported any cases in which "the labor, the diet, the confinement or the regimen of the prison unfavorably affects the health of a prisoner." He could order any alterations to the inmate's treatment necessary to return him to physical and/or mental health. The physician also ensured the sanitation, proper feeding, and proper nursing of all ailing inmates and reported any shortcomings to the warden. He kept a record of all the medicine inmates received, ensured the proper distribution of that medicine, and oversaw all the supplies in the hospital. Finally, he recorded all deaths, the probable cause of death, the age of the inmate, the crime for which the inmate was incarcerated, and the inmate's habits.

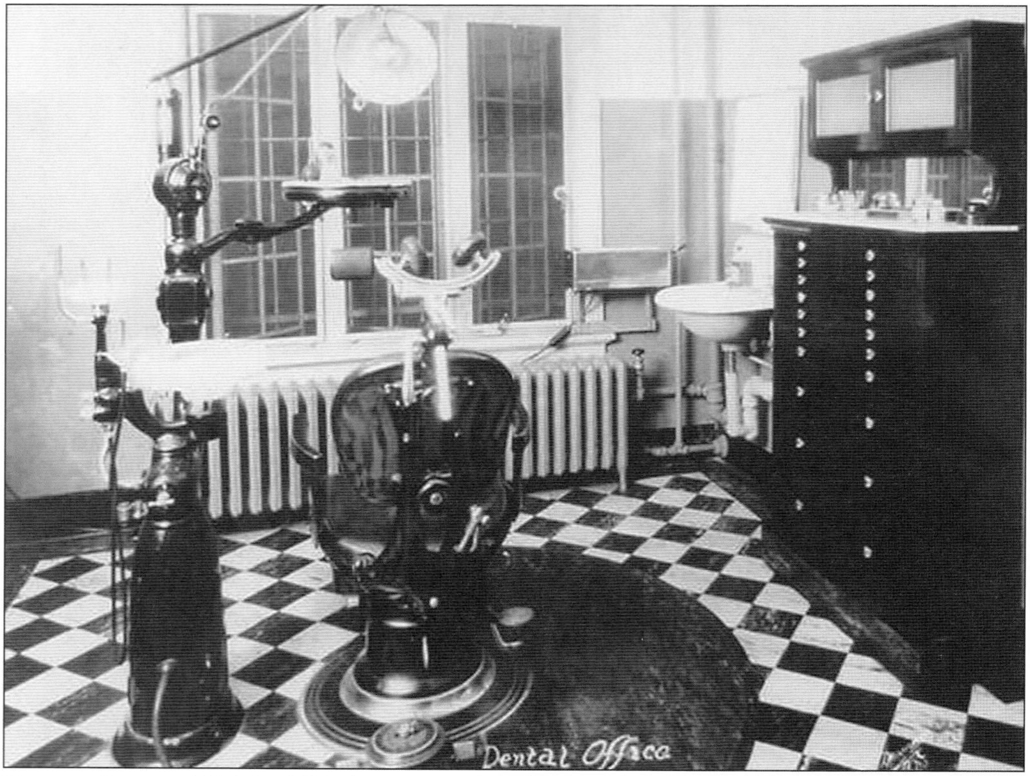

Dental Office, 1928. In 1931, dentist Joseph Osborne reported, "All new prisoners upon arrival at the institution are given a thorough oral examination." He found "a great per cent" of inmates had never been to the dentist and made it his duty to address their needs, educate them on the importance of oral hygiene, and help them overcome their fears of the dentist. In that same report, Osborne noted that he had performed a variety of services for the inmates. These included 3,320 extractions, 2,862 filled teeth, 38 installed bridges, 30 installed dentures, 94 lanced abscesses, and 89 emergency treatments.

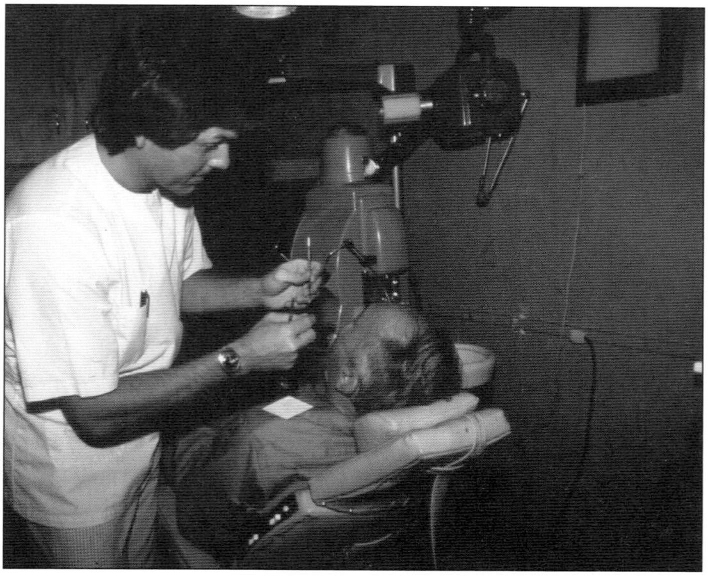

Prison Dentist, 1980s. The prison continually updated its facilities, ensuring that inmates had access to the latest dental technology and trained dentists. For much of the prison's history, medical care of the inmates was an administrative priority.

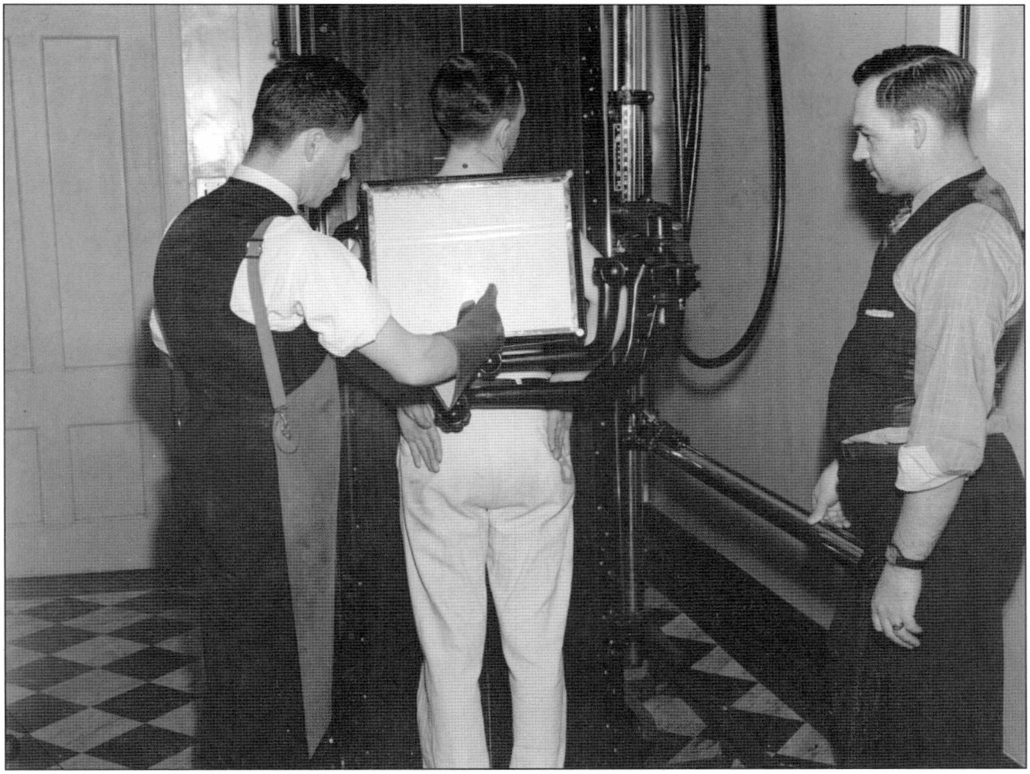

MEDICAL PROCEDURE, X-RAYS, 1941. The 1930 *Report of the Subcommittee on North Carolina's Prison Problem* asserted that inmates deserved the most modern medical treatment the state could offer and recommended the installation of "suitable laboratories, with X-ray and other equipment." Despite the costs, by World War II the prison had modernized its hospital facilities and provided inmates x-ray services and the most up-to-date medical technology.

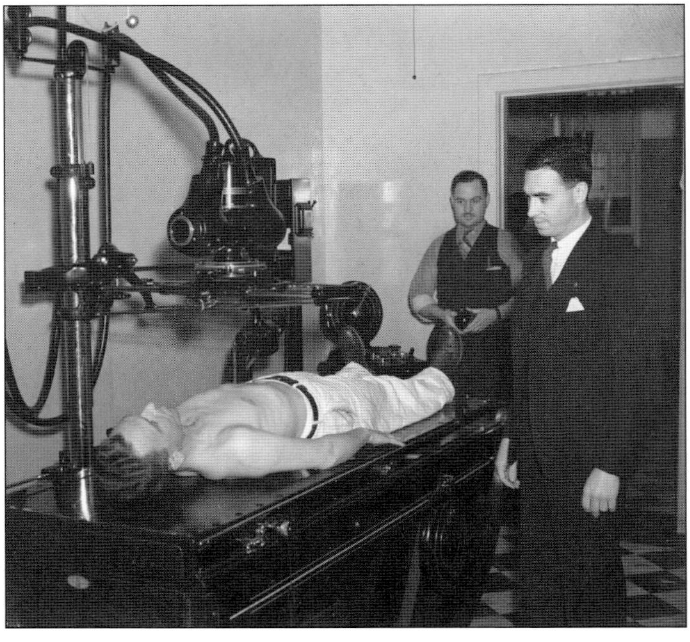

CHEST X-RAYS, 1941. As an additional part of that modernization process and part of a general effort to ensure adequate treatment and prevent the spread of disease, by the 1930s, the penitentiary began to keep a complete medical history of all inmates. That history followed the inmate whenever he was transferred to another facility.

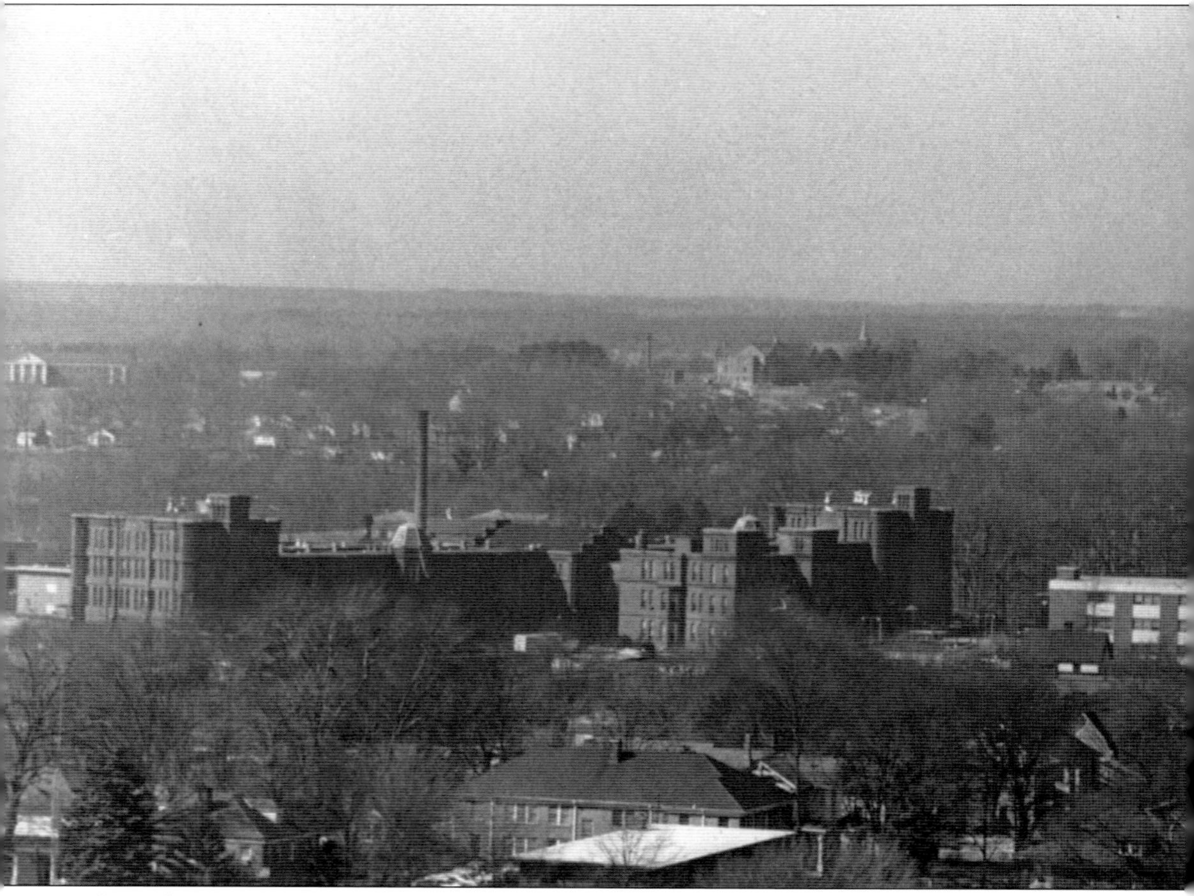

View Showing East Pavilion on the Left and West Pavilion on the Right, 1911. In 1921, there were 30 tubercular inmates segregated on the fourth floor of the east pavilion. They received no special treatment and, due to their location, rarely enjoyed sunshine, exercise, or fresh air. In 1923, the state created the first colony in the United States for the treatment of tubercular prisoners when it sent ailing inmates to a secure facility in the North Carolina Sanatorium for the Treatment of Tuberculosis in present-day McCain, North Carolina. Also segregated were the "dangerous insane" inmates, who originally were housed in the west pavilion. There were no adequate provisions for the proper care of these prisoners, however, so wards for insane white inmates were established at the state hospital in Raleigh and similar wards for African American inmates were established in the state hospital at Goldsboro. In 1970, an on-site mental-health facility was constructed, and in 1973, it began housing all the state's mentally ill inmates.

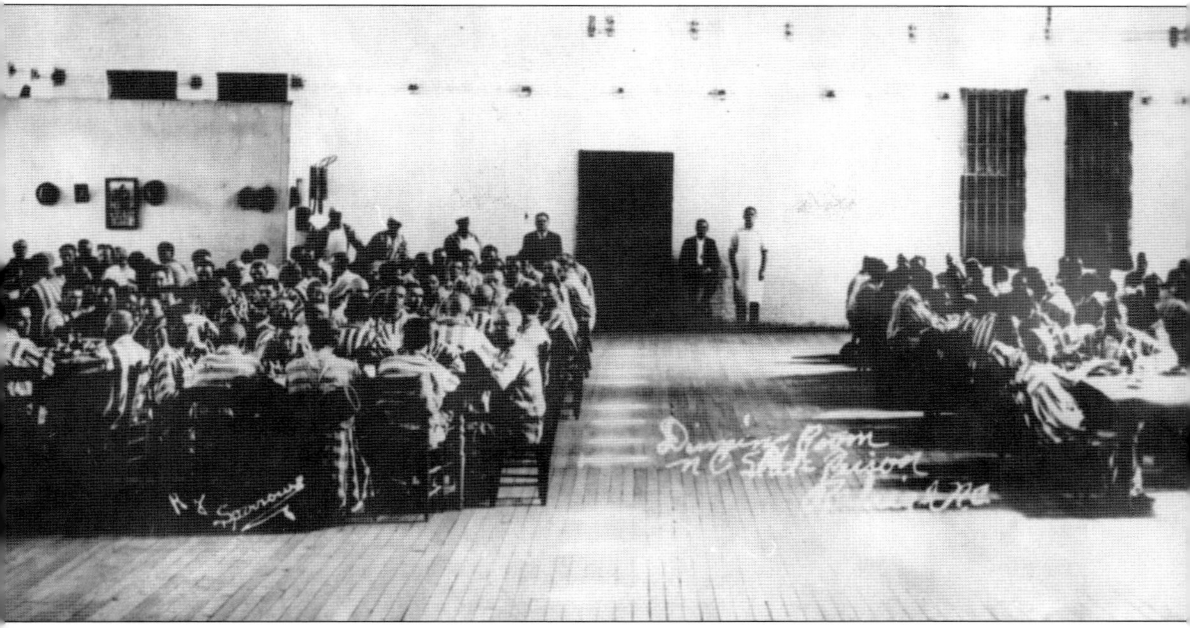

MESS HALL, 1910. The mess hall was located in a portion of the penitentiary originally intended as a cell house. In an effort to minimize the institutional feel of the dining experience, white porcelain table service replaced tin pans and cups in the early 1900s.

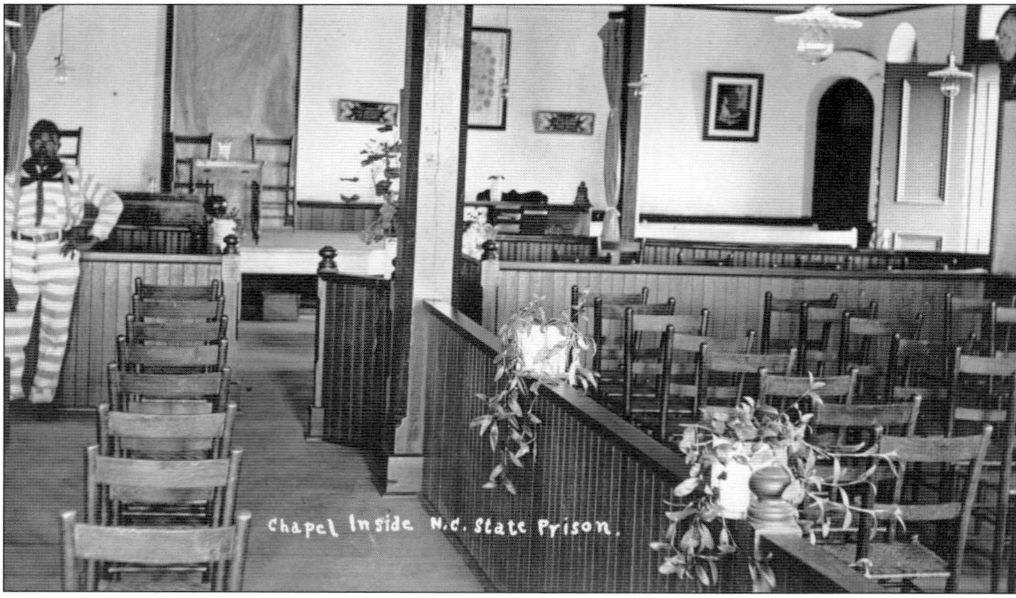

THE CHAPEL, 1910. The chapel was segregated by race and gender. Women sat in the front of the chapel, with whites and African Americans separated by a partition. White men sat behind the white women and African American men sat behind the African American women. The men were separated from each other and from the women by additional partitions. The chapel had electric lights and an organ, which allowed for evening chapel, concerts, and other forms of entertainment.

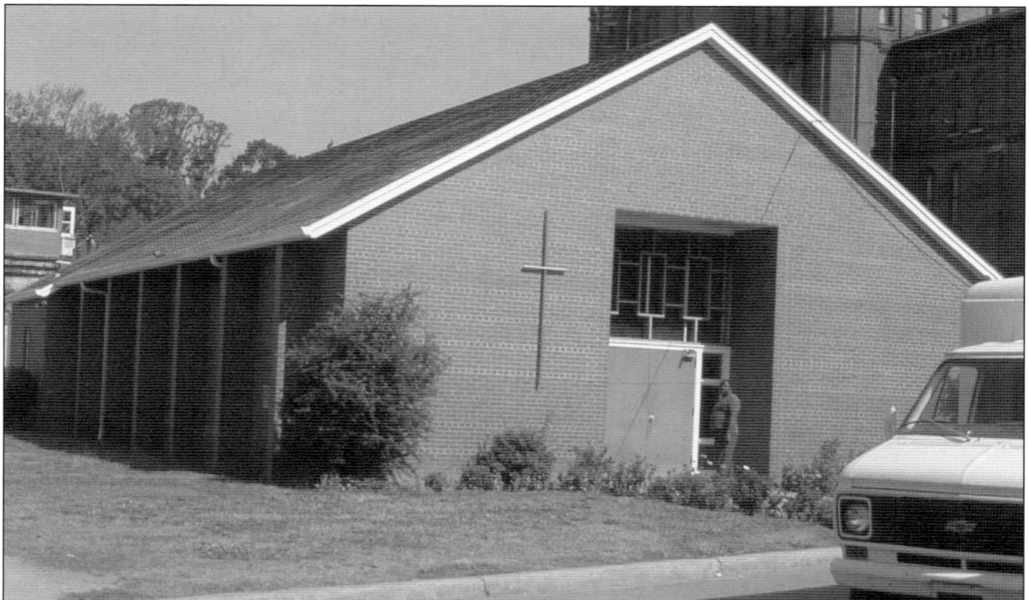

THE CHAPEL, 1980s. As early as 1873, regular church services and Sunday school sessions were provided to the inmates, as ministers of various denominations from nearby Raleigh churches volunteered their time. Such services continued throughout the existence of the penitentiary, and as evidenced by this photograph, renovations to the prison always ensured a continued chapel presence.

Nine

EXECUTIONS IN NORTH CAROLINA

For much of the state's early history, executions were publicly brutal affairs carried out by the counties. In 1909, the state banned local public executions and specified that all those sentenced to death would be electrocuted behind closed doors at Central Prison. The state created a death chamber in the west cell house of the penitentiary and installed an electric chair. The first inmate executed in that chair was an African American man named Walter Morrison, who had been convicted of rape and the attempted murder of a police officer. On March 18, 1910, he was strapped into the chair and had electrodes affixed to his legs and head. He received four jolts of 1,800 volts and subsequently was pronounced dead. Satisfied with the results, the state used the chair 50 times in the ensuing decade.

In 1936, the state began the transition from the electric chair to the gas chamber, as it allowed inmates the right to select their method of execution. On January 24, 1936, Allen Foster, who had been convicted of murder, became the first man executed in the gas chamber. Although his execution proved lengthy and grisly, the state was satisfied with the results. In 1938, the electric chair was removed, and the gas chamber became the sole means of execution. In 1983, inmates again were given an option when they could choose between the gas chamber and lethal injection. In 1998, Ricky Lee Sanderson became the last man in North Carolina executed in the gas chamber, as the state made lethal injection the sole means of execution.

More than 400 inmates have been executed by North Carolina since the imposition of the state death penalty in 1909. Recently, however, judicial, political, cultural, and pharmacological concerns have made North Carolina reluctant to use this power. As of 2015, there were 149 men on death row, but the state has not performed an execution since August 18, 2006, when it executed convicted murderer Samuel Flippen.

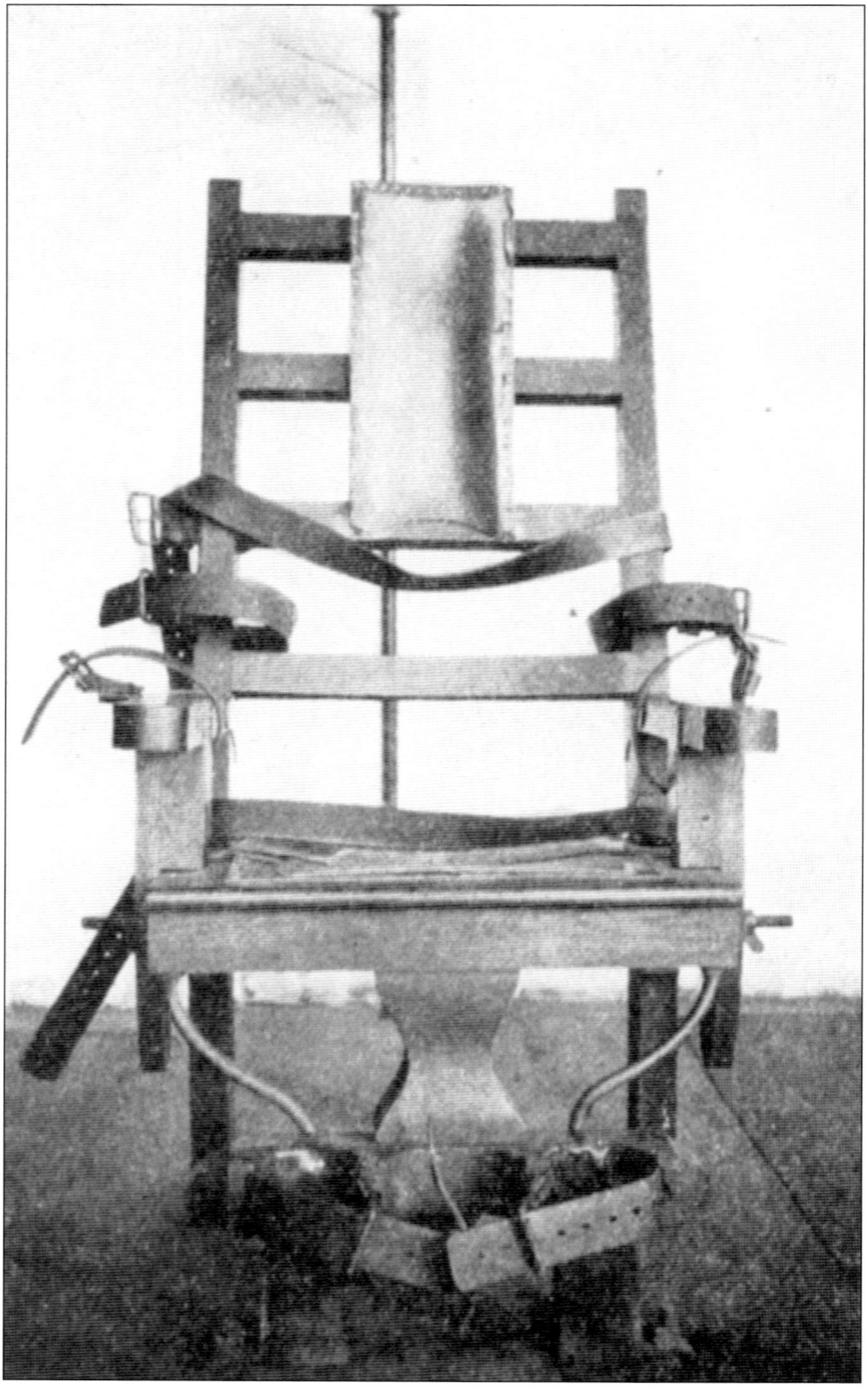

North Carolina's Electric Chair. The first known execution in North Carolina took place in 1726 in Chowan County, when Native American George Sennecca was hanged for murder. For much of the state's history, a wide array of crimes was punishable by death, and as late as 1817, some 28 crimes were capital offenses. That changed when the 1868 state constitution limited capital crimes to murder, rape, arson, and burglary.

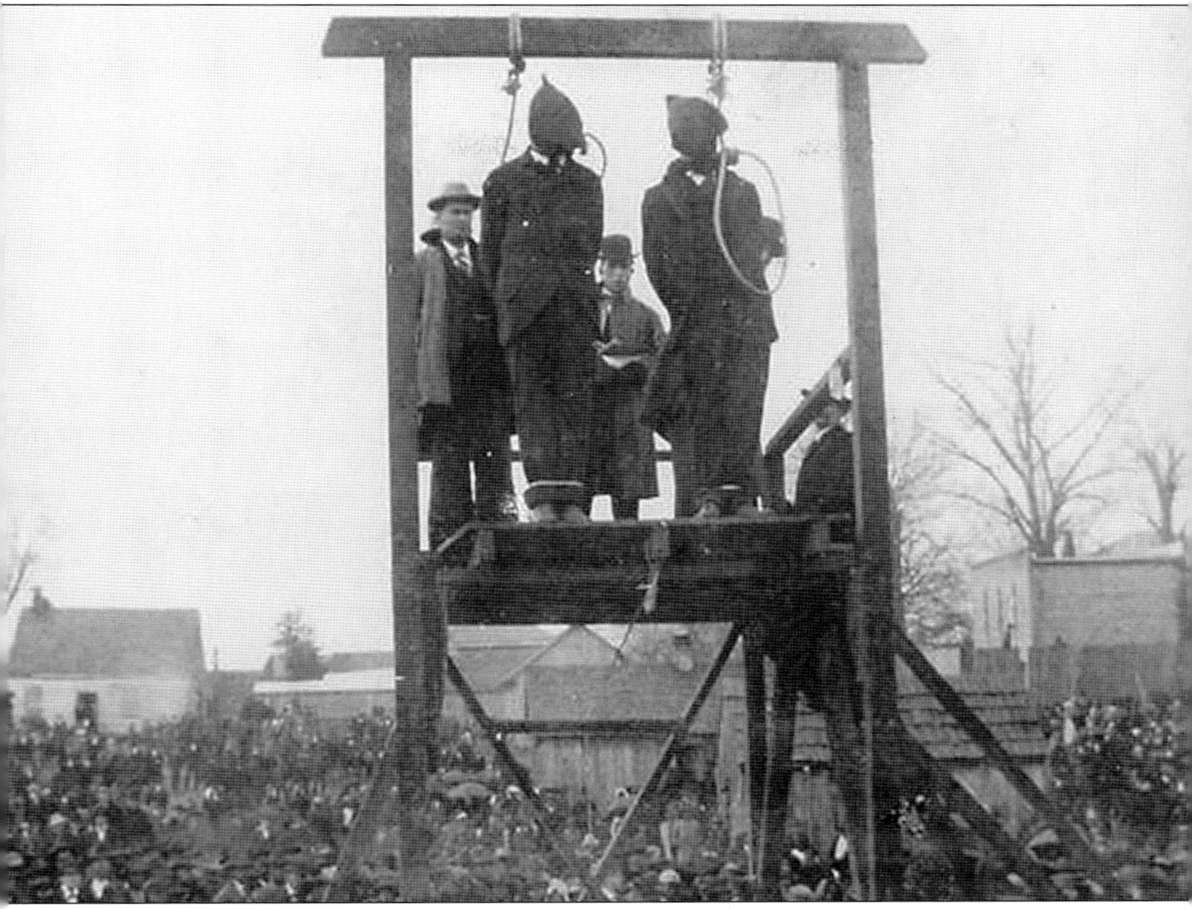

PUBLIC HANGING OF TWO AFRICAN AMERICAN MEN, 1903. The traditional mode of execution by the counties was public hanging via the standard drop method, which employed a fall of between four and six feet designed to break the person's neck. A head cover was applied to the prisoner, a noose was affixed around the neck, and the convicted was placed on a raised and hinged platform.

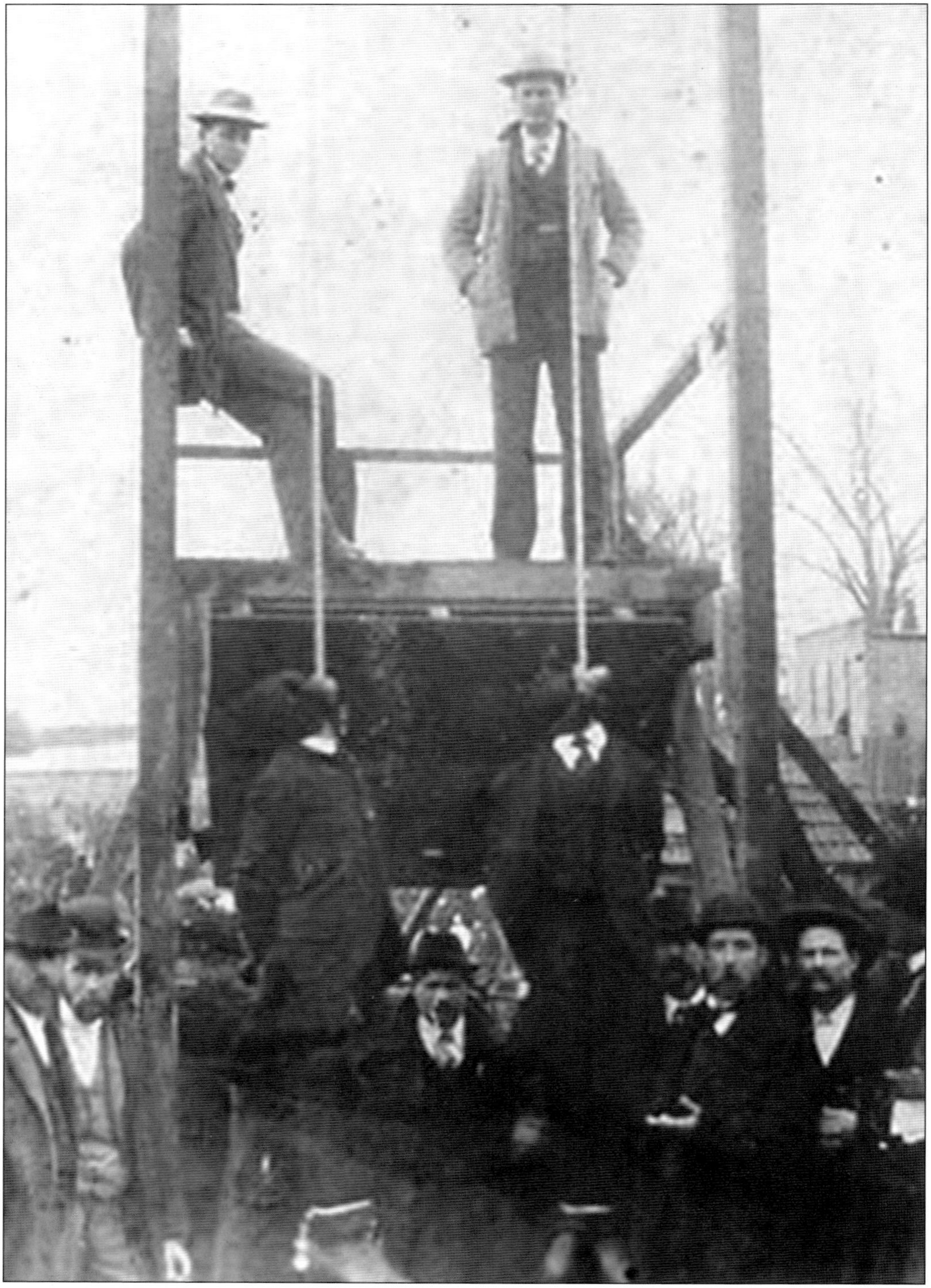

PUBLIC HANGING OF TWO AFRICAN AMERICAN MEN, 1903. The locks holding the platform in place were then released, and the platform swung down, dropping the individual to his death.

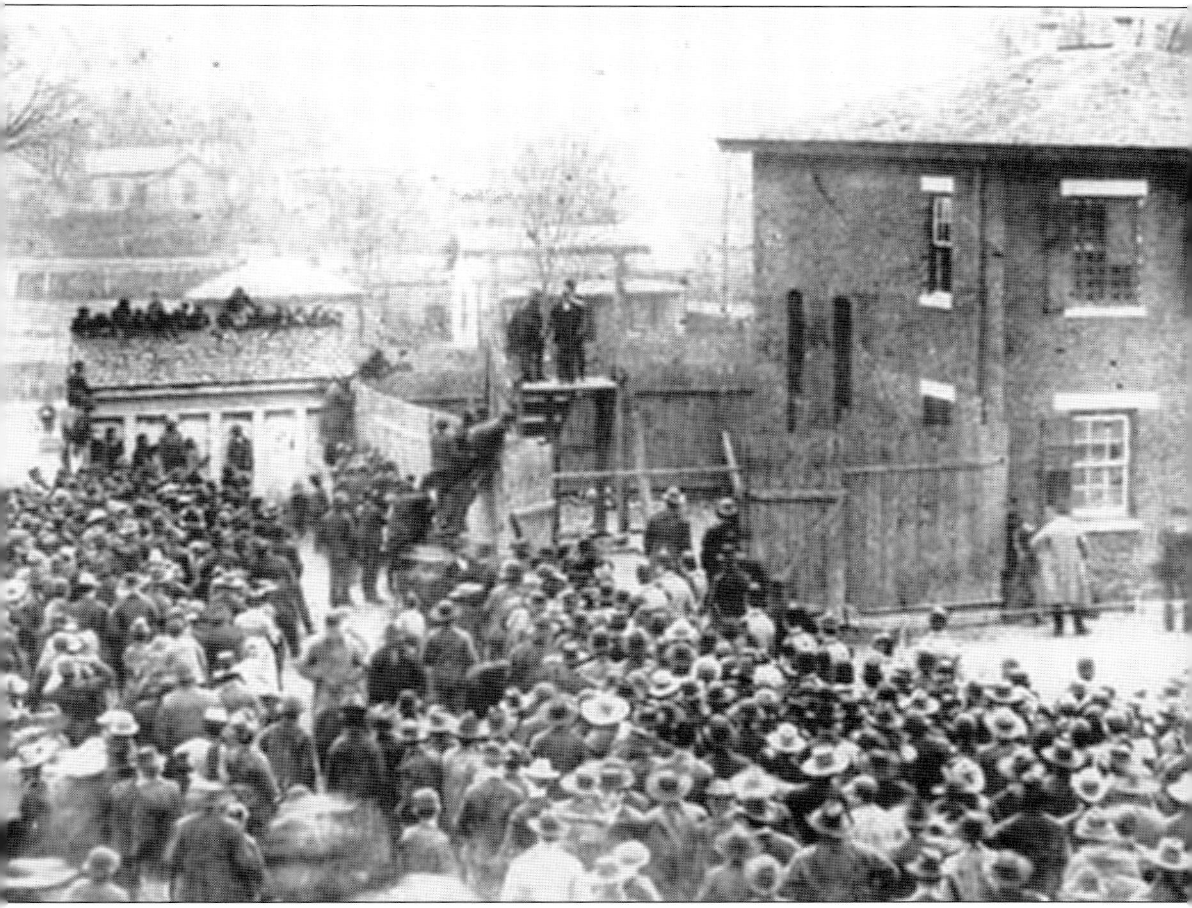

Unidentified Prisoners on the Scaffold, 1900s. Executions of this sort not only were public, they were also spectator events. Entire families attended the executions, local merchants sold food and drinks, and a festive atmosphere pervaded the surrounding area. While a form of entertainment, such spectacles allegedly provided general deterrence, as people witnessed the consequences of lawbreaking.

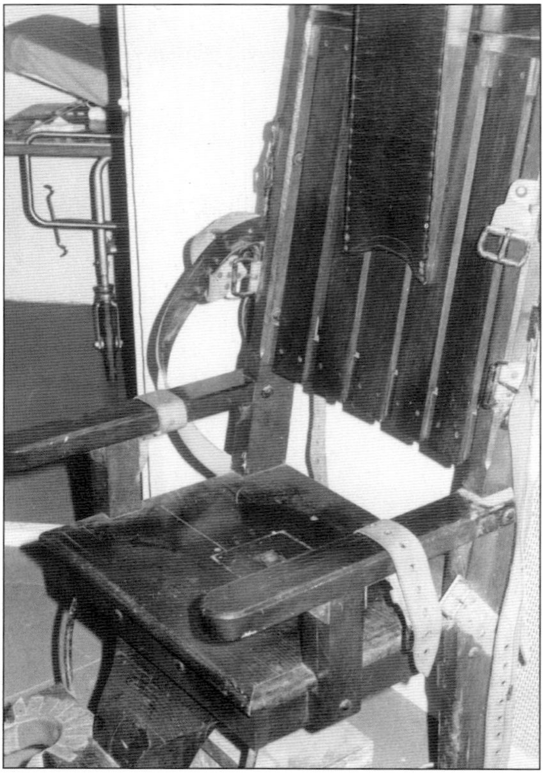

Electric Chair, 1929. In 1909, the state took control of executions and set Central Prison as the location for all subsequent death sentences. That same year, politicians changed the mode of execution from hanging to electrocution, which they deemed more humane. The state paid Edwin F. Davis $1,500 to build and install an electric chair. Davis promised to deliver the chair by September 1909, but technical difficulties hindered his efforts, and he delivered the chair in February 1910.

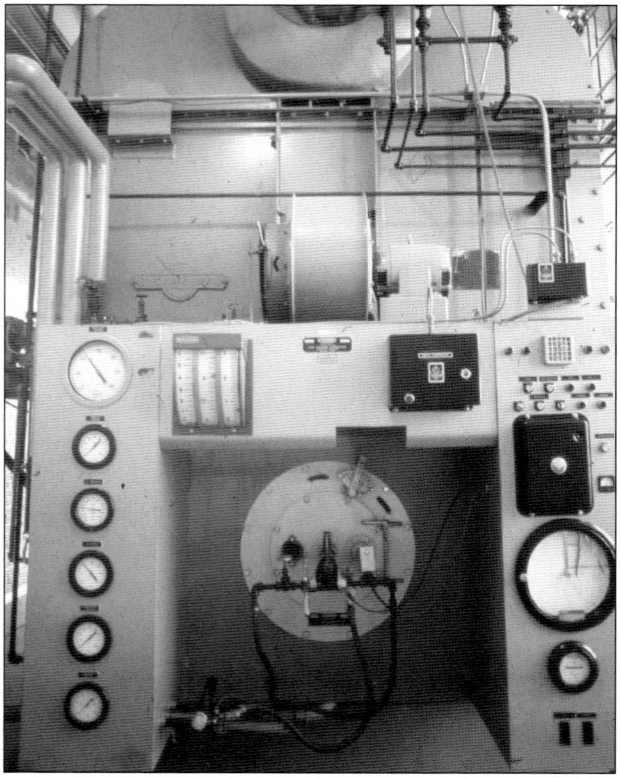

Electric Transformer, 1930s. Walter Morrison was the first person in North Carolina executed by the electric chair. Morrison, a 35-year-old African American man, was convicted of raping a Native American woman in Robeson County and firing upon police. His original execution date was set for September 10, 1909, but Davis's failure to install the chair on time delayed the execution until March 18, 1910.

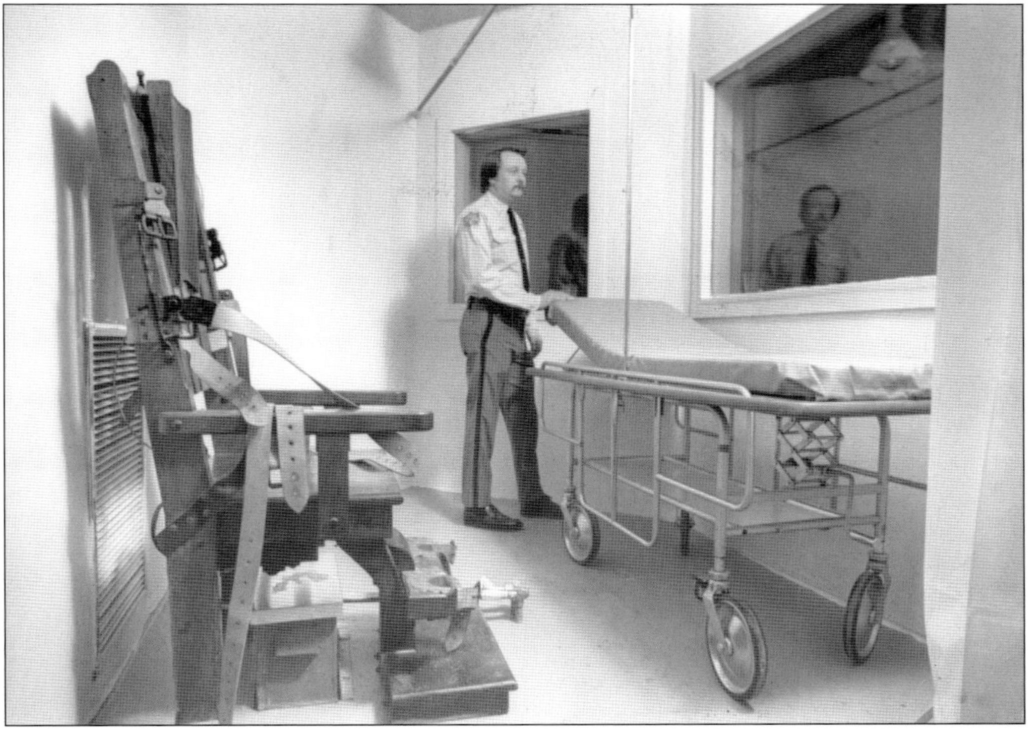

Execution Chamber, February 22, 1984. Lt. Charles Carroll stands in the small gas chamber with the wooden chair used for executions and the hospital gurney used for lethal injections. The window to the witness viewing room is on the extreme right.

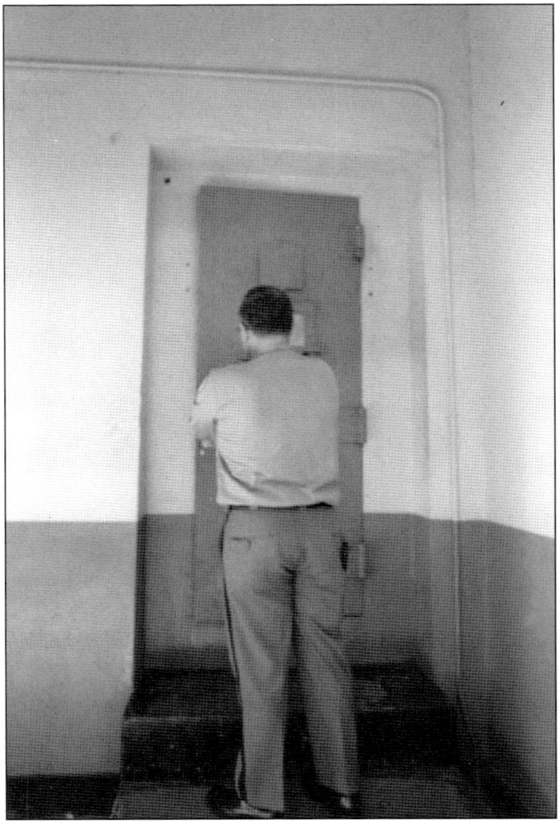

Doorway to the Execution Chamber, 1980s. From 1938 to 1983, the gas chamber was the sole means of execution in the state. Inmates were strapped into the chair, the chamber was sealed, and hydrogen cyanide pellets were activated by dropping them into an open container of sulfuric acid. The resultant poisonous cloud caused death within 15 minutes. As a result of federal judicial proceedings, no executions took place in North Carolina between 1962 and 1983.

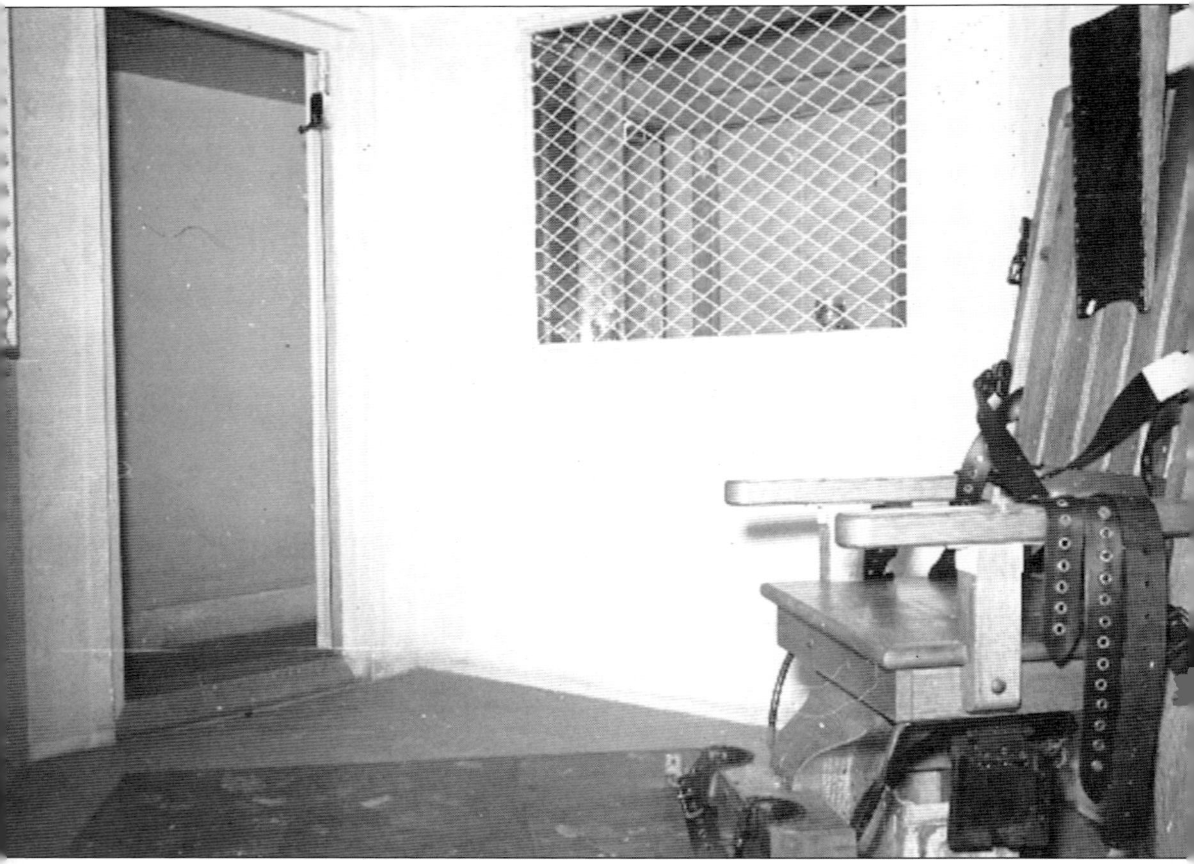

Execution Chamber, 1980s. Between 1910 and 1961, the State of North Carolina executed 360 men and two women. Since the reimposition of the death penalty in 1984, the state has executed 43 inmates. None, however, have been executed since the North Carolina Medical Board banned doctors from participating in executions in 2007. Although the ban was ruled unconstitutional in 2009, the Racial Justice Act gave death row inmates the right to a review hearing if they believed racial bias affected their sentence. The subsequent hearings have prevented any death sentences from being carried out.

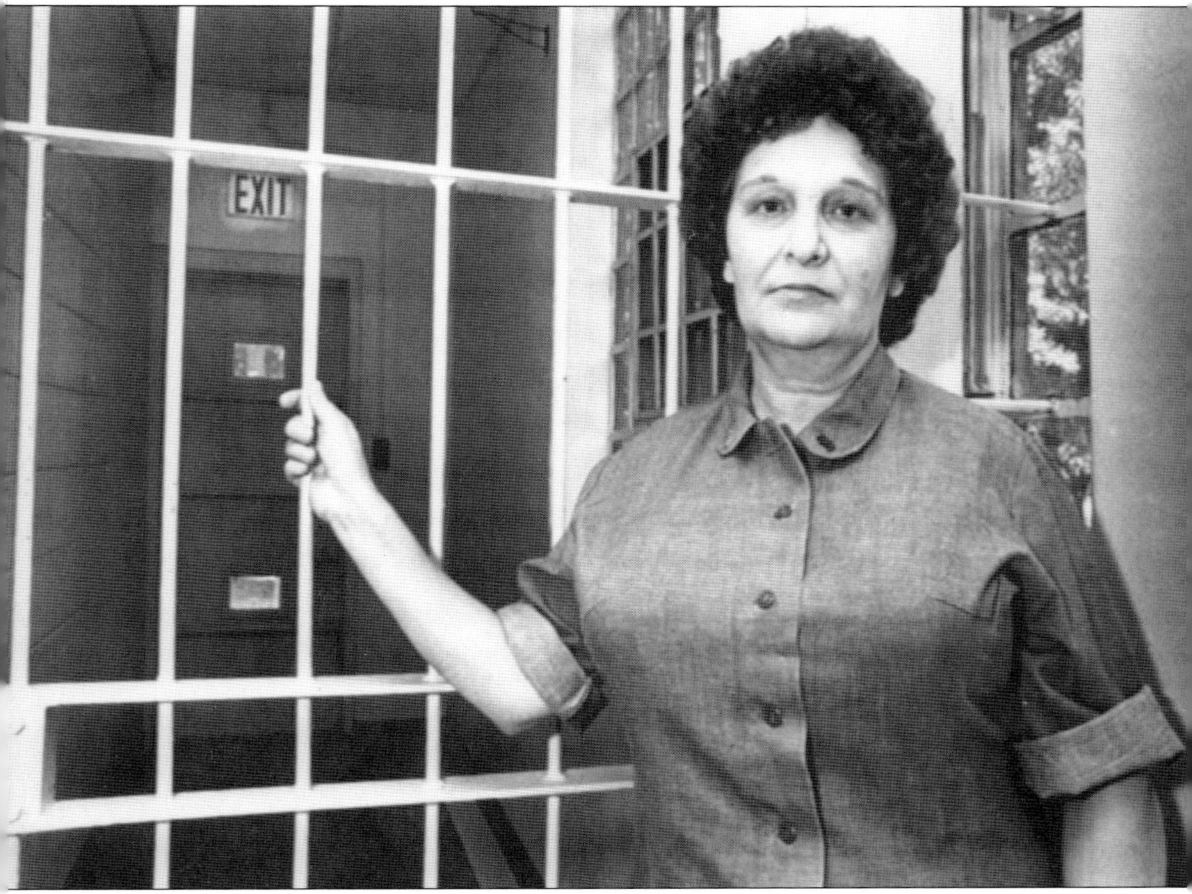

Velma Barfield. In 1943, Rosanna Phillips became the first woman executed by the state of North Carolina. However, the most famous woman executed in North Carolina was Velma Barfield. In 1969, her first husband, Thomas Burke, died. Her second husband, Jennings Barfield, died in 1971, while her mother, for whom she cared, died in 1974. Her boyfriend Stuart Taylor died in 1978. An autopsy on Taylor found the cause of death was arsenic poising, and Barfield was charged with his murder. She pled insanity, but a jury convicted her and sentenced her to death.

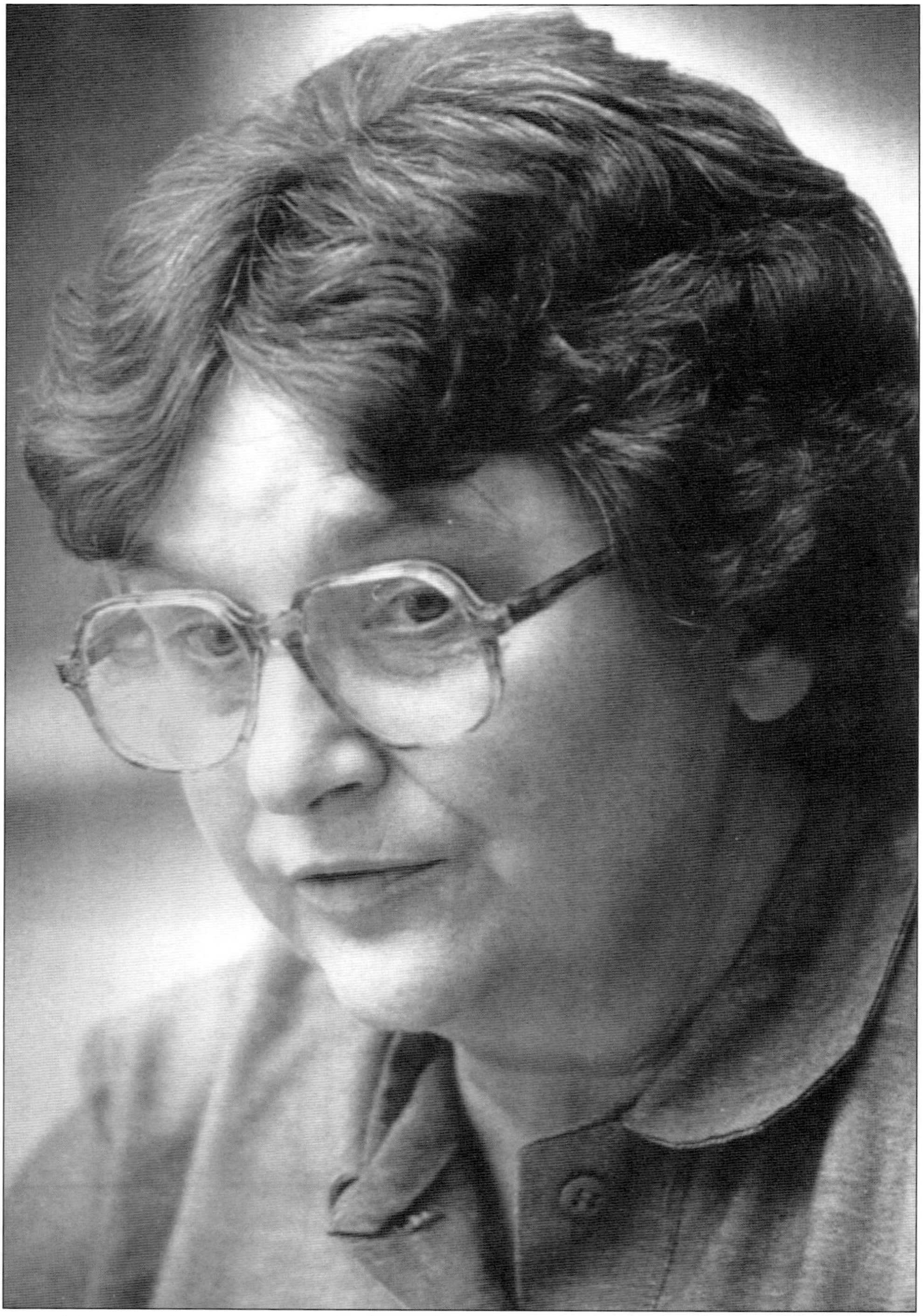

VELMA BARFIELD, JULY 7, 1984. As the only woman on death row at the time, Barfield was housed in Central Prison, where she became a born-again Christian and ministered to inmates. Despite pleas from religious figures and psychologists, who diagnosed her with multiple personality disorder, Barfield was executed by lethal injection on November 2, 1984. She was the first woman executed in the United States since 1962.

Ten

The New Central Prison

After original construction was complete in 1884, the penitentiary underwent several extensive renovations in the 1930s and 1940s. By the 1980s, however, the superstructure was over a century old and needed more than a makeover. Several buildings were in dire need of overhaul, plumbing issues abounded, the cells were outdated and poorly designed, and fears grew that security was compromised. Concerned about health, safety, and security issues, the state razed large portions of the penitentiary and replaced the ancient structures with a modern facility in 1984. The new buildings replaced the majesty and architectural aplomb of the original with a more institutional approach. While its appearance was less impressive, the security features, layout, and internal organization created a more secure institution that today has an inmate capacity of 750.

The security, layout, and organizational elements are obvious both inside and outside the new penitentiary. Within, modern communication devices, control panels, and computers allow officers more efficient control over the inmates. While face-to-face interaction remains a requisite, the opening and closing of doors is now done from secure locations, and the constant monitoring of inmates occurs from specially designed control rooms. The cells themselves also facilitate the custody officers' efforts; the items in the cells are bolted to the floor or walls, while the layout gives custody officers the ability to see every inch of each cell. Unlike the original cells, inmates have no place to escape the custody officers' observation.

From the outside, the new penitentiary is equally distinct from its predecessor. Gone are the cupolas, spires, and castle-like affectations. Instead, the penitentiary has a design focused solely on preventing escape. From the multiple barbed-wire fences and strategically located guard towers to the cleared sight lines and high-powered exterior lighting, architects focused more on functionality than creating visually resplendent structures. Regardless of appearance, the new North Carolina State Prison carries on the century-long tradition of its ancestor and serves the state by securely housing its most dangerous inmates.

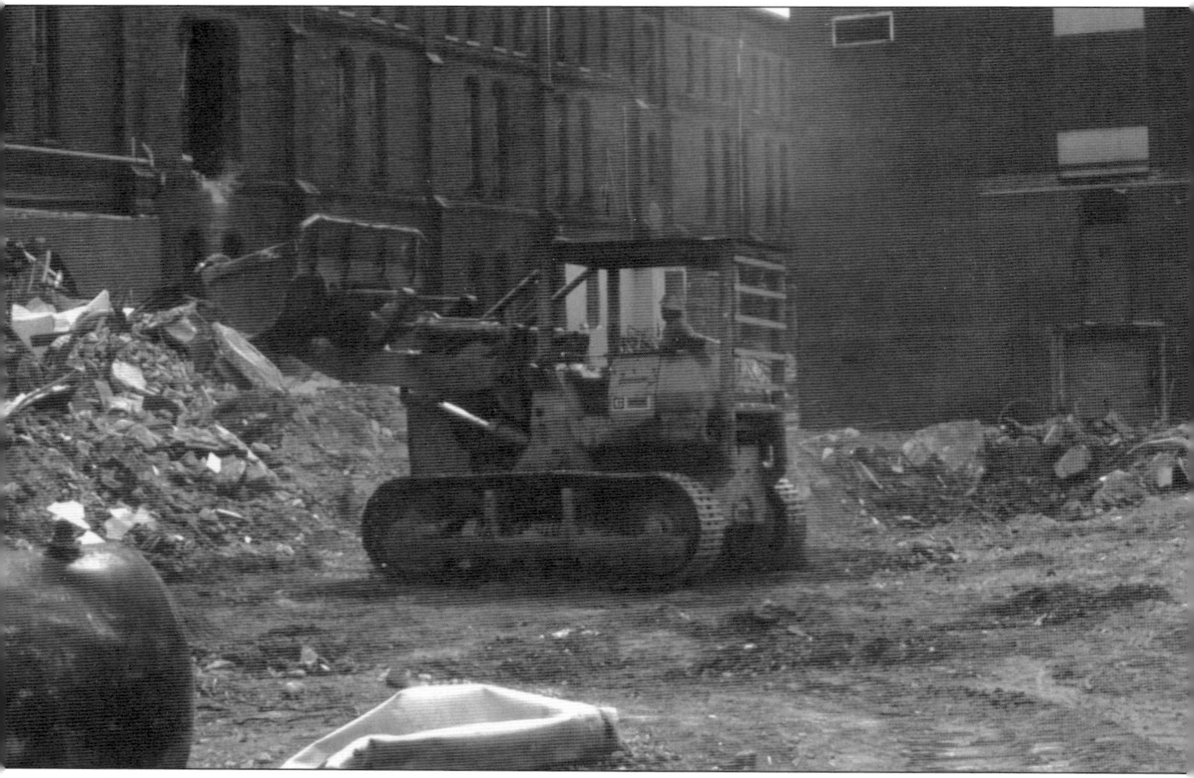

Demolition of Old Central Prison, 1980s. By the 1980s, Central Prison was a century old, and its age was beginning to show. Decorative pieces such as the turrets and spires, which gave the penitentiary its castle-like appearance, were removed for fear of collapse. Those renovations proved insufficient, however, as the buildings themselves were becoming outdated for the needs of a modern maximum-security penitentiary. To address these concerns, the state authorized the expenditure of $38 million for new construction. The original structures were torn down, and a modern facility was built based on the latest penological and architectural models. A new administration building was constructed, a new intake building was added to the grounds, and a new maximum-security complex was built to provide 500 additional cells.

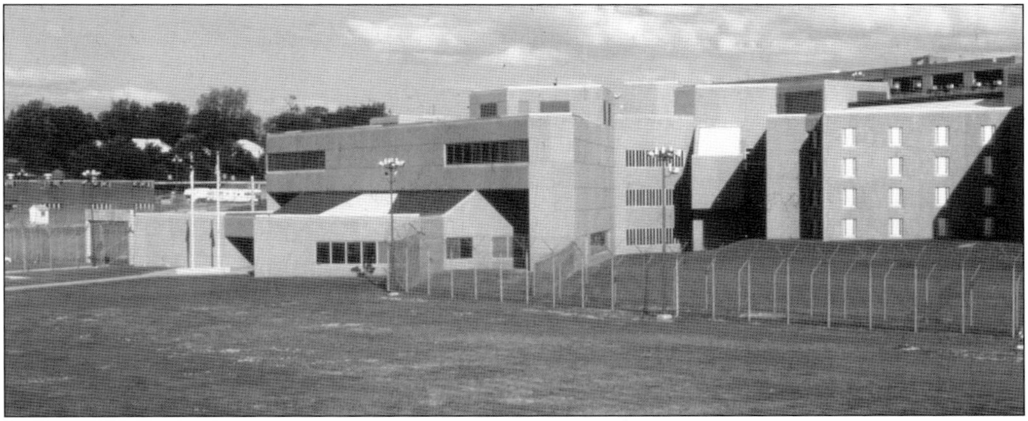

Main Entrance. Not only was the new penitentiary more expensive, it was more institutional and less imperial in appearance than the original. Gone were the castle-like features, replaced by uniform, more utilitarian features. Also gone was the formidable stone fence, replaced by one of barbed wire and chained link. New guard towers, additional cleared land for sight lines, and extensive exterior lighting added to the increased security. Renovations on the inside were notable as well, with new surveillance and monitoring systems built into strategically located control booths.

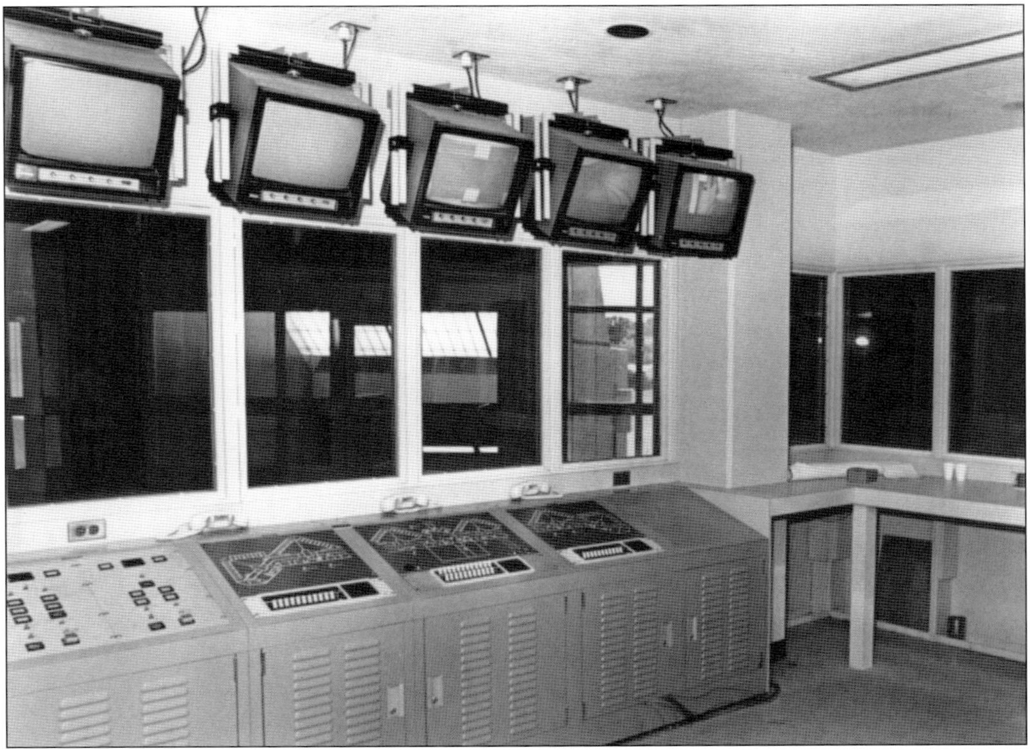

Control Room, 1980s. Television monitors in the security control point of the maximum-custody housing area scan hallways, elevators, and other areas not visible to officers in the booth. From such locations, they can observe inmates at all times and places and are able to lock and unlock doors, tiers, and entire cell houses at the simple touch of a button. Although officers continue to walk the tiers and monitor prisoners up close, these omnipresent security devices make the penitentiary a safer place for inmates and staff.

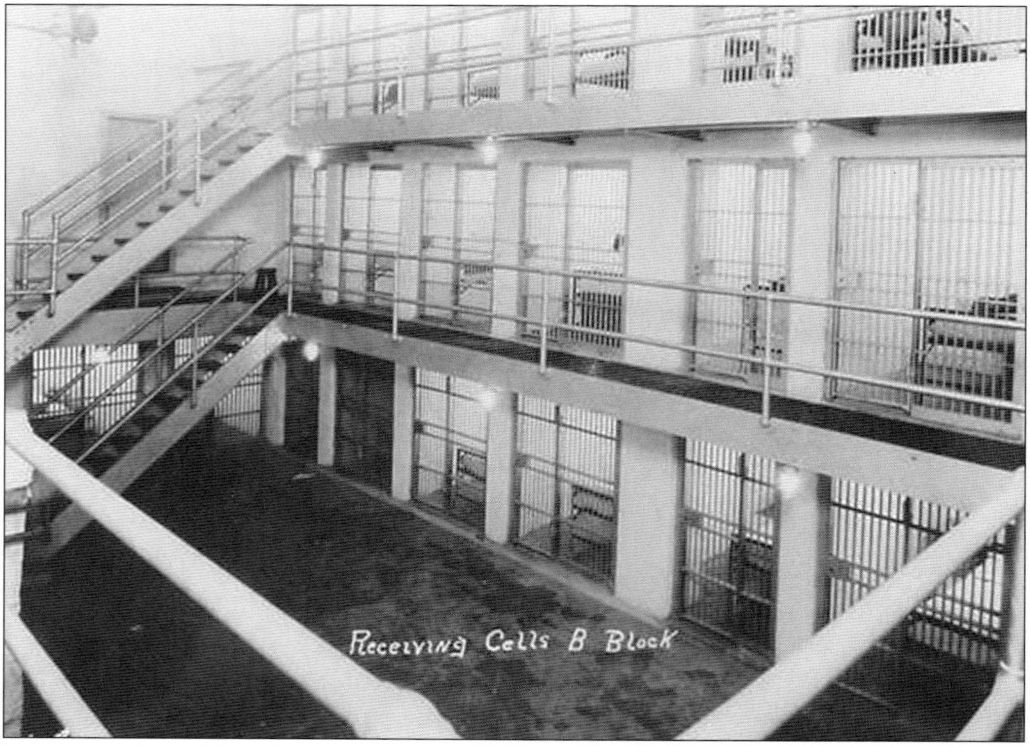

RECEIVING CELLS, NEW CENTRAL PRISON. The new prison houses special populations, including death row inmates and safe-keepers, such as high-risk prisoners awaiting trial as defendants and/or witnesses. While security requires that certain inmates remain in their cells, there are more than 260 job assignments. Inmates work in the kitchen, laundry, or canteen and can serve as barbers, janitors, and clerks.

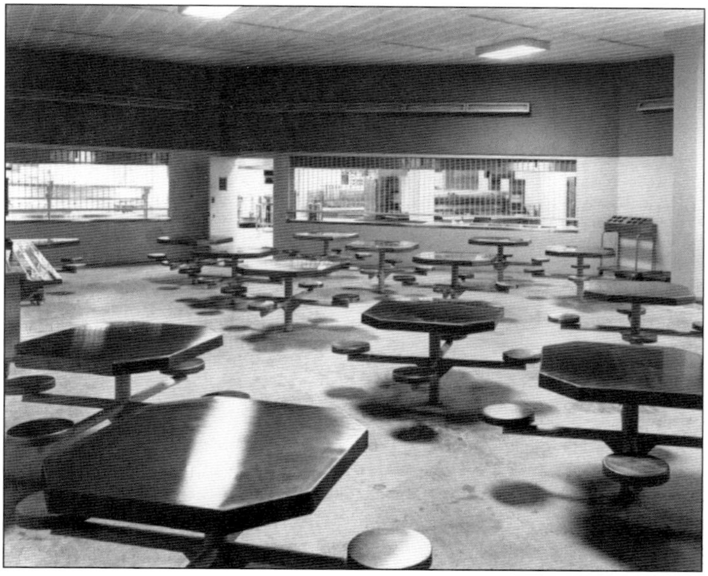

DINING FACILITY, 1990S. This is the view of half of the inmate dining room in the central services building in the new Central Prison. The immovable seats create a natural space between inmates, making it easier for correctional officers to espy any questionable behavior. Most of the sheet metal work in the kitchen (background) was done by inmates employed by Correction Enterprises. (Photograph by Galen Bolin.)

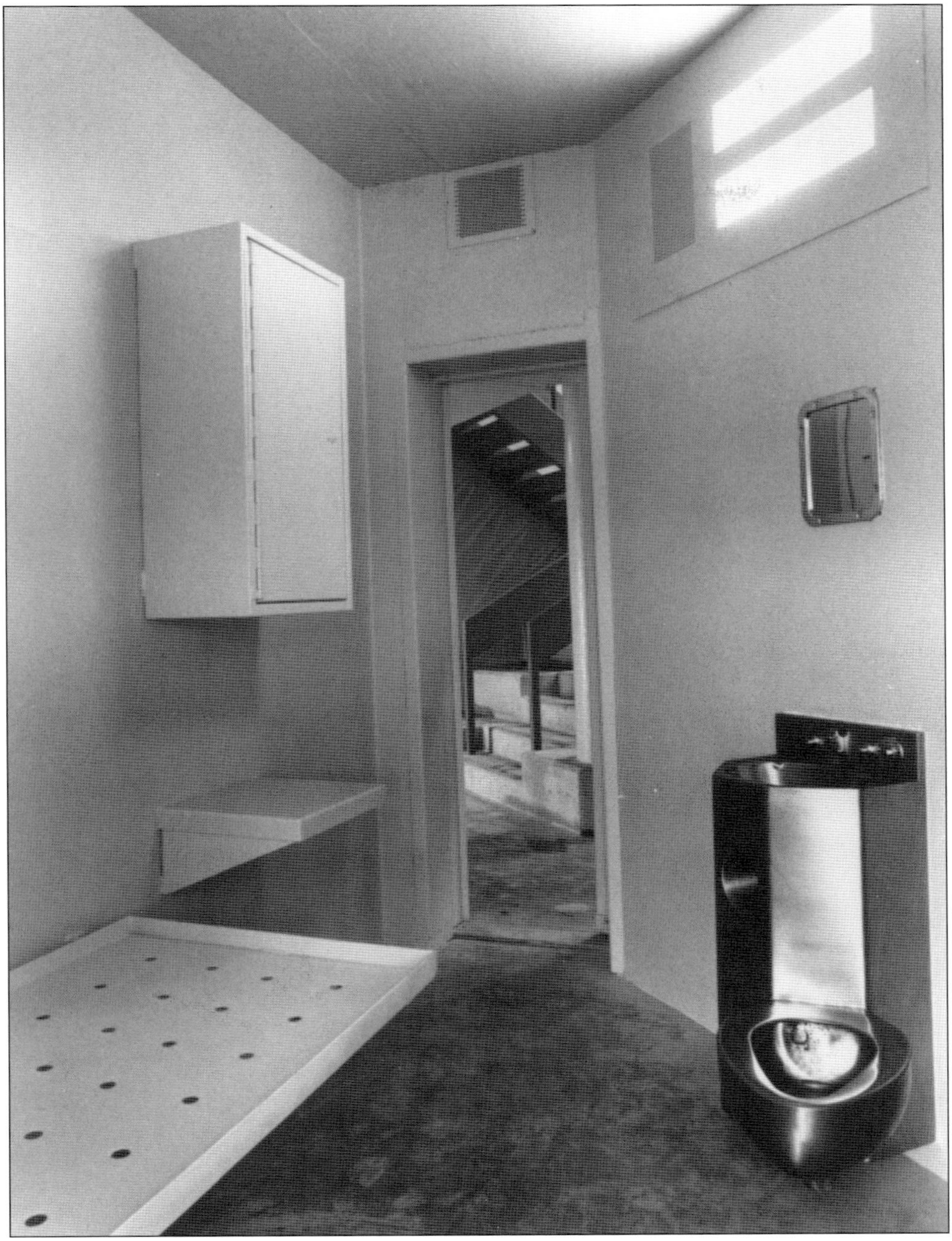

Typical Cell in Maximum-Security Housing, 1980s. In 1934, the prison underwent extensive renovations, including the installation of a plumbed concrete-slab commode and lavatory in each cell. The basic design of the cell remained, however, and its rectangular shape, with the door located to the right front edge, created problems for the custody officers. Inmates often hid behind the wall, making observation and extraction difficult. The new penitentiary solved that problem. This typical single cell in maximum-security housing is a 67-square-foot truncated triangle. With the door at the truncation, every part of the cell is visible from the doorway to prevent a prisoner from lying in wait and attacking a guard. Additionally, all the fixtures are made of metal and firmly secured to the wall.

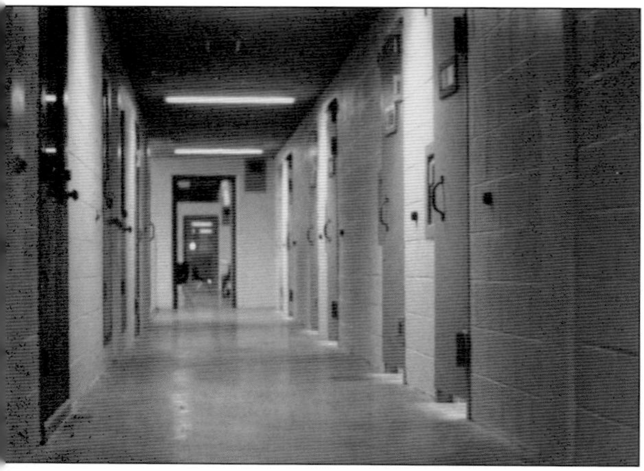

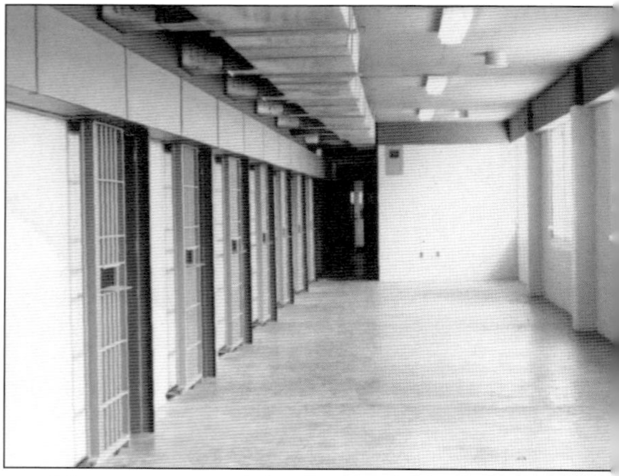

CORRIDORS OF NEW CELL HOUSES, 1990S. Depicted here are two of the new cell blocks. The one on the right continued to employ gated cell doors, while the one on the left introduced the solid cell door for greater officer security.

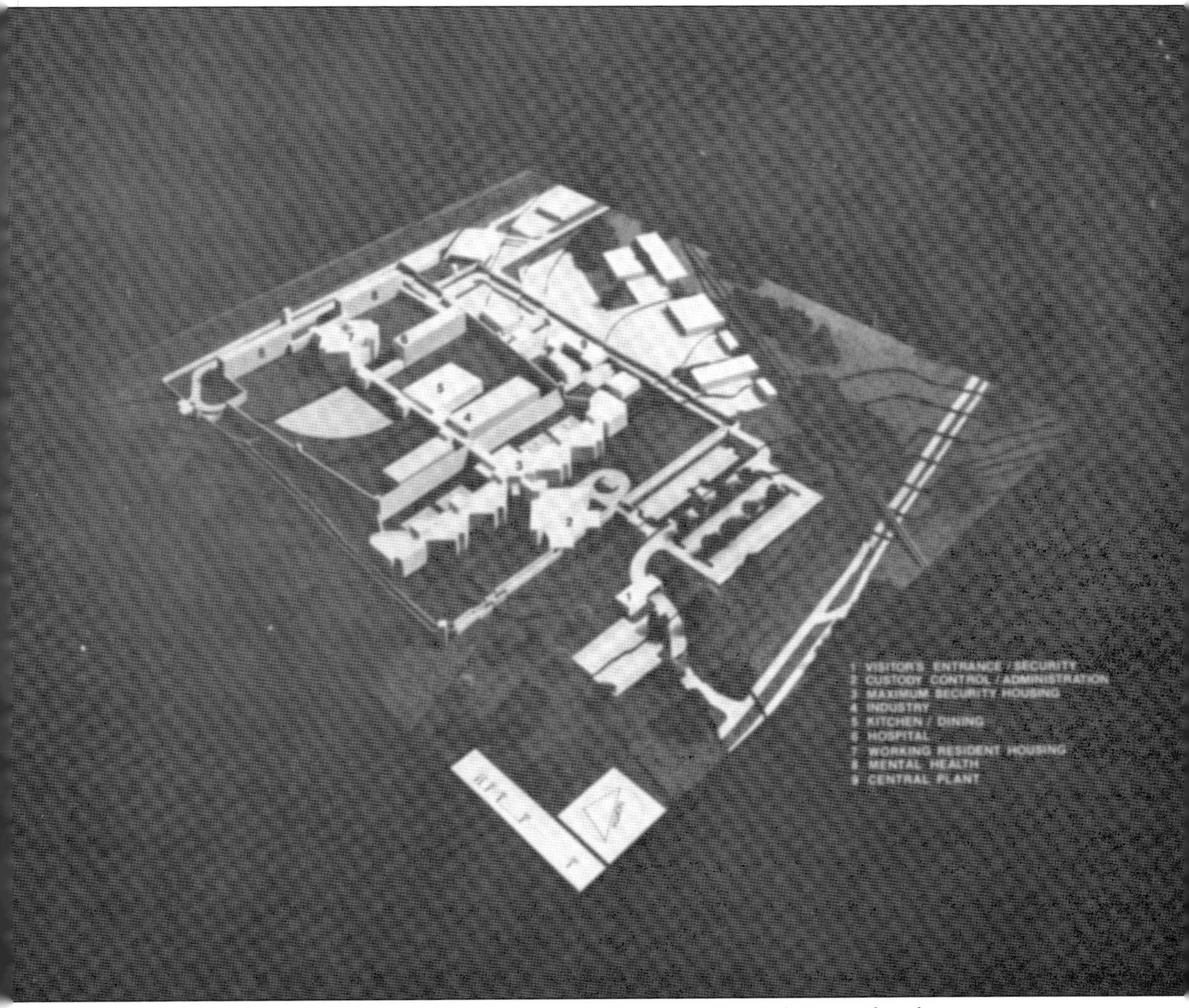

Model of New Central Prison Building with Legend. Central Prison has been in service since 1884. It continues to serve as the admission point into prison for adult male felons sentenced to 20 years or more and is the main medical and mental health center for male inmates.

Consistent with our mission to preserve history on a local level, this book was printed in South Carolina on American-made paper and manufactured entirely in the United States. Products carrying the accredited Forest Stewardship Council (FSC) label are printed on 100 percent FSC-certified paper.

MADE IN THE USA